SCHAUM'S
OUTLINE OF

D0599264

Fundamentals of
SQL
Programming

RAMON A. MATA-TOLEDO, Ph.D.

Associate Professor of Computer Science
James Madison University

PAULINE K. CUSHMAN, Ph.D.

Associate Professor of Integrated Science and Technology
and Computer Science
James Madison University

Schaum's Outline Series

McGRAW-HILL
New York   San Francisco   Washington, D.C.   Auckland   Bogotá   Caracas
Lisbon   London   Madrid   Mexico City   Milan   Montreal   New Delhi
San Juan   Singapore   Sydney   Tokyo   Toronto

RAMON A. MATA-TOLEDO has been teaching since 1971 in the U.S. and overseas high schools and colleges in both mathematics and computer science. He is currently an Associate Professor of Computer Science at James Madison University in Harrisonburg, Virginia. Dr. Mata-Toledo earned his Ph.D. in Computer Science from Kansas State University. He is the author of numerous publications in scientific magazines, national and international congresses, and trade journals. He is coauthor of *Schaum's Outline of Basic Mathematics with Applications to Science and Technology* and *Schaum's Outline of Introduction to Computer Science*. Dr. Mata-Toledo also holds Oracle Masters as Database Administrator and Applications Developer from Oracle Education Services. He has also performed database consultant work for national and international organizations. Dr. Mata-Toledo can be reached at mata1ra@jmu.edu.

PAULINE K. CUSHMAN taught public school at the elementary level for 12 years. She has been teaching computer science and computer information systems courses at the college and university level since 1985. She has taught a variety of computer science courses, including programming, intelligent systems, database design, and multimedia technology. She has done extensive consulting with nonprofit agencies regarding database technology. Currently an Associate Professor of Integrated Science and Technology and Computer Science at James Madison University in Harrisonburg, Virginia. Dr. Cushman earned her Ph.D. in Computer Science and Engineering from the University of Louisville. She is coauthor of *Schaum's Outline of Introduction to Computer Science*. Dr. Cushman can be reached at cushmapk@jmu.edu.

DOS, Notepad, and Windows® 95 are trademarks of Microsoft Corporation.
Oracle™, Personal Oracle™, PO8™ and SQL*Plus™ are trademarks of Oracle Corporation.
Certain portions of Oracle Corporation user documentation have been reproduced herein with the permission of Oracle Corporation. Oracle does not make any representations as to the accuracy or completeness of any information contained in the Work and is not responsible for any errors or omissions contained in the Work.

Schaum's Outline of Theory and Problems of
FUNDAMENTALS OF SQL PROGRAMMING

1 2 3 4 5 6 7 8 9 10 11 12 13 14 15 16 17 18 19 20 PBT PBT 0 9 8 7 6 5 4 3 2 1 0

ISBN 0-07-135953-2

Sponsoring Editor: Barbara Gilson
Production Supervisor: Elizabeth Strange
Editing Supervisor: Maureen B. Walker
Compositor: Keyword Publishing Services Ltd.

Library of Congress Cataloging-in-Publication Data
Mata-Toledo, Ramon A.
    Schaum's outline of fundamentals of SQL programming / Ramon A. Mata-Toledo,
  Pauline K. Cushman.
    p. cm.
    ISBN 0-07-135953-2
    1. SQL (Computer program language) I. Title: Fundamentals of SQL programming. II.
  Cushman, Pauline K. III. Title.
    QA76.73.S67 M325 2000
  005.75'6—dc21   00-033259

McGraw-Hill
A Division of The McGraw-Hill Companies

DEDICATION

Dedicated to the memory of my earthly father, Miguel Jesus Mata and to the glory and praise of my heavenly Father, the Uplifted Savior for the continuous blessing that He offers me through the love and dedication of my wife Anahis and my children Harold, Lys, and Hayley. I dedicate this book to all of them with my deepest love and affection. Last but not least, I dedicate this work to my mother Mami Nina and my friend and aunt Lys Violeta Mata de Gomez for their love, prayers, and support throughout the years.

RAMT

To my husband Jim, as always, for everything, to my entire family for their love and support, and to my granddaughters, Grace and Natalie, for their promise of the future. I also recognize Robert Hutton, who first taught me SQL many years ago.

PKC

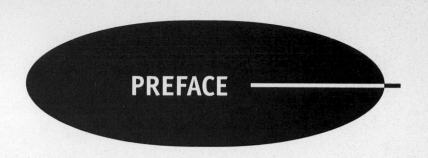

PREFACE

This book has been written for anyone who wants a general introduction to the SQL language, which is the standard computer language used to communicate with relational database management systems. Although particular SQL versions are used by different database management systems vendors, wherever possible, we have used generic SQL. For all illustration purposes, however, we have used Personal Oracle 8i as a database management system running under Windows 95/98/NT because of its popularity and because it is widely available and can be downloaded for free from the main website of the Oracle Corporation (www.oracle.com). All SQL code in this book will work on any platform where Oracle is available. In addition, for the benefit of the reader, all the scripts in this book can be downloaded from www.cs.jmu.edu/sqldata/.

This book can be used with most of the general database books on the market. However, it is intended to be a companion to our book, *Schaum's Outline of Fundamentals of Relational Databases*.

We would like to thank the personnel at McGraw-Hill for their help and support, particularly our sponsoring editor, Barbara Gilson. We hope that this book provides a helpful and informative introduction to the SQL language and relational databases. Enjoy SQL!

RAMON A. MATA-TOLEDO
PAULINE K. CUSHMAN

CONTENTS

Contents

CHAPTER 1

An Introduction to SQL and Relational Database Concepts

1.1 The SQL Language

SQL is the standard computer language used to communicate with relational database management systems (RDBMS). The SQL standard has been defined by the International Standards Organization (ISO) and the American National Standard Institute (ANSI). The official name of the language is International Standard Database Language SQL (1992). The latest version of this standard is commonly referred to as SQL/92 or SQL2. In this book, we will refer to this standard as the ANSI/ISO SQL Standard or just the SQL Standard. The SQL language, initially defined during the early 1970s, was originally called SEQUEL, short for *Structured English QUEry Language*. SEQUEL was first implemented as part of the system R, an IBM's relational database management system prototype. The word *English* was eventually dropped from the original name and the abbreviation changed to SQL. The Oracle Corporation, formerly Relational Software Inc, produced the first commercial implementation of the language in 1979.

   Although most relational database vendors support SQL/92, compliance with the standard is not 100 percent. Currently, there exist several flavors of SQL on the market, since each RDBMS vendor tries to extend the standard to increase the commercial appeal of its product. In this book, we adhere to the SQL/92 standard whenever possible. However, we illustrate the implementations of these features using Personal Oracle 8i, the PC version of the Oracle relational database management system. Wherever there are significant extensions or departures from the standard, we will point out the differences or capabilities of some of the proprietary versions of the language.

One of the main characteristics of the SQL language is that it is a *declarative* or *nonprocedural language*. From the programmer's point of view, this implies that the programmer does not need to specify step-by-step all the operations that the computer needs to carry out to obtain a particular result. Instead, the programmer indicates to the database management system what needs to be accomplished and then lets the system decide on its own how to obtain the desired result.

The statements or commands that compose the SQL language are generally divided into two major categories or *data sublanguages*. Each sublanguage is concerned with a particular aspect of the language. One of these sublanguages, known as the *data definition language*,[1] or DDL, includes statements that support the definition or creation of database objects such as tables, indexes, sequences, and views. Some of the most commonly used DDL statements are the different forms of the **CREATE**, **ALTER**, and **DROP** commands. We will discuss the details of each of these statements later on in the book. The other major sublanguage, the *data manipulation language*, or DML, includes statements that allow the processing or manipulation of database objects. Some of the most commonly used DML statements are the different modalities of the **SELECT**, **INSERT**, **DELETE**, and **UPDATE** statements. This set of instructions will be reviewed further later on. It is important to observe that all objects created in a database are stored in the *data dictionary* or *catalog*.

The SQL language can be used interactively or in its embedded form. *Interactive SQL* allows the user to issue commands[2] directly to the database management system and receive the results back as soon as they are produced. When *embedded SQL* is used, the SQL statements are included as part of a program written in a general-purpose language such as C, C++, or COBOL. In this case, we refer to the general-purpose programming language as the *host language*. The main reason for using embedded SQL is to use additional programming language features that are not generally supported by SQL.

When embedded SQL is used, the user does not observe directly the output of the different SQL statements. Instead, the results are passed back in variables or procedure parameters.

As a general rule, any SQL instruction that can be used interactively can also be used as part of an application program. However, the user needs to keep in mind that there may be some syntactical differences in the SQL statements when they are used interactively or when they are embedded into a program. In this book, we only consider SQL in its interactive form.

Since SQL is exclusively used with relational database management systems, it is necessary to have a basic understanding of this type of database in order to understand better the different features of the language. We will discuss relational database management systems next.

---

[1] The data definition language is also known as the *schema definition language* according to ANSI.

[2] Some authors refer to instructions used in interactive mode as commands and embedded instructions as statements. In this book, we will use these two terms interchangeably.

1.2   Relational Database Management Systems

The software system that allows users to define, create, and maintain a database and provides controlled access to the data is called a *database management system* (DBMS). The term *database* is generally used to refer to the data itself; however, in a computerized database, there are additional components that also form part of the DBMS, such as the hardware, the software itself, and the users. The latter can access or retrieve data on demand using the applications and interfaces provided by the database management system. Users communicate with an RDBMS after logging in with an appropriate username and password whenever this is appropriate. After a successful login, the user is said to start a *session*. This session ends when the user logs out or when the user is disconnected from the database. Appendix A shows how to log in to the Personal Oracle Edition 8 database.

The set of facts represented in a database is called the *universe of discourse* (UOD). The UOD should only include facts that form a logically coherent collection and that are relevant to its users. For this reason, a database should always be designed, built, and populated for a particular audience and for a specific purpose.

A database management system based on the relational data model is called a *relational database management system*, or RDBMS for short. In this type of database, all the information that composes the universe of discourse is represented as *relations*. Although a relation can be defined in mathematical terms, for all practical purposes, we will view relations as two-dimensional tables. Tables or relations are the database objects that hold data. In this book, we will use the terms *tables* and *relations* interchangeably. Each relation consists of a relation name and set of *columns* or *attributes*. The data in the table appears as a set of *rows* or *tuples*. The total number of attributes in the relation is known as the *degree* of the relation. The total number of rows present in the relation at any one time is known as the *cardinality* of the relation. In this book, we use the terms *column* and *attribute* interchangeably. Likewise, we consider the terms *row* and *tuple* as synonyms. In legacy systems, the terms *field* and *record* are used as synonyms of the terms *attribute* and *row*, respectively.

In every relation, as required by ANSI/ISO SQL standard, each column must have a name, and all column names within the same table must be different. However, there is no restriction against two columns in two different tables having identical names. With regard to the degree or cardinality of a relation, the SQL standard does not impose any limit on the number of columns that a table can have or the number of rows that it may contain. Nevertheless, manufacturers usually impose some limit on the number of columns but not on the number of rows. From an operational point of view, it is permissible for a table not to have any rows in it (an empty table). However, it is required that tables have at least one column.

Fig. 1-1 of Example 1.1 shows the basic form of a relation called CUSTOMER_ORDER when viewed as a two-dimensional table.

EXAMPLE 1.1
Identify the degree and cardinality of the CUSTOMER_ORDER relation show below.

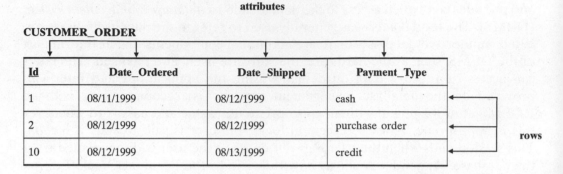

attributes

CUSTOMER_ORDER

Id	Date_Ordered	Date_Shipped	Payment_Type
1	08/11/1999	08/12/1999	cash
2	08/12/1999	08/12/1999	purchase order
10	08/12/1999	08/13/1999	credit

rows

Fig. 1-1.   The CUSTOMER_ORDER relation viewed as a two-dimensional table.

Fig. 1-1 shows that the CUSTOMER_ORDER relation consists of four attributes: `Id`, `Date_Ordered`, `Date_Shipped`, and `Payment_Type`. In addition, there are three different rows in the table. Using the terminology indicated before, we can say that the CUSTOMER_ORDER relation has a degree of four and a cardinality of three.

In this book, we will assume that every entry of a relation has at most a single value. That is, at the intersection of every column and every row, there is at most a single value.[3] For any given relation r, for any attribute A of r, and an arbitrary tuple t of r, we will use the notation $t(A)$ to denote the value of the tuple t under the column A. That is, the value at the intersection of column A and row t.

EXAMPLE 1.2
For the CUSTOMER_ORDER relation of Fig. 1-1, what are the individual values of t(A) if t is the first tuple shown in the table and A is an arbitrary attribute of the relation? If we call t the first tuple shown in the table, we can say that t(Id) = 1, t(Payment_Type) = cash, t(Date_Ordered) = 08/11/1999 and t(Date_Shipped) = 08/12/1999.

Each of the attributes listed in the CUSTOMER_ORDER relation has an associated domain denoted, in general, as Domain(attribute). The *domain* identifies the set of values that may appear as values in a particular column of a given relation r. That is, for every tuple t of relation r and an arbitrary attribute A of r, t(A) must be an element of the Domain(A). This can be expressed in mathematical terms using set theory notation as $t(A) \in$ Domain(A).

EXAMPLE 1.3
Identify the possible domains of the different attributes for the CUSTOMER_ORDER relation of Fig. 1-1.

---

[3] This guarantees that the relation is in first normal form, or 1NF.

In this case, we will assume that the domain of the attribute `Id` may be the set of positive integer numbers. The domain of each of the attributes `Date_Ordered` and `Date_Shipped` is the set of valid dates. Finally, the domain of the attribute `Payment_Type` may be a finite set of characters strings of finite length (not specified here) composed of the following values: {cash, credit, money order, check, purchase order, credit card, debit card, unknown}. Using the notation mentioned above, we could denote these domains as follows:

Domain(id) = Set of positive integers
Domain(Payment_type) = {cash, credit, money order, check, purchase
            order, credit card, debit card, unknown}
Domain(Date_Ordered) = Domain(Date_Shipped) = set of valid dates

Notice that in the table CUSTOMER_ORDER, for every row t and attribute A, t(A) is an element of its corresponding domain.

1.3   Candidate Key and Primary Key of Relation

The notion of a *key* is a fundamental concept in the relational model because it provides the basic mechanism for retrieving tuples within a database. Formally, given a relation r and its attributes $A_1, A_2, A_3 \ldots, A_n$, we will call any subset $K = \{A_1, A_2, \ldots A_k\}$ of these attributes a *candidate key* if K satisfies the following conditions:

1. For any two distinct tuples t_1 and t_2 of the relation r, there exists an attribute B of K such that $t_1(B) \neq t_2(B)$. This implies that no two different tuples of r will have the same value on all the attributes in K. This condition is known as the *uniqueness property of the key*.

2. No proper subset of K' of K satisfies the uniqueness property. In other words, no element of K can be discarded without destroying the uniqueness property. This condition, known as the *minimality property of the key*, guarantees that the number of attributes that compose the key is minimum.

Since in a relation r there may be more than one candidate key, one of these candidate keys may be arbitrarily designated as the *primary key* (PK) of the relation. The values of the primary key can then be used as the addressing mechanism of the relation. Once a primary key has been selected, the remaining candidate keys, if they exist, are sometimes called *alternate keys*. An RDBMS allows only one primary key per table. A primary key may be composed of one single attribute (*single primary key*), or it may be composed of more than one attribute (*composite primary key*). In this book, we will underline the attributes that are part of the primary key. In Example 1.1, the attribute `Id` is the PK of the CUSTOMER_ORDER relation. Notice that `Id` has been underlined. Since `Id` is the PK of the CUSTOMER_ORDER relation, no two orders will have the same Id value.

Since a primary key is used to identify uniquely the tuples or rows of a relation, no value of the attribute or attributes that form the primary key can be NULL. This fact imposes an additional restriction, or *constraint*, on the primary key known as the *integrity constraint*. A NULL value represents missing information, unknown, or inapplicable data. The reader should be aware that a NULL value is not a zero value, nor does it represent a particular value within the computer.[4]

EXAMPLE 1.4

Consider the DEPT table and the rows shown below. Explain whether or not these rows can be inserted into the DEPT table.

DEPARTMENT	NAME	LOCATION	BUDGET
10	Research	New York	1500000
	Accounting	Atlanta	1200000
15	Computing	Miami	1500000

DEPT

DEPARTMENT	NAME	LOCATION	BUDGET
20	Sales	Miami	1700000
10	Marketing	New York	2000000

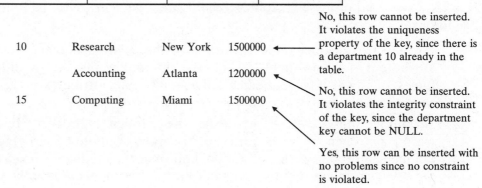

10	Research	New York	1500000
	Accounting	Atlanta	1200000
15	Computing	Miami	1500000

No, this row cannot be inserted. It violates the uniqueness property of the key, since there is a department 10 already in the table.

No, this row cannot be inserted. It violates the integrity constraint of the key, since the department key cannot be NULL.

Yes, this row can be inserted with no problems since no constraint is violated.

1.4   Foreign Keys

Because columns that have the same underlying domain can be used to relate tables of a database, the concept of a foreign key allows the DBMS to maintain consistency among the rows of two relations or between the rows of the same relation. This concept can be formally defined as follows. Given two relations r_1 and r_2 of the same database,[5] a set of attributes FK of relation r_1 is said to be a

---

[4] In SQL, most comparisons between nulls and other values are by definition neither true nor false but unknown.

[5] According to this definition of foreign key, relations r_1 and r_2 could be the same relation.

foreign key of r_1 (with respect to r_2) if the following two conditions are satisfied simultaneously:

- The attributes in FK have the same underlying domain as a set of attributes of relation r_2 that have been defined as the PK of r_2. The FK is said to reference the PK attribute of the relation r_2.
- The FK-values in any tuple of relation r_1 are either NULL or must appear as the PK-values of a tuple of relation r_2.

From a practical point of view, the foreign key concept ensures that the tuples of relation r_1 that refer to tuples of relation r_2 must refer to tuples of r_2 that already exist. This restriction imposed on foreign keys is called the *referential integrity* constraint. Some authors call the table that contains the forcign key a *child table*; the table that contains the referenced attribute or attributes is called the *parent table*. Using this terminology, we can say that the FK-value in each row of a child table is either NULL or it must match the PK or UNIQUE values of a tuple of the parent table.

EXAMPLE 1.5

Consider the tables indicated below. Assume that the attribute EMP_DEPT is a FK of the EMPLOYEE table that references the attribute ID of DEPARTMENT. Indicate if the rows shown below can be inserted into the EMPLOYEE table.

ID	NAME	LOCATION
10	Accounting	New York
40	Sales	Miami

DEPARTMENT

EMP ID	EMP_NAME	EMP_MGR	TITLE	EMP_DEPT
1234	Green		President	40
4567	Gilmore	1234	Senior VP	40
1045	Rose	4567	Director	10
9876	Smith	1045	Accountant	10

EMPLOYEE

9213	Jones	1045	Clerk	30
8997	Grace	1234	Secretary	40
5932	Allen	4567	Clerk	NULL

No, this row cannot be inserted since it violates the referential integrity constraint of the key. There is no department 30 in the department table.

Yes, this row can be inserted with no problem since no constraint is violated.

Yes, this row can be inserted into the table. NULL values are acceptable in the EMP_DEPT column. The NULL value may indicate that the employee has not yet been assigned to a department.

Notice that in the previous example, we use the keyword[6] NULL explicitly to indicate the absence of a department, whereas in Example 1.4 the entry for DEPARTMENT was left blank. The reader should be aware that some systems allow both ways to indicate a NULL value; other systems may require that the NULL keyword be used explicitly.

1.5 Relational Operators

We call *relational operators* a set of operators that allow us to manipulate the tables of the database. Relational operators are said to satisfy the *closure property*, since they operate on relations to produce new relations. When a relational operator is used to manipulate a relation, we say that the operator is "applied" to the relation. In this section, we will discuss only the selection, the projection, and the equijoin relational operators. In Chapter 2, we will consider the implementation of these operators in SQL, as well as some additional relational operators.

1.5.1 THE SELECTION OPERATOR[7]

When applied to a relation r, this operator produces another relation whose rows are a subset of the rows of r that satisfy a specified condition. The resulting relation and r have the same attributes. More formally, we can define this operator as follows. Let r be a relation, A an attribute of r, and a an element of the Domain(A). The Selection of r on attribute A is the set of tuples t of r such that t(A) = a. The <u>Selection of r on A</u> is denoted $\sigma_{A=a}(r)$. The following example illustrates how this selection operator works. Notice that the selection operator is a *unary operator*. That is, it operates on one relation at a time.

EXAMPLE 1.6
Given the EMPLOYEE relation of the previous example, find all the information about the employees that work for department 10.

Since we need to retrieve *all* the information about the employees who work for department 10, it is necessary to determine $\sigma_{EMP\_DEPT=10}(EMPLOYEE)$. Notice that in this example the condition that needs to be satisfied by the tuples of the EMPLOYEE relation is t(EMP_DEPT) = 10. The resulting table is shown below.

$$\sigma_{EMP\_DEPT=10}(EMPLOYEE)$$

EMP ID	EMP_NAME	EMP_MGR	TITLE	EMP_DEPT
1045	Rose	4567	Director	10
9876	Smith	1045	Accountant	10

---

[6] A *keyword* is a word that has a specific meaning to the system and cannot be used outside a specific content.

[7] This operator is also known as the Restrict or Select operator. We do not use the word *select* to avoid any confusion with the SQL command that shares the same name.

1.5.2   THE PROJECTION OPERATOR

The projection operator is also a unary operator. Whereas the selection operator chooses a subset of the rows of the relation, the projection operator chooses a subset of the columns. This operator can be formally defined as follows. The <u>projection of relation r onto a set X of its attributes</u>, denoted by $\pi_X(r)$, is a new relation that we can obtain by first eliminating the columns of r not indicated in X and then removing any duplicate tuple. The columns of the projection relation are the attributes of X. The following example illustrates this.

EXAMPLE 1.7

Using the DEPARTMENT table shown below, what are the locations of the different departments? From the answer to the previous question, can we tell the different locations that there are in this particular table?

DEPARTMENT

ID	NAME	LOCATION
10	Accounting	New York
30	Computing	New York
50	Marketing	Los Angeles
60	Manufacturing	Miami
90	Sales	Miami

Since we need to determine the number of different values that are currently present in the LOCATION column, we need to find the projection of the DEPARTMENT table on the attribute LOCATION. That is, we need to find $\pi_{\text{LOCATION}}(\text{DEPARTMENT})$. In this case, $r = \text{DEPARTMENT}$ and $X = \{\text{LOCATION}\}$. The resulting relation is shown below.

$\pi_{\text{LOCATION}}(\text{DEPARTMENT})$

LOCATION
New York
Los Angeles
Miami

Notice that there is only one occurrence of the values New York and Miami in the resulting table. Observe also that LOCATION is the sole attribute of this table.

In general, the projection of this relation on the attribute LOCATION cannot give us the total number of locations currently present in the DEPARTMENT table, since duplicate values are eliminated. Notice that the projection relation only has three locations, whereas the DEPARTMENT relation has a total of five locations.

> **EXAMPLE 1.8**
> Using the table of the previous example, what are the different departments and their locations?

In this case, $X = \{$NAME, LOCATION$\}$ and $r = $ DEPARTMENT. The resulting relation is shown below.

$\pi_{\text{NAME, LOCATION}}(\text{DEPARTMENT})$

NAME	LOCATION
Accounting	New York
Computing	New York
Marketing	Los Angeles
Manufacturing	Miami
Sales	Miami

The resulting relation does not contain duplicate values, since the different combinations of name and location are unique. Notice that (Manufacturing, Miami) and (Sales, Miami) are different tuples. A similar situation occurs with the departments located in New York.

1.5.3   THE EQUIJOIN OPERATOR

The equijoin[8] operator is a binary operator for combining two relations not necessarily different. In general, this operator combines two relations on all their common attributes. That is, the join consists of all the tuples resulting from concatenating the tuples of the first relation with the tuples of the second relation that have identical values for a common attribute X. Mathematically, this definition can be expressed as follows. Let r be a relation with a set of attributes R and let s be another relation with a set of attributes S. In addition, let us assume that R and S have some common attributes,[9] and let X be that set of common attributes. That is, $R \cap S = X$. The join of r and s, denoted by $r\,Join\,s$, is a new relation whose attributes are the elements of $R \cup S$. In addition, for *every tuple* t of the $r\,Join\,s$ relation, the following three conditions need to be satisfied simultaneously: (1) $t(R) = t_r$ for some tuple t_r of the relation r, (2) $t(S) = t_s$ for some tuple t_s of the relation s, and (3) $t_s(X) = t_r(X)$. The next example illustrates how this operator works.

---

[8] This type of join is also called a *natural join*.

[9] "Common attributes" are not required to have identical names in both tables. However, their underlying meaning and their domains must be the same.

EXAMPLE 1.9

Join the tables shown below on their common attribute DEPT. Write a possible user's request that can be satisfied by the result of this operation. Can these tables be joined on the attribute ID?

DEPARTMENT

ID	DEPT	LOCATION
100	Accounting	Miami
200	Marketing	New York
300	Sales	Miami

EMPLOYEE

ID	NAME	DEPT	TITLE
100	Smith	Sales	Clerk
200	Jones	Marketing	Clerk
300	Martin	Accounting	Clerk
400	Bell	Accounting	Sr. Accountant

The common attribute in this case is the DEPT. The join of these two tables, denoted by DEPARTMENT **Join** EMPLOYEE, is shown below. Since both tables have an attribute called ID, to avoid confusing the attribute ID of the DEPARTMENT table with the attribute ID of the EMPLOYEE table, it is necessary to qualify each attribute by preceding it with its corresponding table name before joining the tables. Observe that this is consistent with the requirement that in any table the column names must be different. Notice that the common column was not duplicated. The results of this join operation could be used to satisfy a user's request to "display all the information about the employees along with their department's ID, name, and location."

DEPARTMENT **Join** EMPLOYEE

DEPARTMENT ID	DEPT NAME	LOCATION	EMPLOYEE ID	EMPLOYEE NAME	TITLE
100	Accounting	Miami	300	Martin	Clerk
100	Accounting	Miami	400	Bell	Sr. Accountant
200	Marketing	New York	200	Jones	Clerk
300	Sales	Miami	100	Smith	Clerk

The tables DEPARTMENT and EMPLOYEE cannot be joined on the attribute `ID` because the attribute `ID` of the EMPLOYEE table and the attribute `ID` of the DEPARTMENT table have different meanings. One is an employee's ID, while the other is a department's ID. This illustrates the fact that two tables cannot be joined just because they have attributes with the same name. To join two tables on their common attributes, these attributes need to have same domain and the same meaning.

We will defer any further discussion of the relational operators until Chapter 2 when we will consider their implementation in SQL.

1.6 Attribute Domains and Their Implementations

As indicated before, the domain of an attribute defines the characteristics of the values that a table column may contain. In any RDBMS, the domain of any given attribute is implemented using a data type. The Standard SQL language names and defines a set of basic data types. These data types, although supported by most of the RDBMS vendors, have implementation details that vary from vendor to vendor. Therefore, it is recommended that the user consult the appropriate SQL reference manual to verify the characteristics of the data types implemented by the RDBMS vendor. Table 1-1 shows some of the basic SQL data types and their implementations for selected RDBMS vendors.

Table 1-1. Some Standard SQL data types and some of the RDBMS vendor's implementations.

Standard SQL	Oracle	Access	DB2
Character(n)—n is number of characters.	**Char(n)**— Fixed length with up to 255 characters maximum.	**Text**—Fixed length with up to 255 characters maximum.	**Character(n)**—same as Oracle Char(n).
Character varying (n)—n characters. Storage fits the size of content.	**Varchar2(n)**— Varying length with up to 2000 characters maximum.	**Text**—Varying length up to 255 characters max or **Memo** varying length up to 64,000 characters maximum.	**Varchar(n)**—Same as Oracle varchar2(n).
Float (p), where **p** is total number of digits.	**Number**—Ranges from 1.0×10^{-130} to 38 9s followed by 88 0s.	**Single or Double**— Depending on range of data values.	**Float**—same as Oracle number.
Decimal(p,s)—at least **p** digits with s defined by vendor.	**Number(p,s) p**— Ranges from 1 to 38, whereas s ranges from −84 to 127.	**Integer or Long Integer**—Depending on range of data values.	**Integer**—same as Oracle number(38).

Columns of data type **Character**(n) or **Character varying**(n), where n is the maximum number of characters that can be stored in the column, are generally used for data containing text or numbers that are not involved in calculations. Examples of this data type are names, addresses, social security numbers, and telephone numbers. The primary difference between the Character(n) and Character varying(n) data types is how they store strings (sequences of characters) shorter than the maximum column length. When a string with fewer than n characters is stored in a Character(n) column, the RDBMS pads blank spaces to the end of the string to create a string that has exactly n characters. When a string with fewer than n characters is stored in a Character varying(n) column, the RDBMS stores the string "as is," and it does not pad it with blank spaces. For this reason, if we know that the contents of a character column may vary in length, it is better to define the column as character varying, since the RDBMS can store this information more efficiently. Text data, whether it is stored as fixed or varying type, is always case-sensitive. For example, the string "abc" is different than the string "aBc". Likewise, the strings " xyz" and "xyz" are different, since the first begins with a pair of blank spaces.

Columns of type **Float**(n), where n is the total numbers of digits, are generally used to represent large numerical quantities or scientific computations. For example, we can use float data types to represent numbers in the range between 1.0×10^{-10} and $1.0 \times 10^{+10}$.

Columns of type **Decimal**(p,s) are used to represent fixed-point numbers. The *precision*, p, is the total number of digits both to the right and to the left of the decimal point. The *scale*, s, is the number of decimal digits to the right of the decimal point. When the number we are representing is a whole number, the scale is set equal to zero. An example of this data type is the number 123.23 that can be specified as Decimal(5,2). Another example is the number 125 that can be specified as Decimal(3,0).

Although not shown on Table 1-1, another data type that is commonly used by all RDBMS is **DATE**. This data type allows users to store date and time information. The date is generally displayed in the default format DD-MM-YY, where *DD* stands for a day, *MM* stands for a month, and *YY* stands for a year. In Chapter 6, we will consider some of the built-in functions used to manipulate date/time information.

1.7 Name Conventions for Database Objects

Database objects, including table names and attribute names, must obey certain rules or conventions that may vary from one RDBMS to another. Failing to follow the naming conventions of a particular RDBMS may cause errors. However, users are generally "safe" if they stay within the following guidelines:

- Names can be from 1 to 30 (64 in MS Access) characters long, with the exception that the database's names may be limited to 8 characters, as is the case of any Oracle database.

- Names must begin with a letter (lower- or uppercase); the remaining characters can be any combination of upper- or lowercase letters, digits, or the underscore character.

1.8   Structure of SQL Statements and SQL Writing Guidelines

Any SQL statement or command is a combination of one or more clauses. *Clauses* are, in general, introduced by keywords. An example of an SQL statement is shown in Fig. 1-2. At this moment, the reader should not be concerned with the inner workings of this statement but only with its structural aspects.

SELECT column-name-1, column-name-2,…column-name-N
FROM table-name
WHERE Boolean-condition
ORDER BY column-name [ASC | DESC][, column-name [ASC | DESC]….];

Fig. 1-2.   Keywords and clauses in the structure of an SQL statement.

In this SQL statement, we can distinguish four keywords and four clauses. The keywords are shown in bold in Fig. 1-2. As indicated before, a keyword is a word that has a specific meaning within the language. Using a keyword other than in its specific context will generate errors. The four clauses of this SQL statement are underlined in Fig. 1-2. Notice that each clause starts with a keyword.[10]

In the preceding statement, the first two clauses (SELECT and FROM) are mandatory and the last two (WHERE and ORDER BY) are optional. When describing the syntax of SQL statements, we will indicate optional keywords or clauses by enclosing them in square brackets. Using this convention, we can rewrite the preceding statement as shown in Fig. 1-3.

SELECT column-name-1, column-name-2,…column-name-N
FROM table-name
[WHERE condition]
[**ORDER BY** column-name [ASC | DESC][, column-name [ASC | DESC]….]];

Fig. 1-3.   Mandatory and optional clauses explicitly indicated in an SQL statement

Notice that in the ORDER BY clause, we have enclosed in square brackets the words ASC and DESC separated by a "|" character. This character, sometimes called a *pipe*, is used to separate the different options that a user can choose

---

[10] Appendix B shows a partial list of SQL keywords.

when writing an SQL statement. The user can choose one and only one from each set of options. Notice also that we have underlined the word <u>ASC</u>. This indicates that this word is a *default value*—that is, a value that will be used by the system when the user does not choose a different option from the set of available choices. In Fig. 1-2, whenever the ORDER BY clause is used and the user does not choose the DESC option, the RDBMS will use the ASC option by default.

When writing SQL statements or commands, it is useful to follow certain rules and guidelines to improve the readability of the statements and to facilitate their editing if necessary. Some of the guidelines that the reader should keep in mind are as follows:

- SQL statements are not case-sensitive. However, keywords that start a clause are generally written in uppercase to improve readability of the SQL statements.

- SQL statements can be written in one or more lines. It is customary to write each clause in its own line.

- Keywords cannot be split across lines and, with very few exceptions, cannot be abbreviated.

- SQL statements end in a semicolon. This semicolon must follow the last clause of the statement, but it does not have to be in the same line.

1.9   Interacting with the Oracle RDBMS through SQL*Plus

As we indicated before, in this book we will concentrate primarily on interactive SQL. Therefore, it is necessary to work with a particular RDBMS that allows the user to enter and execute SQL statements. In this book, we've decided to use Personal Oracle version 8i (PO8) as the main RDBMS. Personal Oracle is a PC version of the full Oracle RDBMS. PO8 was selected because Oracle is widely used across industry and academia and because PO8 can be downloaded for free directly from the Oracle Corporation website (www.oracle.com). At this point, you should already be familiar with the contents of Appendix A, which explains the login procedure to PO8. However, if this is not the case, keep in mind that most of the concepts in this book, with the exception of Appendix E, are very general and apply to most versions of SQL.

The tool that allows us to interact with PO8 is SQL*Plus. This is a tool of the Oracle RDBMS (the server) that recognizes and executes SQL statements. SQL*Plus is neither an extension nor a superset of SQL. However, SQL*Plus includes additional commands to control environment settings, access remote databases, and perform other general functions that facilitates formatting query results and reporting. Fig. 1-4 shows how SQL*Plus interacts with PO8.

From a syntactical point of view, there are no differences between SQL and SQL*Plus commands. However, there is a practical difference that allows us to differentiate between these two types of commands. All SQL commands that the

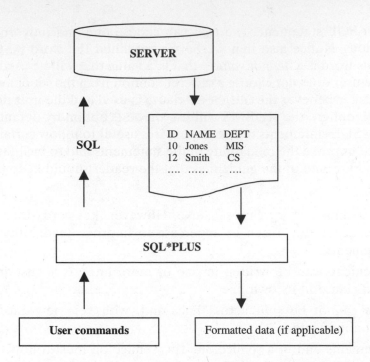

Fig. 1-4.   Interacting with the Oracle server using SQL*Plus.

user types go into a memory area known as the *SQL buffer*. None of the SQL*Plus commands are stored into the SQL buffer. The SQL*Plus command that allows us to view the content of the SQL buffer is the `list` command, or `l` for short. SQL commands are stored one command at a time in the SQL buffer. A single command remains in the SQL buffer until a new command is entered. Unlike SQL commands, SQL*Plus commands do not need to end in a semicolon. After typing a command, the user needs to press the Enter key to execute it. Since it is very easy to forget to type the semicolon after the last clause of the command, the user can execute the command stored in the buffer by typing a single slash followed by the Enter key.

Unless otherwise stated, all database objects in this book will be created using SQL*Plus and PO8.

1.10   Creating Tables

In any RDBMS, tables are the basic unit of data storage. Tables hold all of the user-accessible data. To create a table, it is necessary to name the table and all the attributes that compose it. In addition, for every attribute, the user needs to define its data type and, if necessary, the appropriate constraint or constraints. The name of the table identifies it as a unique object within the RDBMS.[11]

---

[11] Formally, it defines the table as a unique object within the user's tablespace or schema or within the entire system, depending upon whether or not the table has been defined as public.

Column or attribute names serve to differentiate the attributes from one another. Attribute names must be unique within the table. The data type of each attribute defines the characteristics of its underlying domain. The constraint or constraints that may be defined for a column impose conditions that need to be satisfied by all the values stored in the column.

Tables in SQL are created using the **CREATE TABLE** statement or command. Fig. 1-5 shows the basic form of this command. Additional features of the CREATE TABLE command will be examined in Chapter 2. Appendix C shows the syntax diagrams of the subset of the SQL language used in this book. The reader is encouraged to consult this appendix to study additional elements of the SQL language. In this section, we will assume that every time a table is created, there is no other table by the same name previously created by the same user in his or her *schema*.[12] In the database lingo, tables created by a user are said to be "owned" by the user.

```
CREATE TABLE table-name
(
    column-name-1        data-type-1      [constraint],
    column-name-2        data-type-2      [constraint],
          .
    column-name-N        data-type-N      [constraint]
);
```

Fig. 1-5.   A basic syntax of the CREATE TABLE command.

When describing the syntax of the CREATE TABLE command, we will call a *column definition line* every line of the form

```
        column-name         data type      [constraint],
```

where optional elements are enclosed in square brackets. Therefore, according to this notation, every column definition line requires a column name and a data type. Constraints are optional. Usually, when typing a CREATE TABLE command, each column definition line is written in a separate line for readability. Commas separate column definition lines except for the last line that is followed by a parenthesis. As with any other SQL command, a semicolon follows the closing parenthesis.

The SQL standard requires that, whenever a constraint is defined, the constraint be given a name. Constraints can be named explicitly by the user at the time a table is created or modified. Otherwise, the constraint is named

---

[12] This term refers to a collection of logical structures of data or schema objects. Each user owns a single schema whose name is that of its owner. Any user, with the appropriate privileges, can create objects in his or her own schema. Some schema objects are tables, synonyms, indexes, sequences, and views.

internally by the RDBMS. Constraints that are named by the user are called *named constraints*. Constraints named by the RDBMS are vendor-dependent and are called *unnamed constraints*. Although constraint names can follow the conventions indicated in Section 1.7, we will use the following format for *named* constraints:

CONSTRAINT table-name-column-name-suffix

where the clause CONSTRAINT is *mandatory* and the suffix is a one- or two-letter sequence that indicates the type of the constraint. Table 1-2 shows a list of the suffixes that we will use in this book. Unnamed constraints *must not* be preceded by the CONSTRAINT clause.

Table 1-2.   Suffix conventions for named constraints.

SUFFIX	MEANING
PK	Primary key
FK	Foreign key
NN	Not NULL
U	Unique

Some of the constraints that we will consider in this chapter are shown in Table 1-3. A constraint defined as part of a column definition is called a *column constraint*. This type of constraint can be used to impose a single condition on the column in which it is defined. A constraint that is part of a table definition is called a *table constraint*. This type of constraint can be used to define more than one constraint on any column of the table. We will consider table constraints in Chapter 2.

Table 1-3.   Basic column and table constraints.

CONSTRAINT	DEFINITION
NOT NULL (*)	Prevents NULL values from being entered into a column.
UNIQUE (**)	Prevents duplicate values from being entered into a column.
PRIMARY KEY (***)	Requires that all values entered into the column be unique and different than NULL.

* column_constraint.
** column_constraint or table constraint depending upon whether or not it is applied to one or more columns respectively.
*** column_constraint when defining a single PK and a table_constraint when defining a composite PK.

EXAMPLE 1.10
Create the table Calling_ Card with the attributes and assumptions indicated below. Choose the most appropriate data types. *Attributes*: Company_Name, Card_Number, Starting_Value, Value_Left, and Pin_Number.
Assumptions: The attribute Company_Name may have up to 25 characters. The attributes Value_Left and Original_Value are measured in dollars and cents. The attribute Card_Number may have up to 15 digits. The Pin_Number attribute is always 12 characters long. The SQL instruction to create the Calling_Card table is as follows:

```
CREATE TABLE Calling_Card
( Company_Name          VARCHAR2(25),
  Card_Number           VARCHAR2(15),
  Starting_Value        NUMBER(4,2),
  Value_Left            NUMBER(4,2),
  Pin_Number            CHAR(12)
);
```

The attribute Company_Name is obviously of type character. Since not all company names are 25 characters long, the data type of this column is VARCHAR2(25). The Card_Number and Pin_Number columns are both of character type because they are not involved in any type of computation. Since Card_Number may vary in length, its data type is VARCHAR2(15). The data type of Pin_Number is CHAR(12), since this column has a fixed length. The Starting_Value and Value_Left columns are both numerical quantities that may have up to four digits with two decimals. Observe the use of the underscore character to improve the readability of the attribute names.

EXAMPLE 1.11
Rewrite the CREATE TABLE of the previous example with the attribute Card_Number defined as the primary key and the attribute Pin_Number defined as unique. Use unnamed constraints.

In this case, we may use a column constraint to define the attribute Card_Number as the PK. By definition of PK, this attribute is also UNIQUE, and therefore it is not necessary to define it as such. The attribute Pin_Number is only defined as a UNIQUE attribute. The reader should be aware that these two constraints behave a little bit differently. The PRIMARY KEY constraint, in addition to requiring that the values be unique, also guarantees that the values of the Card_Number column cannot be NULL. The UNIQUE constraint of the Pin_Number column does not allow duplicate values in this column, but it does allow NULL values. The new CREATE TABLE command is as follows.

```
CREATE TABLE Calling_Card
( Company_Name          VARCHAR2(25),
  Card_Number           VARCHAR2(15) PRIMARY KEY,
  Starting_Value        NUMBER(4,2),
  Value_Left            NUMBER(4,2),
  Pin_Number            CHAR(12) UNIQUE
);
```

EXAMPLE 1.12

Rewrite the CREATE TABLE of the previous example using named constraints.

Following the convention for naming constraints and using the suffixes of Table 1-2, the constraints associated with the attributes Card_Number and Pin_Number are, respectively, calling_card_card_number_PK and calling_card_pin_number_U.

The corresponding CREATE TABLE command is as follows:

```
CREATE TABLE Calling_Card
(Company_Name       VARCHAR2(25),
 Card_Number        VARCHAR2(15) CONSTRAINT
                    calling_card_card_number_PK
                    PRIMARY KEY,
 Starting_Value     NUMBER(4,2),
 Value_Left         NUMBER(4,2),
 Pin_Number         CHAR(12) CONSTRAINT
                    calling_card_pin_number_U
                    UNIQUE);
```

Notice that the column definition for the attributes Card_Number and Pin_Number have been written in more than one line to fit the width of this page.

1.11   Describing the Structure of a Table

After a table has been created, it may be necessary to determine the name, data type, and some of the constraints of the attributes that compose the table. The SQL*Plus command that allows us to find out this information is the DESCRIBE command. The syntax of this command is as follows:

DESCRIBE table-name

EXAMPLE 1.13

Describe the structure of the table Calling_Card.

The statement that allows us to satisfy this request is as follows:

$$\textbf{DESCRIBE } \texttt{Calling\_Card}$$

The output of this command is

```
Name                         Null?              Type
--------------------         ----------         --------------------
COMPANY_NAME                                    VARCHAR2(25)
CARD_NUMBER                  NOT NULL           VARCHAR2(15)
STARTING_VALUE                                  NUMBER(4,2)
VALUE_LEFT                                      NUMBER(4,2)
PIN_NUMBER                   UNIQUE             CHAR(12)
```

The output of the `DESCRIBE Calling_Card` command consists of three columns: `Name`, `Null?`, and `Type`. The `Name` column contains the name of the different attributes of the table. The `Null?` column indicates whether or not the attribute can accept NULL values. The `Type` column describes the data type of the attributes of the table.

1.12   Populating Tables

After creating a table, the user may add rows to the table using the **INSERT INTO** command. The process of adding rows to a table for the first time is called *populating the table*. In its simplest form, this command allows the user to add rows to a table *one row* at a time. Fig. 1-6 shows the basic syntax of this command. Solved Problem 1.27 considers another variation of this basic form of the INSERT INTO statement. Later on in the book, we will consider another form of this command that will allow us to insert multiple rows from one table into another. (See Chapter 7.)

```
INSERT INTO table-name (column-1, column-2,...column-N)
VALUES (value-1, value-2,...value-N);
```

Fig. 1-6.   Basic form of the INSERT statement.

In Fig. 1-6, `column-1, column-2,...column-N` are the table's columns, and `value-1, value-2, value-3,...value-N` are the values that will be inserted into their corresponding columns. Notice that the value to be inserted into a column must be of the same data type that was specified for that column when its table was created. It is important to keep in mind that we *must* specify a value in the VALUES clause for each column that appears in the column list.

EXAMPLE 1.14
Insert into the Calling_Card table the data indicated below.

Company_Name, Card_Number, Starting_Value, Value_Left, Pin Number

ACME	1237096435	20.00	12.45	987234569871
Phone Card, Inc	5497443544	15.00	11.37	433809835833

Since the basic form of the INSERT INTO command only allows the insertion of one row at a time, it is necessary to use two consecutive INSERT INTO commands to add these two tuples to the Calling_Card table. Notice that all character data has been enclosed in single quotes.

```
INSERT INTO Calling_Card (Company_Name, Card_Number,
                          Starting_Value,Value_Left,Pin_Number)
VALUES ('ACME', '1237096435', 20.00, 12.45, '987234569871');

INSERT INTO Calling_Card (Company_Name, Card_Number, '
                          Starting_Value,Value_Left,Pin_Number)
VALUES ('Phone Card, Inc', '5497443544', 15.00, 11.37,
'433809835833');
COMMIT;
```

The COMMIT command that follows the last INSERT INTO command is necessary to make the changes to the table permanently. The COMMIT command will be explained in the next section.

The reader should be aware that the order of the columns following the INTO clause is immaterial provided that their corresponding values appear in the same order in the VALUES clause. This allows us to fill in the columns of a row in any order. Example 1.15 illustrates this.

EXAMPLE 1.15
Insert into the Calling_Card table the rows shown below, and fill in the columns
in the following sequence: Pin_Number, Card_Number, Company_Name,
Starting_Value, and Value_Left.

Company_Name, Card_Number, Starting_Value, Value_Left, Pin_Number

ACM	2137096435	20.00	20.00	125234569871
Mobile Phone, Inc	3817443544	20.00	20.00	632809835833

As in the previous example, we need two consecutive INSERT statements to add these rows to the Calling_Card table. The new INSERT statements are as follows:

```
INSERT INTO Calling_Card (Pin_Number,Card_Number,Company_Name,
                          Starting_Value,Value_Left)
VALUES ('125234569871', '2137096435', 'ACM', 20.00,
        20.00);

INSERT INTO Calling_Card (Pin_Number, Card_Number,Company_Name,
                          Starting_Value,Value_Left)
VALUES ('632809835833', '3817443544', 'Mobile Phone, Inc',
        20.00, 20.00);
COMMIT;
```

1.13　The COMMIT and ROLLBACK Commands

To make permanent all changes made to a table through the use of an INSERT, UPDATE, or DELETE operation, the user needs to commit these changes. The instruction that allows a user to record these changes permanently into the database is the COMMIT statement. The basic syntax of this statement is this:

COMMIT [WORK];

Notice that the keyword WORK is optional.

The reader should be aware that prior to the execution of a COMMIT command, all changes made to the rows of a table are stored in a *database buffer* or working storage area in main memory. If, for some reason, the user quits the database *before* committing the changes, no data will be written to the database files and the changes will be lost. If the user making changes to a table is working in a multi-user environment and this table is shared by other users, no changes made to the table will be accessible to the other user unless the person making the changes issues a COMMIT command. This happens because whenever a user modifies the rows of a table, he or she has exclusive access to these rows *until* the changes have been committed. By "exclusive access of a row," we mean that no other user can view the current contents of the row that have been changed. The affected rows are said to be *locked*. At this time, any other user accessing the same table will not notice that the table has changed. When the user commits the changes, the modified rows are written to the database files and the locks on all affected rows are released. Users whose transactions started *after* the data was committed can view the modified rows with their new content.

Assuming that the changes made to a table (insertions, updates, or deletions) have not been committed, the user can cancel all the intermediates changes made to a table by issuing a **ROLLBACK** statement or by ending the session. These actions cause the RDBMS to ignore all changes made to any table or any other database object since the last commit or since the user began his or her interactive session.

Technically, a **ROLLBACK** statement is used to cancel or terminate the current transaction. A *transaction* is a *logical unit of work* that, in general, involves several database operations. *All operations of a transaction succeed or fail as a group*. In other words, if one operation fails, then *all* operations fail. In this sense, the transactions are said to be *atomic*. In addition to this, transactions are said to be *durable*. What this implies is that once a transaction is committed, the changes made to the tuples are guaranteed to be written to the database files even if there are system failures. A transaction begins with the first executable SQL statement after a COMMIT, a ROLLBACK, or a connection to the database. A transaction ends after a COMMIT, a ROLLBACK, or a disconnection from the database. Most databases issue an implicit COMMIT statement after processing a DDL statement.

Sometimes it is desirable to go back to a particular point in time during an interactive session. For instance, we can imagine a user that has made several uncommitted changes to a table and realizes that the last few changes are incorrect or unnecessary. If at this moment the user issues a ROLLBACK statement, all changes made to the table will be ignored, including the changes that were correct. It would be nice if the user could go back to a prior state of the database buffer right before where he or she began making the incorrect changes. The SQL command that can be used to accomplish this is the SAVEPOINT command.

A *savepoint* identifies a point in the transaction to which we can go back to (i.e., roll back), provided that the transaction has not been committed. In this sense, we can think of a SAVEPOINT statement as a "bookmarker" within the database buffer. Savepoints allow us to undo only a part of the current transaction by allowing the user to go back to a particular point in time.

The basic form of this statement is as follows:

SAVEPOINT savepoint-name;

where savepoint_name is a unique name within the transaction. Generally, savepoint names are single letters, but they can be longer. Savepoints follow the same naming rules of any other object in the database. Savepoints are useful in interactive programming because they give the user some degree of control over the execution of the program. To go back to a previous and uncommitted state of the database buffer, it is necessary to issue the following command:

ROLLBACK savepoint-name;
Or
ROLLBACK TO SAVEPOINT savepoint-name;

Fig. 1-7 illustrates the combined use of the SAVEPOINT and ROLLBACK commands. The sequence of actions depicted in Fig. 1-7 shows the effect of rolling back to a savepoint. In this case, we assume that the user begins the operation by issuing a SAVEPOINT A command. The user then inserts a new tuple and issues a SAVEPOINT B command. The process continues, and the user deletes the first tuple of the table and issues a SAVEPOINT C command. Finally, the user issues a ROLLBACK TO SAVEPOINT A command. Notice that the effect of ROLLBACK TO SAVEPOINT A is to return the table to the state that it had when the user issued the SAVEPOINT A command. By rolling back to savepoint A, the user has ignored all changes made to the table after issuing the SAVEPOINT A command.

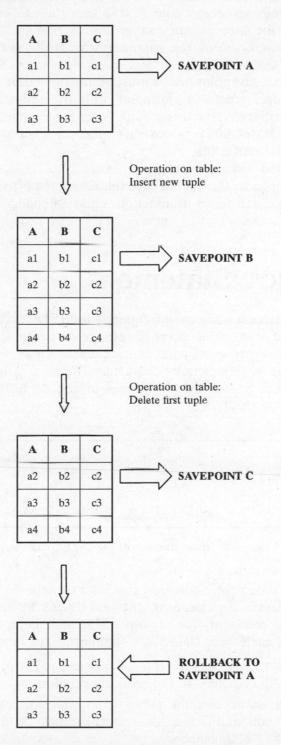

Fig. 1-7.   SAVEPOINT and ROLLBACK TO SAVEPOINT statements.

Obviously, this example assumes that the user never issued a COMMIT statement between savepoint A and savepoint C. Had the user committed the data after savepoint C, it would have been impossible for the user to return to any of the previous savepoints A or B. It is important to keep in mind that, at the same time, the user cannot change his or her mind after returning to savepoint A. That is, he or she cannot return (roll forward) to any of the savepoints B or C.

Also notice that savepoint names must be unique within a given transaction. Whenever the user creates a savepoint with the same name of an earlier savepoint, the earlier savepoint is erased. After the changes are committed, the user can reuse any of the previous savepoint names, provided that they are unique within the transaction.

As we indicated before, when a user issues a ROLLBACK command without the SAVEPOINT clause, the net effect of this command is to end the transaction, erase all SAVEPOINTS in the transaction, undo all changes in the transaction, and release any locks.

1.14   The SELECT Statement

The SELECT statement is the most frequently used SQL statement. The SELECT statement is used primarily to *query* or retrieve data from the database. For this reason, it is customarily to call a SELECT statement a *query*. In this book, we will refer to any SELECT statement by this name. The basic syntax of this statement is shown in Fig. 1-8. Additional features of the SELECT statement will be considered in later chapters.

```
SELECT column-1, column-2, column-3,...,column-N
FROM table-1,..., table-N
[WHERE condition]
[ORDER BY column-1 [ASC|DESC][,column-2 [ASC|DESC]...]];
```

Fig. 1-8.   Basic structure of the SELECT statement.

The SELECT statement is formed by at least two clauses: the **SELECT** clause and the **FROM** clause. The clauses **WHERE** and **ORDER BY** are optional. Observe that the SELECT statement, like any other SQL statement, ends in a semicolon. The functions of each these clauses are summarized as follows:

- The **SELECT** clause lists the columns to display. The attributes listed in this clause are the columns of the resulting relation.

- The **FROM** clause lists the tables from which to obtain the data. The columns mentioned in the SELECT clause must be columns of the tables listed in the FROM clause.

- The **WHERE** clause specifies the condition or conditions that need to be

satisfied by the rows of the tables indicated in the FROM clause.
- The **ORDER BY** clause indicates the criterion or criteria used to sort rows that satisfy the WHERE clause. The ORDER BY clause only affects the display of the data retrieved, not the internal ordering of the rows within the tables.

As a mnemonic aid to the basic structure of the SELECT statement, some authors summarize its functionality by saying that "you **SELECT** columns **FROM** tables **WHERE** the rows satisfy certain condition, and the result is **ORDERED BY** specific columns."

The WHERE clause is what gives real power to the SELECT command, since it provides the ability to display data that meets a specified condition. For instance, you might want to print out all the names of people in a certain zip code area, or you might want to see the names of all employees that work for a given department. The condition that accompanies the WHERE clause defines the criterion to be met. The types of condition that we consider in this chapter are of the following form:

```
Column-name   comparison-operator   single-value
```

Column-name is the name of one of the columns of the table indicated in the FROM clause. The comparison-operator is one of the operators shown in Table 1-4. By single-value, we mean a numeric quantity or a character string. In Chapter 3 we will consider more-complex queries using compound conditions using the Boolean operators AND, OR, and NOT.

Table 1-4.   Comparison operators for the WHERE clause.

Comparison Operator	Description
=	equal to
<>	not equal to
<	less than
<=	less than or equal to
>	greater than
>=	greater than or equal to

The following example illustrates the use of the SELECT command.

EXAMPLE 1.16
Using the EMPLOYEE table of Example 1.9, display the name and title of all the employees who work in the accounting department.

To retrieve this data from the EMPLOYEE table, we use the following statement:

```
SELECT name, title, dept        Columns to display
FROM employee                 Table from which to retrieve the data
WHERE dept = 'Accounting';        Criterion to be satisfied
```

The resulting table is as follows:

NAME	TITLE	DEPT
Martin	Clerk	Accounting
Bell	Sr. Accountant	Accounting

Notice that in the resulting table the attribute names and their corresponding values are displayed in the same order in which they were listed in the SELECT statement. All the retrieved tuples satisfy the condition indicated in the WHERE clause. That is, for any tuple t of the resulting relation, t(DEPT) = Accounting. Observe that the rows retrieved are not sorted by alphabetical name. However, if we want to display the table with the names ordered alphabeticallly, we can proceed as indicated in Example 1.17. Observe also that in the SELECT clause the attribute names are not case-sensitive. That is, we can write the attributes in either lower- or uppercase and obtain the same result. However, the condition indicated in the WHERE clause requires some consideration. Since dept is a character column, the condition has been enclosed in single quotes. In addition, we need to remember that character data is case-sensitive. Had the condition of the WHERE clause be written as DEPT = 'ACCOUNTING', then no tuple would have satisfied it. Observe that the strings 'Accounting' and 'ACCOUNTING' are different strings.

EXAMPLE 1.17
Display the result of the previous query in alphabetical order by the employee's name.

In this case, the SELECT statement needs to indicate to the RDBMS that the results need to be sorted in alphabetical order. Since we want to sort the resulting table according to the attribute NAME, it is necessary to mention this attribute in the ORDER BY clause. By default, the sorting of rows is done in ascending order[13] according to the column or columns that defines the order—in this case, the attribute NAME. The SELECT statement to accomplish the desired result is shown next.

---

[13] By "ascending order," we mean from lower values to higher values according to the coalescence sequence of the ASCII characters.

```
SELECT name, title, dept
FROM employee
WHERE dept = 'Accounting'
ORDER BY name;
```

The resulting table is shown here:

NAME	TITLE	DEPT
Bell	Sr. Accountant	Accounting
Martin	Clerk	Accounting

The rows of this table have been sorted in
alphabetical order by last name.

1.15   The Sample Database

In the remainder of this chapter, unless otherwise stated we will be working with
the Sporting Goods (SG) database. The scripts to create two different versions
of this database in Oracle are shown in Appendix D. This database is based on
the Sporting Goods database frequently used in the training courses offered by
the Oracle Corporation. The modified version of the SG database has been
reproduced with permission of the Oracle Corporation.

The Sporting Goods is an American wholesale company that operates
worldwide to fill orders of retail stores specializing in sporting goods. The
customers of the company are both domestic and international. Each customer
is assigned a unique identification number. For each customer or client, the
company must keep track of the store name and phone number. Some additional
information that may be kept for each customer includes his or her address, city,
state, country, zip code, credit rating, and general comments about customer
preferences. In general, customers place their orders by phone or fax. For each
order, the company needs to track its identification number, the date ordered,
and the type of payment. The date the order is shipped to the customer needs
to be kept in the database. To speed up the process of all incoming orders,
customers are assigned to specific regions of the world. Currently, there are six
different regions: Central America/Caribbean, North America, South America,
Africa/Middle East, Asia, and Europe. Every region has a unique name and
identification number. Each region has a warehouse from which the products are
shipped to the customer. For every warehouse, SG keeps track of its identification number and some additional information that may include the address, city,
state, country, zip code, manager ID, and phone number. For each item that the
company has in stock, it is necessary to track its unique identification number.
In addition to this information, SG may also track the item price, quantity

ordered, and the quantity shipped. To increase customer satisfaction, SG maintains a specialty product line. For each of these products, SG must know its unique product identification number and its name. Occasionally, it is necessary to have a short description of a product, its suggested price, and the unit sale.

The company has several employees or sales representatives to attend to its customers' requests. Employees may be assigned to more than one region. For every employee, the company maintains information about first name, last name, unique identification number, and his or her computer user ID. Additional information about employees may include the date the employee started working for the company, comments, title, salary, and the commission percent. For each warehouse and the products that it stores, SG maintains an inventory that may include the amount in stock for each product, the reorder point, the maximum number that can be in stock at any one time, the restock date, and an out-of-stock explanation when necessary. Tables 1-5 through 1-13 describe the attributes of the tables that compose the SG database and the constraints imposed on these attributes.

1.15.1   TABLES OF THE SPORTING GOODS DATABASE

Table 1-5.   Attributes of the S_customer table.

Column Name	Description/Data Type
Id	Customer unique identification number. Maximum is 3 characters.
Name	Name of the customer. Maximum is 20 characters.
Phone	Telephone number of customer. Maximum is 20 characters.
Address	Address of customer. Maximum is 20 characters.
City	City where customer is located. Maximum is 20 characters.
State	State where customer resides. Maximum is 15 characters.
Country	Country where customer resides. Maximum is 20 characters.
Zip_code	Zip code of customer. Maximum is 15 characters.
Credit_rating	Credit standing of customer. Maximum is 9 characters.
Sales_rep_id	Sales representative of customer. Maximum is 3 characters.
Region_id	Region in which the country of the customer is located. Maximum is 3 characters.
Comments	Product preferences of customer. Maximum is 255 characters.

Table 1-6.   Attributes of the S_dept table.

Column Name	Description/Data Type
Id	Unique identification number assigned to each department. Maximum is 3 characters.
Name	Name of the department. Maximum is 20 characters.
Region_id	Region ID in which the department is located. Maximum is 3 characters.

Table 1-7.   Attributes of the S_emp table.

Column Name	Description/Data Type
Id	Unique identification number assigned to each employee. Maximum is 3 characters.
Last_name	Last name of employee. Maximum is 20 characters.
First_name	First name of employee. Maximum is 20 characters.
Userid	Login ID of employee. Maximum is 8 characters.
Start_date	Date in which employee started working in the company. Date data type.
Comments	Information about employee. Maximum is 25 characters.
Manager_id	ID of the employee's manager. Maximum is 3 characters.
Title	Title of the employee in the company. Maximum is 25 characters.
Dept_id	ID of the employee's department. Maximum is 3 characters.
Salary	Salary of the employee. 11 digits including 2 decimals.
Commision_pct	Percentage of commission earned by employee. 4 digits including 2 decimals.

Table 1-8.   Attributes of the S_region table.

Column Name	Description/Data Type
Id	Unique identification assigned to each region. Maximum is 3 characters.
Name	Unique name of each region. Maximum is 20 characters.

Table 1-9.   Attributes of the S_inventory table.

Column Name	Description/Data Type
Product_id	Unique identification number of the specialty product. Maximum is 7 characters.
Warehouse_id	ID of the warehouse where the product is stored. Maximum is 7 characters.
Amount_in_stock	Amount of items in stock. Maximum is 9 digits.
Reorder_point	Minimum number of items in stock before reordering. Maximum is 9 digits.
Max_in_stock	Maximum number in stock. Maximum is 9 digits.
Out_of_stock_explanation	Reason why product is not in stock. Maximum is 255 characters.
Restock_date	Date when product will be again in stock. Date data type.

Table 1-10.   Attributes of the S_item table.

Column Name	Description/Data Type
ord_id	ID of the order associated with this item. Maximum is 3 characters.
item_id	Unique identification number assigned to each item. Maximum is 7 characters.
Product_id	ID of the product associated with this item. Maximum is 7 characters.
Price	Price of item. Maximum is 11 digits including 2 decimals
Quantity	Quantity of this item. Maximum is 9 digits.
Quantity_shipped	Quantity shipped of this item on this order for a given product. Maximum is 9 digits.

Table 1-11.   Attributes of the S_product table.

Column Name	Description/Data Type
Id	Unique identification number assigned to each product. Maximum is 7 characters.
Name	Name of the product. Maximum is 25 characters.
Short_desc	Description of the product. Maximum is 255 characters.
Suggested_whlsl_price	Suggested wholesale price of product. Maximum is 11 digits including 2 decimals.
Whlsl_ units	Units of product for wholesale. Maximum is 10 characters.

Table 1-12.   Attributes of the S_warehouse table.

Column Name	Description/Data Type
Id	Unique identification number assigned to each warehouse. Maximum is 7 characters.
Region_id	Id of the region where the warehouse is located. Maximum is 3 characters.
Address	Address of the warehouse. Maximum is 20 characters.
City	City in which the warehouse is located. Maximum is 20 characters.
State	State in which the warehouse is located. Maximum is 15 characters.
Zip_code	Zip code of the city where the warehouse is located. Maximum is 15 characters.
Country	Country in which the warehouse is located. Maximum is 20 characters.
Phone	Telephone number of the warehouse. Maximum is 20 characters.
Manager_id	ID of the manager of the warehouse. Maximum is 3 characters.

Table 1-13.   Attributes of the S_ord table.

Column Name	Description/Data Type
Id	Unique identification number assigned to each order. Maximum is 3 characters.
Customer_id	Customer unique identification number. Maximum is 3 characters.
Date_ordered	Date in which order was placed. Date data type.
Date_shipped	Date in which order was shipped. Date data type.
Sales_rep_id	Unique identification number of sales representative that took the order. Maximum is 3 characters.
Total	Total amount of this order. Maximum is 11 digits, including 2 decimals.
Payment_type	Form of payment. Maximum is 6 characters.
Order_filled	Indicator of whether or not the order has been filled. Maximum is 1 character.

1.15.2 REFERENTIAL INTEGRITY CONSTRAINTS OF THE SG DATABASE

The referential integrity constraints that need to be satisfied by the tables of the SG database are shown in Table 1.14.

Table 1.14.   Integrity constraints of the SG database.

Table Name	Foreign Key	Referenced Attribute/Table
S_DEPT	region_id	id of table S_REGION
S_EMP	manager_id	id of table S_EMP
S_EMP	dept_id	id of table S_DEPT
S_EMP	title	title of table S_TITLE
S_CUSTOMER	sales_rep_id	id of table S_EMP
S_CUSTOMER	region_id	id of table S_REGION
S_ORD	customer_id	id of table S_CUSTOMER
S_ORD	sales_rep_id	id of table S_EMP
S_ITEM	ord_id	id of table S_ORD
S_ITEM	product_id	id of table S_PRODUCT
S_WAREHOUSE	manager_id	id of table S_EMP
S_WAREHOUSE	region_id	id of table S_REGION
S_INVENTORY	product_id	id of table S_PRODUCT
S_INVENTORY	warehouse_id	id of table S_WAREHOUSE

1.15.3 ADDITIONAL CONSTRAINTS OF THE SG DATABASE

The following constraints also hold in the SG database:

- The credit rating of a customer can only take the values of EXCELLENT, GOOD, or POOR.
- The combination of name and region_id should be unique in the S_DEPT table. This guarantees that departments are unique within regions.

- The commission percentage of any employee must be one of the following: 10, 12.5, 15, 17.5, and 20.
- The combination of attributes `product_id` and `warehouse_id` is unique within the table S_INVENTORY.

1.16   Updating and Deleting Rows of a Table

Sometimes it is necessary to modify the existing values of one or more rows in a table as a result of the normal activities that occur in a database. Remember that a database is intended to capture a representation of the real world and some of its dynamics.

1.16.1   THE UPDATE TABLE COMMAND

As the name of this command suggests, its primary function is to update the rows of a table. The basic syntax of this SQL command to update one or more values of a single row is as follows:

```
UPDATE table-name SET col-1 = new-val1 [...,...col-N = new-valN]
[WHERE condition];
```

where `col-1...,col-N` stand for column names and `new-val1,...new-valN` stand for the new values that will be stored in their corresponding columns. The WHERE clause allows us to change the values of selected rows. The following example illustrates the use of this command.

EXAMPLE 1.18
Assume that BJ Athletics has moved to a new location in Melbourne, Florida. The new address, zip code, and telephone number are 2905 Havens Avenue, 32901, and 407-345-1265, respectively. Update the information of the BJ Athletics retail store in the S_CUSTOMER table of the SG database.

To change the information of this client in the database, it is necessary to update its corresponding row in the S_CUSTOMER table. Since the user may or may not know or remember the attributes of this table, the user can describe the S_CUSTOMER table to determine its structure. The structure of this table is as follows:

```
DESC s_customer;

Name                          Null?          Type
--------------------          ----------     ----------------
ID                            NOT NULL       VARCHAR2(3)
NAME                          NOT NULL       VARCHAR2(20)
PHONE                         NOT NULL       VARCHAR2(20)
ADDRESS                                      VARCHAR2(20)
CITY                                         VARCHAR2(20)
STATE                                        VARCHAR2(15)
COUNTRY                                      VARCHAR2(20)
ZIP_CODE                                     VARCHAR2(15)
CREDIT_RATING                                VARCHAR2(9)
SALES_REP_ID                                 VARCHAR2(3)
REGION_ID                                    VARCHAR2(3)
COMMENTS                                     VARCHAR2(255)
```

The UPDATE command to reflect the new changes in the S_CUSTOMER table is shown next.

```
UPDATE s_customer SET
phone='407-345-1265',
address = '2905 Fairway Dr.',
city = 'Melbourne',
state='FL',
zip_code='32901'
WHERE name = 'BJ Athletics';
```

The user can verify that the changes are correct by issuing the following query:

```
SELECT phone, address, city, state, zip_code
FROM s_customer
WHERE name = 'BJ Athletics';
```

Notice that there was no need to inquire about any other attributes because no other values were changed.

The user needs to be careful when executing an UPDATE command, since it is very easy to make mistakes. For instance, had the user issued the following UPDATE command, the result would have been an incorrect update of all the rows of the S_CUSTOMER table.

```
UPDATE S_customer SET
phone='407-345-1265',
address = '2905 Fairway Dr.',
city = 'Melbourne',
state='FL',
zip_code='32901';
```

The reason for this is the failure to qualify the query with the appropriate WHERE clause. The user could have recovered from this error very easily by issuing a SAVEPOINT A command *prior* to executing the UPDATE. A simple ROLLBACK TO A command would have restored the table to its previous state. The authors encourage this practice of issuing SAVEPOINT commands prior to any table update.

1.16.2   THE DELETE AND THE TRUNCATE COMMANDS

As part of the normal operation, one or more rows may need to be removed or deleted from the database. For instance, in the SG database, a customer may go out of business or an employee may resign. The SQL command that allows the user to delete rows from a table is the DELETE command. This command can be used to remove rows that meet certain conditions, or it can be used to remove all rows from a particular table. The syntax of this command to remove rows that meet certain condition is shown here:

DELETE FROM table-name **WHERE** condition;

The syntax of the DELETE command to remove all rows of a table is as follows:

DELETE table-name;

EXAMPLE 1.19
Assume that a particular supplier is no longer producing the product whose ID is 32779. Remove this tuple from the table S_INVENTORY table.

Assuming that the only information that we have about this product is its product_id, the DELETE command to remove it from the database is as follows:

```
DELETE FROM s_inventory WHERE product_id= '32779';
```

The user has to be careful when executing this command because it is so easy to make a mistake and delete more rows than what was intended. For instance, if the user omits the WHERE clause in the previous DELETE command, then all the rows of the S_INVENTORY table are deleted.

The reader should be aware that it is not always possible to delete a particular row from a table, as the following example illustrates.

EXAMPLE 1.20
Assume that customer One Sport has gone out of business. Delete this customer from the S_CUSTOMER table.

Assuming that the only information that we have about this customer is its name, the command to delete it from the database is as follows:

```
DELETE FROM s_customer WHERE name = 'One Sport';
```

However, instead of deleting the corresponding rows from the S_CUS-TOMER table, the user gets an integrity violation error. The reason for this error is that the user is trying to delete a row that is referenced by the foreign key of another table. The general format of this type of error may look like this:

Manufacturer internal ID error number

```
ERROR AAAA integrity constraint (table_name_column_name_fk)
violated - child record found
```

To delete the One Sport customer, the user needs to use the DELETE or UPDATE commands to delete or update the corresponding foreign key. Deleting or adding an FK is a topic that we will consider in the next chapter. Therefore, we will postpone any further discussion of this topic until then.

An easier and faster way of removing *all* rows from a table is using the TRUNCATE command. The basic syntax of this command is as follows:

TRUNCATE TABLE table-name;

The reader should be aware that there are some limitations in the use of this command. First, we cannot truncate the rows of a table if there are referential integrity constraints for which this table is the parent table. Second, we cannot roll back a TRUNCATE statement. This limitation is illustrated in the next example.

EXAMPLE 1.21
Create a new set of tables running the script SG_NO_CONSTRAINTS.sql[14] (see Appendix D), and perform the following actions:
1. Display the titles stored in the table S_TITLE.
2. Create a savepoint called before_update.
3. Insert into the table S_TITLE the new title "Warehouse Inspector". Do not commit the changes.
4. Display the titles stored into the S_TITLE table.
5. Roll back to the savepoint before_update.
6. Display the titles stored into the S_TITLE table.
7. Create the savepoint before_truncate.
8. Truncate the S_TITLE table.
9. Insert into the table S_TITLE the new title "Warehouse Inspector". Do not commit the changes.
10. Roll back to the savepoint before_truncate.

This sequence of instructions produce the following results:

---

[14] This script is the same script that produces the SG database except that all the foreign constraints have been removed. Make sure to take the constraints out before running the script.

```
SQL> SELECT title FROM S_title;                          (1)

TITLE
--------------------------
President
Sales Representative
Stock Clerk
VP, Administration
VP, Finance
VP, Operations
VP, Sales                                        (2)
Warehouse Manager
8 rows selected.                                 (3)
SQL> SAVEPOINT before_update;
Savepoint created.
SQL> INSERT INTO S_title (title) VALUES('Warehouse Inspector');
1 row created.
SQL> SELECT title FROM S_title;                  (4)
TITLE
--------------------------
President
Sales Representative
Stock Clerk
VP, Administration
VP, Finance
VP, Operations
VP, Sales
Warehouse Manager
Warehouse Inspector
9 rows selected.
SQL> ROLLBACK TO SAVEPOINT before_update;        (5)
Rollback complete.
SQL> SELECT title FROM S_title;                  (6)
TITLE
--------------------------
President
Sales Representative
Stock Clerk
VP, Administration
VP, Finance
VP, Operations
VP, Sales
Warehouse Manager
8 rows selected.                                 (7)
SQL> SAVEPOINT before_truncate;                  (8)
Savepoint created.
SQL> TRUNCATE TABLE S_title;                     (9)
Table truncated.
SQL> INSERT INTO S_title (title) VALUES('Warehouse Inspector');
1 row created.
SQL> ROLLBACK TO before_truncate;                (10)
rollback to before_truncate
*
ERROR at line 1:
ORA-01086: savepoint 'BEFORE_TRUNCATE' never established
```

Notice that the error generated by the RDBMS indicates that the savepoint `before_truncate` does not exist even though we have clearly created it. The reason for getting this error is that TRUNCATE TABLE is a DDL command, and no rollback information is generated for it. In addition, like in any other DDL command, the RDBMS issues an implicit COMMIT statement.

1.16.3   THE DROP TABLE COMMAND

Sometimes it is necessary to remove a table and all its data from a database. The SQL command that allows us to do this is the DROP TABLE command. The basic format of this instruction is shown here:

DROP TABLE table-name [**CASCADE CONSTRAINTS**];

The optional clause CASCADE CONSTRAINTS is used whenever there are referential integrity constraints that refer either to a primary key or to a unique attribute in the table that we are trying to drop. That is, if we try to delete a particular table and this table is the parent table for some other table, we will get an error unless we use the CASCADE CONSTRAINTS clause.

The DROP TABLE CASCADE CONSTRAINTS command is commonly issued *before* a CREATE TABLE command. The reason for this is to avoid any error generated by the RDBMS when trying to create a table that has the same name of another table that already exists in the schema owned by the user.

 Solved Problems

1.1. Given the information shown below, write the SQL instruction to create the PROGRAMMER table. Assume that the attributes of this table satisfy the conditions stated below.

Attribute Name	Description/Data Type/Constraint
EmpNo	Programmer's unique ID. Maximum is 3 characters.
Project	Project in which programmer participates. Maximum is 3 characters.
TaskNo	Number of the task associated with the project. Numeric column, 2 digits maximum.
Last_Name	Surname of employee. Maximum is 25 characters. Required.

First_Name	Employee's first name. Maximum is 25 characters.
Hire_Date	Date in which employee was hired. Date data type.
Language	Programming language used by programmer. Maximum is 15 characters.
Clearance	Type of clearance given to programmer. Maximum is 25 characters.

The attributes EmpNo and Project may be up to three characters long. The attribute TaskNo is a numeric column with two digits maximum. Attributes Last_Name, First_Name, and Clearance may be up to 25 characters long. The Language attribute can be up to 15 characters long. Each programmer is issued a unique EmpNo. Last names are required.

EmpNo	Last Name	First Name	Hire Date	Project	Language	TaskNo.	Clearance
201	Campbell	John	1/1/95	NPR	VB	52	Secret
390	Bell	Randall	1/05/93	KCW	Java	11	Top Secret
789	Hixon	Richard	08/31/98	RNC	VB	11	Secret
134	McGurn	Robert	07/15/95	TIPPS	C++	52	Secret
896	Sweet	Jan	06/15/97	KCW	Java	10	Top Secret
345	Rowlett	Sid	11/15/99	TIPPS	Java	52	
563	Reardon	Andy	08/15/94	NITTS	C++	89	Confidential

The corresponding CREATE TABLE instruction is the following:

```
DROP TABLE programmer CASCADE CONSTRAINTS;
CREATE TABLE Programmer
   (EmpNo          Varchar2(3)      PRIMARY KEY,
   Last_Name       Varchar2(25)     NOT NULL,
   First_Name      Varchar2(25),
   Hire_Date       Date,
   Project         Varchar2(3),
   Language        Varchar2(15),
   TaskNo          Number(2),
   Clearance       Varchar2(25)
);
```

Notice that we have placed a DROP TABLE programmer CASCADE CONSTRAINTS command *before* the CREATE TABLE command to remove any other table with the same name that may be owned by the user. The embedded blanks in each attribute name have been replaced by an underscore to comply with the naming guidelines of Section 1.7. The attribute employee number has been defined as the primary key of this table. The attribute Last_Name has been defined as NOT NULL, since it is a required attribute.

1.2. Create a script to populate the PROGRAMMER table with the data indicated above. How many instructions are necessary to populate the table with this particular data?

The script that we need to write is a simple text file that contains all the instructions to populate the data. If we call the script *programmer.sql* and assume that it is located in drive A:, we can run it from PO8 typing @"A:programmer.sql" at the SQL prompt. Since the INSERT INTO command allows us to add to a table only one tuple at a time, it is necessary to have an INSERT INTO command per every row of data. Therefore, we need seven INSERT INTO commands to populate the table. Notice that it was necessary to change the data of the HIRE_DATE attribute to avoid errors. This is necessary since, by default, the date format is "DD-MM-YY," where *DD* is a day of the month (1-31), *MM* is the abbreviated name of a month as indicated by the first three letter of its name (JAN, FEB, DEC), and *YY* are the last two digits of the year. This implies that a date such as 1/1/95 needs to be changed to '1-JAN-95'. Remember to surround the date with single quotes.

Observe the use of the NULL value to fill in the attribute Clearance for the employee Sid Rowlett. The script to populate the programmer table is as follows:

```
INSERT INTO programmer
(EmpNo, Last_Name, First_Name, Hire_Date, Project, Language,
TaskNo, Clearance)
Values('201','Campbell', 'John', '1-JAN-95','NPR', 'VB',52,
'Secret');
INSERT INTO programmer
(EmpNo, Last_Name, First_Name, Hire_Date, Project, Language,
TaskNo, Clearance)
Values('390', 'Bell', 'Randall', '1-MAY-93', 'KCW', 'Java', 11,
'Top Secret');
INSERT INTO programmer
(EmpNo, Last_Name, First_Name, Hire_Date, Project, Language,
TaskNo, Clearance)
Values('789', 'Hixon', 'Richard', '31-AUG-98', 'RNC', 'VB', 11,
'Secret');
INSERT INTO programmer
(EmpNo, Last_Name, First_Name, Hire_Date, Project, Language,
TaskNo, Clearance)
Values('134','McGurn','Robert', '15-JUL-95', 'TIP','C++',
52, 'Secret');
INSERT INTO programmer
(EmpNo, Last_Name, First_Name, Hire_Date, Project, Language,
TaskNo, Clearance)
Values('896','Sweet', 'Jan', '15-JUN-97', 'KCW', 'Java',10,
'Top Secret');
INSERT INTO programmer
(EmpNo, Last_Name, First_Name, Hire_Date, Project, Language,
TaskNo, Clearance)
Values('345','Rowlett', 'Sid', '15-NOV-99', 'TIP','Java',
52, NULL);
```

```
INSERT INTO programmer
(EmpNo, Last_Name, First_Name, Hire_Date, Project, Language,
TaskNo, Clearance)
Values('563', 'Reardon', 'Andy', '15-AUG-94', 'NIT', 'C++', 89,
'Confidential');
```

1.3. Update the PROGRAMMER table to change the clearance for the employee with EmpNo = 345 from NULL to Secret.

Using the employee's number as the qualifier of the desired tuple, the corresponding SQL command to update the CLEARANCE attribute is as follows:

```
UPDATE programmer
SET clearance ='Secret'
WHERE empno ='345';
```

1.4. Insert the following tuples into the programmer table, and then display the last name, first name, clearance, and hire date of all employees. Sort the result by clearance.

EmpNo	Last Name	First Name	Hire Date	Project	Language	TaskNo.	Clearance
597	Campbell	Alan	1/1/00	NPR	VB	52	Secret
390	Bell	Greg	1/1/00	KCW	Java	11	Top Secret

The instructions to insert these two tuples are as follows:

```
INSERT INTO programmer
(EmpNo, Last_Name, First_Name, Hire_Date, Project, Language,
TaskNo, Clearance)
Values('198','Campbell', 'Alan', '1-JAN-00','NPR', 'VB',52,
'Secret');
INSERT INTO programmer
(EmpNo, Last_Name, First_Name, Hire_Date, Project, Language,
TaskNo, Clearance)
Values('834', 'Bell', 'Greg', '1-MAY-00', 'KCW', 'Java', 11,
'Top Secret');
```

The statement to display the information required and the result that it produces is this:

```
SELECT last_name, first_name, hire_date, clearance
FROM programmer
ORDER by clearance;

LAST_NAME       FIRST_NAME      HIRE_DATE       CLEARANCE
Reardon         Andy            15-AUG-94       Confidential
Campbell        John            01-JAN-95       Secret
Hixon           Richard         31-AUG-98       Secret
McGurn          Robert          15-JUL-95       Secret
Campbell        Alan            01-JAN-00       Secret
```

```
Rowlett      Sid          15-NOV-99    Secret
Bell         Randall      01-MAY-93    Top Secret
Bell         Greg         01-MAY-00    Top Secret
Sweet        Jan          15-JUN-97    Top Secret
```

1.5. Write the SQL command to reflect the fact the employee EmpNo = 789 has resigned.

Since we want to remove a tuple from the table, we need to use the DELETE command. The corresponding SQL command is shown here:

```
DELETE FROM programmer
WHERE empno='789';
```

1.6. Run the script SG.SQL to refresh the contents of the database. What is the degree of the S_EMP table? What is its cardinality? What SQL instructions would you use to answer these questions?

The *degree* is the number of attributes or columns in the S_EMP table. The *cardinality* is the number of tuples currently stored in the table. To determine the degree, we can "describe" the table. That is, we issue the command DESCRIBE s_emp and count the number of attributes.

```
Name                          Null?          Type
----------------------------  -----------    ----------------
ID                            NOT NULL       VARCHAR2(3)
LAST_NAME                     NOT NULL       VARCHAR2(20)
FIRST_NAME                                   VARCHAR2(20)
USERID                        NOT NULL       VARCHAR2(8)
START_DATE                    NOT NULL       DATE
COMMENTS                                     VARCHAR2(255)
MANAGER_ID                                   VARCHAR2(3)
TITLE                                        VARCHAR2(25)
DEPT_ID                                      VARCHAR2(3)
SALARY                                       NUMBER(11,2)
COMMISSION_PCT                               NUMBER(4,2)
```

Since there are 11 attributes listed, the degree of S_EMP is 11.

To determine the cardinality we need to issue a SELECT statement where we list all the attributes of the table. This SELECT statement may look like this:

```
SELECT id, last_name, first_name, userid, start_date, comments,
       manager_id, title, dept_id, salary, commission_pct
FROM s_emp;
```

The resulting table shows 25 rows; therefore, the cardinality of this table is 25. Observe that after all the rows of the SELECT statements are displayed, Oracle shows the total number of rows that were retrieved. This is known in Oracle as the *feedback*. By default, this feedback information is shown only if more than six rows are retrieved. This environment setting can be changed at any time during a session by using the following command at the SQL prompt:

```
SET feedback No_of_rows
```

where `No_of_rows` is an integer number that indicates the minimum number of rows that need to be retrieved *before* we can see this feedback message.

1.7. In the S_EMP table, how many employees work in department 41? Who are they?

To answer this question, we need to issue a `SELECT` statement that allows us to know the last name, first name, and ID of all the employees who work in department 41. The corresponding `WHERE` clause is `WHERE dept_id = '41'`. The complete `SELECT` statement may look like this:

```
SELECT id, last_name, first_name
FROM s_emp
WHERE dept_id ='41';
```

The resulting relation is this:

```
ID      LAST_NAME           FIRST_NAME
2       Smith               Doris
6       Brown               Molly
15      Hardwick            Elaine
16      Brown               George
4 rows selected
```

1.8. Is there an easier way to retrieve all the columns of a single table without having to mention all the attributes of the table?

The answer to this question is yes! There is a shorthand notation within the `SELECT` statement that allows us to do just that. However, without formatting the columns of the table, the results on the screen may look messy. The general format of this statement is as follows:

```
SELECT *
FROM table-name
[WHERE condition]
[ORDER BY];
```

1.9. Sort the contents of the table of Solved Problem 1.7 in alphabetical order according to the employee's last name.

Since we want to sort the rows of the S_EMP table that satisfy the `WHERE` condition, we need to use the `ORDER BY` clause of the `SELECT` statement. The corresponding `SELECT` statement may look like this:

```
SELECT id, last_name, first_name
FROM s_emp
WHERE dept_id ='41'
ORDER by last_name;
```

The resulting table is shown here:

```
ID     LAST_NAME      FIRST_NAME
6      Brown          Molly
16     Brown          George
15     Hardwick       Elaine
2      Smith          Doris
```

1.10. The result of the previous exercise has been sorted by the employee's last name. However, notice that for a given last name, the employees are not sorted by their first name. For instance, Brown George should come *before* Brown Molly. Is it possible to do this?

Yes! it is possible. The instruction to do this is as follows:

```
SELECT id, last_name, first_name

FROM s_emp

WHERE dept_id ='41'

ORDER by last_name, first_name;
```

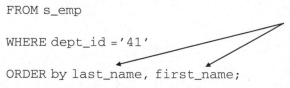 The rows of the resulting table will be ordered by last_name first and for identical last_names by first_name. Observe the order in which the attributes are written in the WHERE BY clause is important.

Observe that we have added the `first_name` column to the ORDER BY clause and that we have separated the column names with commas. Notice also that the order of the attributes is important. In this case, we sort first by last name and for identical last names by first name. The resulting table is shown below.

```
ID     LAST_NAME      FIRST_NAME
16     Brown          George
6      Brown          Molly
15     Hardwick       Elaine
2      Smith          Doris
```

These two rows are sorted by last name and for identical names by first name.

Had we had another column such as `middle_name` and we wanted to sort by this column too, the ORDER BY clause would have looked like this:

```
ORDER by last_name, first_name, middle_name;
```

The effect on the resulting table would have been to order by last name first, and for identical last names by first name, and for identical first names by middle name.

1.11. Write a script to create the Product table for the retail store Waves-R-Us with the attribute list shown below. Use named constraints if it is appropriate to do so, and confirm that the table was created correctly.

ATTRIBUTE NAME	DESCRIPTION
ID	Unique product identifier. 5 chars max. Required.
NAME	Name of the product. Max length 25 characters. Required.
DISCOUNT PERCENTAGE	Percentage of the price discounted to preferred customer. 1 digit max.
PRICE	Retail price of the product. 6 digits total with 2 decimals

ID	NAME	PRICE	DISCOUNT PRCNTG
111	Surfing board	225.95	5
200	Ear plugs	10	2
345	Goggles	35	1

The SQL instruction to create this table is shown below. The constraints defined for the attributes ID and NAME follow the conventions of Table 1.2.

```
CREATE TABLE Product

(
 id   Varchar2(5)    CONSTRAINT Products_id_pk    PRIMARY KEY,
 Name Varchar2(25)   CONSTRAINT Products_name_nn  NOT NULL,
 Discount_prcntg     Number(1),
 Price               Number(6,2)
);
```

To verify if the table has been created correctly, it is necessary to determine its structure through the use of the DESCRIBE product command.

```
DESCRIBE product;

Name                        Null?          Type
--------------------        -----------    ----------------
 ID                         NOT NULL       VARCHAR2(5)
 NAME                       NOT NULL       VARCHAR2(25)
 DISCOUNT_PRCNTG                           NUMBER(1)
 PRICE                                     NUMBER(6,2)
```

1.12. The output of the DESCRIBE product command shows the structure of the table. However, it does not show the attribute constraints. How can I find out if the constraints have been named correctly?

To find out if the constraints for the Product table have been named correctly, it is necessary to consult the USER_CONSTRAINTS data dictionary view.[15] This view, as its name indicates, contains information about all the constraints defined on a particular table.

A general query to determine the constraint name and type defined on a particular table is as follows:

```
SELECT constraint_name, constraint_type

FROM user_constraints

WHERE table_name = 'TABLE-ON-WHICH-CONSTRAINTS-ARE DEFINED';
```

Table names must be written in capital letters.

The corresponding SELECT command for the Product table is shown below.

```
SELECT constraint_name, constraint_type

FROM user_constraints

WHERE table_name='PRODUCT';
```

Notice that in the WHERE clause the table name *must* be written surrounded by single quotes and in capital letters. The reason for this is that in the data dictionary, table names are stored in capital letters. The result of this query is as follows:

```
CONSTRAINT_NAME                C    TABLE_NAME
--------------------           -    --------------------
PRODUCTS_NAME_NN               C    PRODUCT
PRODUCTS_ID_PK                 P    PRODUCT
```

The column constraint_type, shown as column C, in the resulting table deserves some consideration. The values of this column and their meaning are as follows:

C indicates that the constraint is of type CHECK. In this case, the RDBMS checks for non-null values.
P indicates that the constraint is associated with a Primary key.
U indicates that the constraint is associated with a UNIQUE constraint.
R indicates that the constraint is associated with a FoReign key.

---

[15] Views will be considered in Chapter 8.

1.13. What are the columns of the USER_CONSTRAINTS view? What is the meaning of each column?

    The structure of the USER_CONSTRAINTS view can be obtained by using the command DESCRIBE USER_CONSTRAINTS. A partial list of the columns of this view is shown below.

```
Name                            Null?          Type
------------------------------  -------------  -------------
OWNER                           NOT NULL       VARCHAR2(30)
CONSTRAINT_NAME                 NOT NULL       VARCHAR2(30)
CONSTRAINT_TYPE                                VARCHAR2(1)
TABLE_NAME                      NOT NULL       VARCHAR2(30)
SEARCH_CONDITION                               LONG
R_OWNER                                        VARCHAR2(30)
R_CONSTRAINT_NAME                              VARCHAR2(30)
DELETE_RULE                                    VARCHAR2(9)
STATUS                                         VARCHAR2(8)
LAST_CHANGE                                    DATE
```

    The meaning of each of the selected columns of the USER_CONSTRAINTS view is indicated as follows:

COLUMN	DESCRIPTION
OWNER	User who defined (owns) the constraint.
CONSTRAINT_NAME	Name of the constraint.
CONSTRAINT_TYPE	Type of the constraint.
TABLE_NAME	Name of the table where the constraints are defined.
SEARCH_CONDITION	Text of the search condition of a CHECK constraint.
R_OWNER	User who created the parent table (owner) referenced in a FK.
R_CONSTRAINT_NAME	Name of the PK or UNIQUE attribute referenced in the parent table.
DELETE RULE	Action to take with FKs that reference a deleted PRIMARY or UNIQUE key; supported actions are CASCADE and NO ACTION.
LAST_CHANGE	Date in which the constraint was last modified.

1.14. For a given table, how do I find out the names of columns on which the constraints are defined?

To find the names of the constraints and the columns on which they are defined use the USER_CONS_COLUMNS data dictionary view. The structure of this view is as follows:

```
SQL> DESC USER_CONS_COLUMNS;

    Name                          Null?           Type
    ----------------------        -----------     ----------------
    OWNER                         NOT NULL        VARCHAR2(30)
    CONSTRAINT_NAME               NOT NULL        VARCHAR2(30)
    TABLE_NAME                    NOT NULL        VARCHAR2(30)
    COLUMN_NAME                                   VARCHAR2(4000)
    POSITION                                      NUMBER
```

The corresponding SELECT statement for the PRODUCTS table and its output are shown here:

```
SELECT column_name, constraint_name
FROM user_cons_columns
WHERE table_name= 'PRODUCTS';

CONSTRAINT_NAME                   COLUMN_NAME
----------------------            --------------------
PRODUCTS_ID_PK                    ID
PRODUCTS_NAME_NN                  NAME
```

1.15. As a user, how can I find out the total number of tables that I have created or the tables that I can have access to?

To answer this question, query the data dictionary view USER_TABLES. The names of the tables that any user can have access to or that he or she has created can be displayed with the following query:

```
SELECT table_name
FROM user_tables;
```

1.16. Using the S_EMP table, display the last name, userid and title of all employees. The corresponding SQL query is this:

```
SELECT last_name, userid, title
FROM s_emp;
```

A partial output of this query is shown below. Notice that the output has been formatted.

```
LAST_NAME                    USERID          TITLE
--------------------         -----------     ----------------------
Martin                       martincu        President
Smith                        smithdj         VP, Operations
Norton                       nortonma        VP, Sales
Quentin                      quentiml        VP, Finance
Roper                        roperjm         VP, Administration
```

```
Brown           brownmr    Warehouse Manager
Hawkins         hawkinrt   Warehouse Manager
Burns           burnsba    Warehouse Manager
Catskill        catskiaw   Warehouse Manager
Jackson         jacksomt   Warehouse Manager
Henderson       hendercs   Sales Representative
Gilson          gilsonsj   Sales Representative
Sanders         sanderjk   Sales Representative
Dameron         dameroap   Sales Representative
Hardwick        hardwiem   Stock Clerk
Brown           browngw    Stock Clerk
Washington      washintl   Stock Clerk
Patterson       patterdv   Stock Clerk
Bell            bellag     Stock Clerk
Gantos          gantosej   Stock Clerk
Stephenson      stephebs   Stock Clerk
Chester         chesteek   Stock Clerk
Pearl           pearlrg    Stock Clerk
Dancer          dancerbw   Stock Clerk
Schmitt         schmitss   Stock Clerk
25 rows selected.
```

1.17. Display the query of the previous question in alphabetical order by title in descending order.

The corresponding SQL query is shown here:

```
SELECT last_name, userid, title
FROM s_emp
ORDER BY title DESC;
```

The output of this query is shown here:

```
LAST_NAME            USERID         TITLE
-------------------- ------------   -----------------------
Brown                brownmr        Warehouse Manager
Hawkins              hawkinrt       Warehouse Manager
Burns                burnsba        Warehouse Manager
Jackson              jacksomt       Warehouse Manager
Catskill             catskiaw       Warehouse Manager
Norton               nortonma       VP, Sales
Smith                smithdj        VP, Operations
Quentin              quentiml       VP, Finance
Roper                roperjm        VP, Administration
Hardwick             hardwiem       Stock Clerk
Brown                browngw        Stock Clerk
Bell                 bellag         Stock Clerk
Patterson            patterdv       Stock Clerk
Washington           washintl       Stock Clerk
Gantos               gantosej       Stock Clerk
Chester              chesteek       Stock Clerk
Dancer               dancerbw       Stock Clerk
```

```
Pearl              pearlrg      Stock Clerk
Schmitt            schmitss     Stock Clerk
Stephenson         stephebs     Stock Clerk
Henderson          hendercs     Sales Representative
Sanders            sanderjk     Sales Representative
Dameron            dameroap     Sales Representative
Gilson             gilsonsj     Sales Representative
Martin             martincu     President
25 rows selected.
```

1.18. For all employees of the S_EMP table, list their titles, last names, and departments in this order. Make sure that the different titles are listed in alphabetical order and that the employees who have the same title are in listed in reverse alphabetical order.

The corresponding query is this:

```
SELECT title, last_name, dept_id
FROM s_emp
ORDER BY title, last_name DESC;
```

The output of this query is as follows:

```
TITLE                      LAST_NAME          DEP
------------------------   ----------------   ----
President                  Martin             50
Sales Representative       Sanders            33
Sales Representative       Henderson          31
Sales Representative       Gilson             32
Sales Representative       Dameron            35
Stock Clerk                Washington         42
Stock Clerk                Stephenson         45
Stock Clerk                Schmitt            45
Stock Clerk                Pearl              34
Stock Clerk                Patterson          42
Stock Clerk                Hardwick           41
Stock Clerk                Gantos             44
Stock Clerk                Dancer             45
Stock Clerk                Chester            44
Stock Clerk                Brown              41
Stock Clerk                Bell               43
VP, Administration         Roper              50
VP, Finance                Quentin            10
VP, Operations             Smith              41
VP, Sales                  Norton             31
Warehouse Manager          Jackson            45
Warehouse Manager          Hawkins            42
Warehouse Manager          Catskill           44
Warehouse Manager          Burns              43
Warehouse Manager          Brown              41
25 rows selected.
```

1.19. Display the last name and salary of all the employees who work in department 41.

The corresponding SQL query is this:

```
SELECT last_name, salary
FROM s_emp
WHERE dept_id = '41';
```

The output of this query is as follows:

```
LAST_NAME               SALARY
Smith                   2450
Brown                   1600
Hardwick                1400
Brown                    940
4 rows selected.
```

1.20. Increase the salary of all the employees of department 41. Verify the result. Make sure that all changes can be discarded in case the user makes a mistake. If the operation is incorrect, how can the user undo the changes?

To increase the salary of the employees of department 41, it is necessary to update the appropriate rows in the S_EMP table. However, before making any changes to this table, let's define a savepoint. This way, we know that we can undo the changes.

```
SAVEPOINT before_update;
```

The current salary for all the employees of department 41 is shown here.

```
LAST_NAME               SALARY
--------------------    --------
Smith                   2450
Brown                   1600
Hardwick                1400
Brown                    940
4 rows selected.
```

The SQL command to update the salary of employees of department 41 is as follows:

```
UPDATE S_emp
SET salary = salary + 1000
WHERE dept_id = '41';
```

We can verify that the changes are correct by issuing the following query.

```
SELECT last_name, salary
FROM s_emp
WHERE dept_id = '41';
```

The output of this query is shown here:

```
LAST_NAME           SALARY
Smith               3450
Brown               2600
Hardwick            2400
Brown               1940
4 rows selected.
```

If the update is incorrect, the user can undo the changes by issuing the following command:

```
ROLLBACK TO SAVEPOINT before_update;
```

1.21. In Oracle, how can I save to a file the commands that I type in an interactive session?

To save one interactive command to a particular file, use the following SQL*Plus command:

```
SAVE filename
```

To accumulate more than one interactive command to the *same* file, use the following SQL*Plus command. In all cases, a full path description may precede the filename.

```
SAVE filename REPLACE
```

If no path name is indicated, the file will be saved in the default directory. If the user indicates no extension, the system will use the default extension .SQL.

1.22. How can I execute a query that was previously saved with the SAVE command?

To execute the command stored in a file, use the following SQL*Plus command:

```
START filename
```

where the file must be preceded by its full path name and extension if the latter is not the default value.

1.23. Run the script to refresh the PROGRAMMER table of Solved Problem 1.2. Assume that due to completion of the project KCW, all the employees that worked in that project are transferred back to their company headquarters. Remove these employees from the PROGRAMMER table.

The SQL instruction to remove the employees from the PROGRAMMER table is as follows:

```
DELETE FROM programmer WHERE project = 'KCW';
```

1.24. Refresh the PROGRAMMER table and display the names and project of all programmers that have a Secret clearance.

The query to produce this information is as follows:

```
SELECT last_name, project, clearance
FROM programmer
WHERE clearance = 'Secret';
```

The output of this query is shown here.

```
LAST_NAME                    PRO     CLEARANCE
------------------------     ----    ----------------
Campbell                     NPR     Secret
Hixon                        RNC     Secret
McGurn                       TIP     Secret
3 rows selected.
```

1.25. Due to job requirements, all employees of the PROGRAMMER table who have a `Secret` clearance have been granted a `Top Secret` clearance. Write the corresponding SQL instruction to reflect this upgrade of clearance in the PROGRAMMER table.

The corresponding SQL instruction is shown below.

```
UPDATE programmer SET clearance = 'Top Secret'
WHERE clearance = 'Secret';
```

1.26. A table called TOOL has been created with three numerical attributes of varying precision.

```
CREATE TABLE tool
(
  Id                 NUMBER,
  Manufacturer_id    NUMBER (5),
  Price              NUMBER (5,2)
);
```

Show the values stored in each column as result of the execution of the INSERT INTO commands shown in the table on the following page.

The attribute `Id` allows any number of digits to be entered either to the left or to the right of the decimal. The attribute Manufacturer_id allows no more than 5 digits to the left of the decimal. If any digits are inserted to the right of the decimal, the number will be rounded off. The attribute `Price` allows no more than 5 digits total. With 2 specified to the right of the decimal point, that leaves only 3 possible to the left of the decimal point. The results of the INSERT INTO commands are as follows:

INSERT INTO commands	Id	Manufacturer_id	Price
INSERT INTO tool (Id, Manufacturer_id, Price) VALUES (987, 987, 987);	987	987	987
INSERT INTO tool (Id, Manufacturer_id, Price) VALUES (987.222, 987.225, 987.225);	987.222	987	987.23
INSERT INTO tool (Id, Manufacturer_id, Price) VALUES (98.55, 98.55, 98.55);	98.55	99	98.55
INSERT INTO tool (Id, Manufacturer_id, Price) VALUES (98765, 98765, 98765);			Insert fails because too many digits for this attribute.

1.27. When populating a table, is it always necessary to write the column names in the INSERT INTO clause?

No, it is not necessary to write the column names in the INSERT INTO clause, provided that the data items in the VALUES clause are written in the same order in which the attributes of the table are listed in the CREATE TABLE command. We illustrate this using the first of three INSERT INTO commands of the previous solved problem. Notice that in the CREATE TABLE tool command, the attributes are listed in the following order: Id, Manufacturer_id, and Price.

No column names are mentioned in this INSERT INTO command

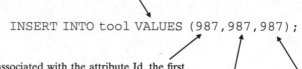

INSERT INTO tool VALUES (987,987,987);

This data item is associated with the attribute Id, the first attribute mentioned in the CREATE TABLE tool command.

This data item is associated with the attribute Manufacturer_id, the second attribute mentioned in the CREATE TABLE tool command.

This data item is associated with the attribute price, the third attribute mentioned in the CREATE TABLE tool command.

Likewise, we could write the second and third INSERT INTO statements as follows:

INSERT INTO tool VALUES(987.222,987.225,987.225);

INSERT INTO tool VALUES(98.55, 98.55, 98.55);

Before using this form of the INSERT INTO command, the user should make sure that the data items are listed in the correct order.

Supplementary Problems

1.28. Write the SQL statement to create a five-field table to contain sample climate information. The constraints that need to be satisfied by the attributes of this table are as follows: 1) the attribute `City name` is mandatory and can have up to 13 characters, 2) the attribute `Sample_Date` is of type `date` and mandatory, 3) the temperatures at noon and midnight can be at most 3 digits, with 1 decimal place, and 4) the `Precipitation` attribute can have at most 5 digits, including 1 decimal digit.

1.29. Create a table named STAFF with the attributes and constraints indicated below. Use the most appropriate data type for each of the attributes, and name any necessary constraint. Use any attribute length that you consider necessary.

Attributes	Constraints
First Name	Required
Last Name	Required
Title	Can be up to 15 characters long
Id	Key, can have up to 5 characters
Salary	Numeric (6 digits maximum with 2 decimals)
Department	Required, can have up to 10 characters

1.30. When deleting tuples from a table, the DELETE and the DROP TABLE commands seem to have the same effect. Is there any difference between these two instructions when removing tuples from a table?

1.31. Assuming the following table definition, what value is stored in each attribute following the execution of the INSERT INTO commands shown in the following?

```
CREATE TABLE trynum

(
 first number,
 second number (2),
 third number (2,2)
);

INSERT INTO trynum (first, second, third)
        VALUES (.00005, .00005, .00005);
INSERT INTO trynum (first, second, third)
        VALUES (1.9, 1.9, 1.9);
INSERT INTO trynum (first, second, third)
        VALUES (10, 10, 10);
```

1.32. Run the script World_Cities.sql, and display the attributes in the following order: continent, country, and city. Make sure that the continents are listed in reverse alphabetical order, that countries located in the same continent are listed in alphabetical order, and that the cities in the same country are listed in reverse alphabetical order.

1.33. In the World_City table, display the name of the cities that are not located in Asia. Order the output by continents, by country within continents, and by cities within a country.

1.34. Display the name and all the latitude and longitude information for all the European cities of the World_Cities table in reverse alphabetical order by city.

1.35. Run the script SG.sql, and display the last name, user ID, and start date for all employees hired on March 8, 1990.

1.36. Display the last name, first name, and the department ID for all employees who do not work in department 44.

1.37. Describe the data dictionary view USER_OBJECTS, and display the name of all the tables owned by the user.

1.38. Display the last name, first name, and salary of all the employees who are stock clerks. Order the result in ascending order by salary.

1.39. Display the last name, first name, and hire date of all employees who were hired after August 31, 1991.

1.40. Display the last name, first name, and salary of all employees whose salary is less than $1200.

1.41. Drop the table S_EMP using the `DROP TABLE` command. What happens and why?

 # Answers to Supplementary Problems

1.28.

```
CREATE TABLE climate (
City            Varchar2(13) not null,
Sample_Date     DATE not null,
Noon            Number(3,1),
Midnight        Number(3,1),
Precipitation   Number(5,1)
);
```

1.29.

```
DROP TABLE staff CASCADE CONSTRAINTS;
CREATE TABLE staff (
First_Name Varchar2(20)  CONSTRAINT  staff_first_name_nn
                         NOT NULL,
Last_Name  Varchar2(20)  CONSTRAINT  staff_last_name_nn
                         NOT NULL,
Title      Varchar2(15),
Id         Varchar2(5)   CONSTRAINT  staff_id_pk PRIMARY KEY,
Salary     Number(6,2),
Department Varchar2(10)  staff_department_nn NOT NULL);
```

1.30. Yes, there is a difference. The DELETE FROM command may remove one or more tuples from a table, depending upon the WHERE condition. However, this instruction preserves the structure of the table. The DROP TABLE command removes a table and all its content. If the execution of a DROP TABLE is successful, the table no longer exists in the database.

1.31. After the first INSERT INTO command, the values stored in the attributes of the table are shown below. Notice that the values of attributes SECOND and THIRD are both 0 because the values are rounded off with 0 and 2 decimal places, respectively.

```
FIRST        SECOND       THIRD
----------   ----------   ----------
.00005       0            0
```

The second INSERT INTO generates an error because of the precision of the attribute THIRD. If, at most, two digits are allowed and two decimals are needed, any value with any digit to the left of the decimal point will be too large. The error may read "Value larger than specified precision allows for this column."

The third INSERT INTO command also fails. The RDBMS generates the same error it generated for the previous INSERT INTO command.

1.32.
```
SELECT continent, country, city
FROM World_Cities
ORDER BY continent DESC, country, city DESC;
```

1.33.
```
SELECT continent, country, city
FROM World_Cities
WHERE Continent <> 'ASIA'
ORDER BY Continent, country, city;
```

1.34.
```
SELECT City, Latitude, NorthSouth, Longitude, EastWest
FROM World_cities
WHERE Continent = 'EUROPE'
ORDER BY City DESC;
```

1.35.
```
SELECT last_name, userid, start_date
FROM s_emp
WHERE start_date = '08-MAR-90';
```

1.36.
```
SELECT last_name,first_name,dept_id
FROM S_emp
WHERE dept_id <> '44';
```

1.37.

```
DESCRIBE USER_OBJECTS;
```

Results may vary depending on the tables that have been created by the user. However, the query to answer this question is as follows:

```
SELECT object_name
FROM user_objects
WHERE object_type = 'TABLE';
```

1.38.

```
SELECT last_name, first_name, salary
FROM s_emp
WHERE title = 'Stock Clerk'
ORDER by salary;
```

1.39.

```
SELECT last_name, first_name, start_date
FROM s_emp
WHERE start_date > '31-AUG-91';
```

1.40.

```
SELECT last_name,last_name,salary
FROM s_emp
WHERE salary < 1200;
```

1.41. The table S_EMP cannot be dropped because some of its attributes are referenced by the FK of some other tables. The error generated reads "Unique/primary keys in table referenced by foreign keys." To drop this table the user needs to use the command DROP TABLE s_emp CASCADE CONSTRAINTS.

CHAPTER 2

Implementation of the Relational Operators in SQL

In the previous chapter, we considered several of the basic operational aspects of the SQL language. In the remaining sections of this chapter, we concentrate on studying the implementation of the theoretical relational operators that were explained in Chapter 1, Section 1.5. In addition, we explore other features of the `CREATE TABLE` and `SELECT` commands and consider new DDL statements that allow us to enforce integrity constraints and manipulate table structures.

2.1 Implementation of the Selection Operator

The *selection* operator on a given relation *r* produces a new relation that has the same attributes of *r* and whose rows are these rows of r that satisfy a specified condition. As all other relational operators, this operator is also implemented using the `SELECT` statement. In this section, we will consider some variations of this statement to illustrate the implementation of the selection operator in SQL.

EXAMPLE 2.1
Display all the information of the Operations department that is contained in the S_DEPT table of the Sporting Goods database.

To answer this query, we need to show all columns of the S_DEPT table for every row that satisfies the condition NAME = 'Operations'. The SELECT statement to display the required information is as follows:

```
SELECT region_id, name, id
FROM S_dept
WHERE NAME = 'Operations';
REG NAME                     ID
--- -------------------- ---

1   Operations           41
2   Operations           42
3   Operations           43
4   Operations           44
5   Operations           45
5 rows selected.
```

The result of this operation shows that the column headings are written in capital letters and listed in the same order in which they are mentioned in the SELECT clause. One intriguing aspect of this result is how the heading of the column region_id is displayed. Only the first three characters of this column name are shown, even though the entire column name is used in the SELECT command. This occurs because when the S_REGION table was created, the region_id attribute was defined as VARCHAR2(3). By default, the Oracle RDBMS displays the content of any column using as many characters as there are characters in the column definition. We can verify this by describing the S_DEPT (see below). The columns ID and NAME are displayed in their entirety because they were defined as VARCHAR2(3) and VARCHAR2(20), respectively. The width of these columns is big enough to display the entire column name as a heading.

Name	Null?	Type
ID	NOT NULL	VARCHAR2(3)
NAME	NOT NULL	VARCHAR2(20)
REGION_ID		VARCHAR2(3)

Another way of displaying the entire contents of a table was already mentioned in Chapter 1 (See Solved Problem 1.8). In this variation of the SELECT statement, we use an asterisk in lieu of the column names. The next example illustrates this.

EXAMPLE 2.2
Display all the information of the Operations department that is contained in the S_DEPT table of the SG database without writing explicitly the column names.

The query to obtain this information using the * in lieu of all column names is shown below.

```
SELECT *
FROM s_dept
WHERE NAME = 'Operations';
ID  NAME                  REG
___ _____  ___
41  Operations            1
42  Operations            2
43  Operations            3
44  Operations            4
45  Operations            5
5   rows selected.
```

Observe that the display of the result of this query is slightly different from the one we obtained in the previous example. In particular, the order in which the column names are displayed is different. Whenever we use an asterisk to display the columns of a table, Oracle displays the columns in the same order in which they were defined in the CREATE TABLE command of the table mentioned in the FROM clause. We can verify this by observing the structure of the S_DEPT table. According to this, when the S_DEPT table was created, the first column that was defined was ID, then NAME, and finally REGION_ID. This is precisely the order, from left to right, in which the SELECT statement displays the columns of the S_DEPT.

A generalization of the selection operator that allows us to display every column and every row of a table is shown next.

```
SELECT *
FROM table-name;
```

This statement is equivalent to a selection operation with an unspecified WHERE condition that is satisfied by every row of the table mentioned in the FROM clause. The following example illustrates this.

EXAMPLE 2.3
Display the entire content of the S_DEPT table.

The query and a partial output are shown in the following:

```
SELECT *
FROM s_dept;
ID  NAME                  REG
___ _____  ___
10  Finance               1
31  Sales                 1
.
.
12 rows selected.
```

Observe also that the use of the * displays the columns in the same order in which they were defined in the CREATE TABLE s_dept command.

2.2 Using Aliases to Control Column Headings

In all the queries that we have considered so far, we have allowed the RDBMS to display the data using default values. For instance, in Example 2.1, we saw that the heading of the attribute region_id was displayed using only three characters. Letting the RDBMS display results using the default values may result in column headings that are not meaningful. There are times when we would like to control how the column headings are displayed. For instance, we may have a query where we do not want the users to know the column names of a particular table. In cases like this, we would like to use substitute headings. The alternative name that we may select to replace a column heading is called a *column alias*.

Column headings are changed in the SELECT clause of the SELECT statement. There are two basic methods for creating a column alias. First, we follow the column name with the keyword **AS** and the column alias enclosed in double quotes. Second, we follow the column name with its alias enclosed in double quotes without using the keyword AS. These two methods of creating aliases are equivalents, but the use of the keyword AS seems to make the alias more explicit and the SELECT statement easier to read. In this book, we will create aliases using both methods. We also advocate the use of double quotes to enclose an alias even if the alias is just a single word. However, if the alias contains upper- and lowercase letters, consists of more than one word separated by spaces, or includes special characters such $ or #, we *must* enclose the alias in double quotes. The reader should keep in mind that by using aliases the user *does not change* the column names inside a table. Aliases act as headings for display purposes only.

In cases where we need to override the Oracle restriction of not displaying more characters than the number of characters in a column definition, we may format the column using the COLUMN command SQL*Plus. The following example illustrates the use of aliases and the COLUMN command.

EXAMPLE 2.4
Display the last name, first name, and salary of all employees of the Sporting Goods database. Use Last Name, First Name, and Salary as column headings.

Since each of the new headings Last Name and First Name consists of two words separated by a space, it is necessary to enclose these aliases in double quotes. This is also necessary for the heading Salary because it has mixed cases. The SELECT statement and the headings that it produces are shown below. Notice that only the first two rows of the result of this query are displayed.

```
SELECT last_name AS "Last Name", first_name AS "First
Name", salary AS "Salary"
FROM s_emp;

Last Name                First Name              Salary
-------------------- -------------------- ---------
Martin                   Carmen                    4500
Smith                    Doris                     2450
.
.
.
25 rows selected.
```

The SQL*Plus COLUMN command allows us not only to override the RDBMS default values to display headings but also to format the display of data. In this book, we will use the following syntax of this command.

COLUMN column-name HEADING new-heading FORMAT [format-mask]

The optional format-mask specifies how the column data is displayed. Table 2-1 shows some of the format masks used throughout this book and their effect on the displayed data.

Table 2-1. Formatting masks.

Mask	Effect	Example	Description
An	Display column using a column width of n characters.	A10	Display 10 characters. Truncate extra characters for longer columns.
9	Display a significant digit.	999	Display three significant digits. Leading zeros are displayed as blanks.
0	Display a leading zero or a value of zero in this position.	0999	If all 9s digits are zero, display a zero or display a leading zero at this position.
,	Display a comma in this position.	9,999	Value of 2456 is displayed as 2,456
.	Display a period in this position.	9,999.99	Value 2456 is displayed as 2,456.00
$	Display a floating dollar sign.	$999.99	Value 25 is displayed as $25.00

The following example illustrates the use of this formatting command.

EXAMPLE 2.5
Display the region, name, and ID of all the Operations departments of the Sporting Goods database. Use the headings `Region Number`, `Department Name`, and `Department Id`.

The query to display the information requested is almost identical to that of Example 2.1. However, the use of the COLUMN command allows us to display the headings a little bit differently. The query, the headings displayed, and the first two rows of the results are shown in the following:

```
COLUMN region_id HEADING "Region|Number" FORMAT A10
COLUMN id HEADING "Department|Id" FORMAT A10
SELECT region_id, name AS "Department Name", id
FROM S_dept
WHERE NAME = 'Operations';
Region                            Department
Number          Department Name   Id
----------      ------------------- ----------
1               Operations        41
2               Operations        42
.
.
.
5 rows selected.
```

Notice the use of the heading separator character, |, to split some of the headings into two lines. Observe also how we have combined the COLUMN command and a column alias to change the headings. It is important to notice that in this particular example, we must use the COLUMN command to produce these headings. If we do not use the COLUMN command, the RDBMS would have used the column length definition to display the column names or their aliases, and the headings would have been truncated as we saw in Example 2.1.

The reader should be aware that whenever a COLUMN command is used to format the heading of a particular column name, that heading format remains in effect until a new COLUMN command changes it or the column heading is CLEARed. Alias names defined with the AS option of the SELECT clause are temporary in nature and are for display purposes only. Column aliases no longer exist after the SELECT statement is executed.

To clear the heading of a particular column, use this SQL*Plus command:

COLUMN column-name CLEAR

To clear all columns headings, use this SQL*Plus command:

CLEAR COLUMNS

To display the current settings of all columns use this SQL*Plus command:

COLUMN

2.3   Implementation of the Projection Operator

The *projection* operator, when applied to a relation *r* and a set *X* of its attributes, produces a new relation where there are no duplicate rows and whose attributes are the elements of *X*. This operator is implemented in SQL using the DISTINCT option of the SELECT clause of the SELECT command (see Fig. 2-1). The use of the DISTINCT option suppresses *the display* of duplicate rows. The attributes that participate in the projection of table are mentioned in the SELECT clause in the usual way. Observe that in the syntax of the SELECT command, the default of the SELECT clause is ALL. That is why the SELECT command, unless the user explicitly indicates otherwise, displays all rows, including duplicates.

```
SELECT [ALL | DISTINCT] col-1, col-2,col-3,.........,col-N
FROM table-1,........., table-N
[WHERE condition]
[ORDER BY column_1 [ASC|DESC][,column_2 [ASC|DESC]...]];
```

Fig. 2-1. SELECT statement showing the DISTINCT option and the default value ALL.

EXAMPLE 2.6
How many different departments are in the S_DEPT table?

Since we do not want to duplicate department names, it is necessary to use the DISTINCT option of the SELECT clause. The query to obtain this information and the result that it produces are shown in the following:

```
SELECT DISTINCT name
FROM s_dept;
NAME
-------------------
Administration
Finance
Operations
Sales
4 rows selected.
```

Observe that there are no duplicate rows in the result of the query.

The reader should be aware that when the projection is on more than one column of the relation, the uniqueness of the rows is determined by the values of all their columns. The following example illustrates this.

EXAMPLE 2.7
For all the different countries contained in the World_Cities table, display their names and the continent in which they are located. Make sure that no country name is duplicated.

```
SELECT DISTINCT country, continent
FROM World_Cities;
COUNTRY                           CONTINENT
-------------------------- --------------
ARGENTINA                         SOUTH AMERICA
AUSTRALIA                         AUSTRALIA
BRAZIL                            SOUTH AMERICA
CANADA                            NORTH AMERICA
CHILE                             SOUTH AMERICA
CHINA                             ASIA
COLOMBIA                          SOUTH AMERICA
ECUADOR                           SOUTH AMERICA
EGYPT                             AFRICA
ENGLAND                           EUROPE
FRANCE                            EUROPE
GREECE                            EUROPE
INDIA                             ASIA
ITALY                             EUROPE
JAPAN                             ASIA
LIBYA                             AFRICA
PERU                              SOUTH AMERICA
POLAND                            EUROPE
RUSSIA                            EUROPE
SPAIN                             EUROPE
UNITED STATES                     NORTH AMERICA
VENEZUELA                         SOUTH AMERICA
22 rows selected.
```

Notice that there are 22 different rows in the resulting table. As mentioned before, it is the combination country-continent that should be considered unique and not the values of any single column. Observe that EUROPE is repeated several times under the CONTINENT column, but there are no duplicate rows in the resulting table. The effect of the DISTINCT option in this query is significant. If this option is not used in the query, the resulting table shows 32 rows instead of 22. It should be clear that without the DISTINCT option, this query does not implement a projection on the attributes country and continent of the World_Cities table.

2.4 Implementation of the Join Operator

The *join* operation allows us to bring data from two or more tables together into a single table. The tables that participate in the join are "connected" through their common attributes according to the condition specified in the WHERE clause. Very frequently, these common attributes are in a key-foreign key relationship. Joins are classified based upon the type of condition involved (equality versus nonequality), the number of tables involved (only one table or more than one table), and the type of rows that are retrieved (with or without a direct match in some other table). In this chapter, we are only going to consider the types of join indicated in Table 2-2.

Table 2-2. Partial list of types of join.

Type	Description
Equijoin	A join between two tables connected through common equal values.
Self join	A join between a table and itself.
Outer join	Joins between two tables to determine all the rows of one table that do not have a match in the other table.

2.4.1 THE EQUIJOIN

An *equijoin* is the join of two tables through their common equal values. The syntax of the SELECT command to implement this type of join is shown in Fig. 2-2. This command can easily be generalized to join more than two tables.

```
SELECT table-1.col1,...,table-1.colN...,table-2.col1,...,table-2.colN
FROM table-1, table-2
WHERE table-1.common-column = table-2.common-column;
```

Fig. 2-2. General format of the SELECT statement for joining two tables.

Notice that in the SELECT clause, we have preceded each column name with the name of its table. This is necessary if the same column name appears in more than one table. Columns whose names are preceded by the name of their tables are said to be *qualified*. If there are no common names in the two tables, there is no need to qualify the columns. However, to improve the system performance it is better to qualify the columns.

It should be obvious by now that the column names that appear in the SELECT clause must appear as columns of at least one of the tables mentioned in the FROM clause.

EXAMPLE 2.8
Select the last name, first name, and department name of all the employees of the S_DEPT table.

To answer this query, we need to bring together into one table—the Join table—data from two other tables—namely, the S_DEPT and S_EMP tables. The attributes last name and first name can be obtained from the S_EMP table. The department name can be obtained from the S_DEPT table. The common attributes are dept_id (of S_EMP) and id (of S_DEPT). It is through these common attributes that we can join the tables and bring the required pieces of information together into a single table. The condition in the WHERE clause that defines the equijoin is shown in the following:

$$s\_emp.dept\_id = s\_dept.id$$

Notice that in this case, the attribute dept_id is an FK of the S_EMP table that refers to the PK ID of the table S_DEPT.

The SELECT command to implement this equijoin is this:

```
SELECT s_emp.last_name, s_emp.first_name,s_dept.name AS
      "Department"
FROM s_emp,s_dept
WHERE s_emp.dept_id = s_dept.id;
```

Observe that in this query we have qualified all the attributes mentioned in the SELECT and WHERE clauses even though there are no common column names shared by these two tables. Since these attribute names are not duplicated in any of the tables, we could have written this query as shown below without confusing the RDBMS.[1]

```
SELECT last_name, first_name, name AS "Department"
FROM s_emp,s_dept
WHERE s_emp.dept_id = s_dept.id;
```

The result of this query is shown next.

```
LAST_NAME            FIRST_NAME           DEPARTMENT
-------------------- -------------------- -------------------
Martin               Carmen               Administration
Smith                Doris                Operations
Norton               Michael              Sales
Quentin              Mark                 Finance
.
.
.
25 rows selected.
```

2.4.2   USING TABLE ALIASES TO SIMPLIFY QUERIES

In some occasions, we would like to simplify the writing of queries that involve qualified attributes. Qualifying column names can be a time-consuming and error-prone activity, particularly when joining tables that have lengthy names. To

---

[1] In this sense, qualifying the columns is said to avoid any ambiguity on the part of the RDBMS.

simplify this task, we can use table aliases instead of the table names. A *table alias* is a temporary name that we can give to a table within a SELECT command. The table alias follows the table name in the FROM clause of the SELECT statement. No special punctuation is necessary to write a table alias. After the SELECT statement is executed, the alias no longer exists. By choosing a short table alias we can reduce the amount of typing that is necessary to write a query. It is important to keep in mind that once an alias is assigned to a table in the FROM clause, that alias *must* be used throughout SELECT command. The following example illustrates the use of an alias.

EXAMPLE 2.9

Select the last name, first name, and department name of all the employees of the SG database. Use table aliases.

This query is identical to the query of Example 2.8. For sake of comparison, we reproduce the query of this example next.

```
SELECT s_emp.last_name, s_emp.first_name,s_dept.name
FROM s_emp,s_dept
WHERE s_emp.dept_id = s_dept.id;
```

The same query using aliases (shown in bold) may look like this:

```
SELECT A.last_name, A.first_name, B.name
FROM s_emp A ,s_dept B
WHERE A.dept_id = B.id;
```
⟵ Alias names are assigned in the FROM clause. The alias for the table s_EMP is A and the alias for the table s_DEPT is B.

Notice that the table aliases follows each of the individual table names in the FROM clause. The alias of the S_EMP table is **A**. Likewise, the alias of the S_DEPT table is **B**. Therefore, throughout the entire table we must use A in lieu of S_EMP and B in lieu of S_DEPT.

Table aliases can be up to 30 characters long. However, using aliases this long defeats their purpose of simplifying queries. The authors believe that, as far as table aliases is concerned, "the shorter, the better."

2.4.3 USING LITERALS AND THE CONCATENATION OPERATOR TO MODIFY QUERY RESULTS

The use of column aliases has allowed us to control the headings of the result of a query but not how the rows are displayed. To do the latter, we need to use the concatenation operator, which is denoted by two consecutive vertical bars ||. The *concatenation* operator combines or puts together columns or character strings or both to form a character expression. A *character string* is a sequence of characters enclosed in single quotes. To enhance the display of queries, we use the concatenation operator in conjunction with one or more literal characters.

CHAPTER 2   Relational Operators in SQL

By a *literal* we mean any character string, expression, or number included in the SELECT clause that is not a column name or an alias. The following examples illustrate the use of the concatenation operator and literal characters to modify simple query results. In Chapter 4, we will consider further uses of the concatenation operator

EXAMPLE 2.10
Display the first name, last name, and title of all the employees of the S_EMP table.

The following SELECT command shows how we can concatenate column names and literal characters to form a character expression. Notice that character expression is treated as a single column that we can rename using an alias. Observe also the use of blank spaces to separate the character strings from the column values to improve the readability of the result of the query. The query and its partial output are shown below.

```
SELECT first_name || ' ' || last_name || ' ' || 'is a ' ||
title || ' of the company' AS "Employees and their titles"
FROM s_emp;

Employees and their titles
-------------------------------------------------
Carmen Martin is a President of the company
Doris Smith is a VP, Operations of the company
Michael Norton is a VP, Sales of the company
.
.
.
25 rows selected.
```

2.4.4   SELF JOIN

A *self join* is the join of a table with itself. It is easier to work with this type of join if we give to the same table two different aliases. This way, we can treat the same table as two different tables. The following example illustrates this.

EXAMPLE 2.11
For every employee of the SG database, display the employee's name and the name of his or her manager.

To answer this query, we need to join the table to itself. As mentioned previously, this type of query is easier to work with if we use two different aliases for the same table. In this case, we have assigned to the S_EMP table the aliases E (for employee) and M (for manager). The query to retrieve the information requested and its output are shown in the following:

```
SELECT M.last_name ||' works for ' || E.last_name ||' '||
E.first_name AS "Employees and their managers"
FROM s_emp M, s_emp E
WHERE E.id = M.manager_id;
```

```
Managers and their employees
----------------------------------------
Smith works for Martin Carmen
Norton works for Martin Carmen
Quentin works for Martin Carmen
Roper works for Martin Carmen
.
.
.
24 rows selected.
```

2.4.5   Outer Join

Given the join of two tables, sometimes we would like to know the rows of one of the tables that do not meet a specified condition in the other table. For instance, we would like to know the employees who do not have a manager. The operator that allows us to answer this type of question is the *outer join* operator. The syntax of this operator is shown in Figs. 2-3a and 2-3b.

```
SELECT table1.col1,...table1,colN, table1.col1,...table2.colN
FROM table1, table2
WHERE table1.column-name(+) - table2.column-name;
```

Fig. 2-3a.   Outer join to calculate these rows of Table 1 that do not have a match in Table 2.

```
SELECT table1.col1, ...table1,colN, table1.col1,....table2.colN
FROM table1, table2
WHERE table1.column-name = table2.column-name(+);
```

Fig. 2-3b.   Outer join to calculate these rows of Table 2 that do not have a match in Table 1.

The outer join operator is indicated by a plus sign enclosed in parentheses. The operator is used in the WHERE clause and follows the column name on that side of the join condition that does not have matching rows in the other table. Therefore, according to the syntax of this operator, the (+) can be placed on either side of the WHERE condition but not in both. The following example illustrates how this operator works.

EXAMPLE 2.12
List all the employees who do not have a manager.

The query to answer this question and a partial result are shown in the following:

```
SELECT M.last_name || ' ' || 'works for' ||' '|| E.last_name ||' '||
E.first_name AS "Managers and their employees"
FROM s_emp M, s_emp E
WHERE e.id (+)= M.manager_id;

Managers and their employees
--------------------------------
Martin works for          ◄——————   Notice that Martin has no manager.

Smith works for Martin Carmen
Norton works for Martin Carmen
Quentin works for Martin Carmen
.
.
.
25 rows selected.
```

Observe that this query is almost identical to the query of the previous example except for the outer operator that appears in the condition of the WHERE clause. The outer join operator creates one or more *null rows* that can be joined with one or more rows of the other table. Notice that the result includes a tuple that was not there before. In particular, the tuple that shows that Martin Carmen does not have a manager.

2.5 Creating Foreign Keys

In Chapter 1, we considered the CREATE TABLE command and saw how to define a simple primary key and how to specify attributes that are NOT NULL or UNIQUE. However, we did not consider how to enforce integrity constraints. As indicated in Section 1.4, foreign keys are used to maintain consistency among the rows of two relations or between the rows of the same relation. Foreign keys can be defined at the time a table is being created or after the table has been created. Let's consider both of these cases.

2.5.1 DEFINING FOREIGN KEYS AT THE TIME A TABLE IS CREATED

A foreign key within a table can be defined at the column level or at the table level. As we indicated in Chapter 1, only one constraint can be defined at the column level for any attribute of the table. The syntax to define a foreign key at the column level is shown below. The reader should keep in mind that in any table there may be one or more attributes defined as FK. Before creating any FK, the user needs to make sure that the column referenced in the parent table is either a PK or it has been defined as UNIQUE. The syntax to define FKs at the column level is shown next.

```
CREATE TABLE table-name
(
column-name-1      data type-1 [CONSTRAINT constraint-name]
                   REFERENCES Parent-Table(column-of-parent-
                   table),
 column-name-2     data type-2 [constraint],
                        .
                        .
 column-name-N     data type-N [constraint],
);
```

EXAMPLE 2.13

Create a table CUSTOMERS based on the information shown below. Define SalesRep as an FK that references the attribute AssociateId of the SalesAssociates table (not shown here). What assumptions need to be made?

Customer Id	City	Credit	SalesRep	Last Order
0109	Miami	Good	9012	1/12/00
0245	Caracas	Good	9786	1/15/99
0345	London	Poor	9873	1/26/99

The command to create this table may look like this:

```
CREATE TABLE customer(
  CustomerId   Varchar2(5) NOT NULL,
  City         Varchar2(25),                   Name of parent table
  Credit       Varchar2(4),
  SalesRep     Varchar2(4) REFERENCES SalesAssociate
               (AssociateId),    Column referenced in the parent table
  LastOrder    Date);
```

Before adding this foreign constraint, it is necessary to know that the attribute AssociateId has been defined as a PK or as a UNIQUE attribute in the SalesAssociate table.

2.5.2   DEFINING FOREIGN KEYS IN AN EXISTING TABLE

To define a foreign key constraint in a table that has already been created, we need to use the ALTER TABLE command. To define a single FK constraint with the ALTER TABLE command, we will use the following variation of this command:

```
ALTER TABLE table-name
ADD [CONSTRAINT constraint-name] FOREIGN KEY (column-name)
REFERENCES parent-table (parent-table column);
```

> **EXAMPLE 2.14**
> Using the CUSTOMERS table of the previous example, add an FK to this table so that the attribute Credit references the attribute Credit_Standing of the CreditType table. Assume that the latter table has been previously defined, but it is not shown here. What assumptions are necessary to ensure that a foreign key can be defined in the CUSTOMERS table?

To add a constraint to an existing table, we need to use the ALTER TABLE command. To add the required constraint, the ALTER TABLE command may look like this:

```
ALTER TABLE customer
ADD CONSTRAINT CreditType_Credit_FK FOREIGN KEY (CREDIT)
REFERENCES CreditType (CreditStanding);
```

To ensure that the FK can be created, the attribute CreditStanding must be either a PK or a UNIQUE attribute in the CreditType table.

2.6   Defining Primary Keys in an Existing Table

After a table has been created, a single or composite primary key can be defined for that table using the ALTER TABLE command. The syntax of this command to add a PK constraint is as follows:

```
ALTER TABLE ADD [CONSTRAINT constraint-name]
PRIMARY KEY (column-1 [,column-2 [,column-3]]...] );
```

Notice that if the primary key, is a composite key more than one attribute can be mentioned inside the parentheses, provided that these attributes are separated by commas. The use of this command is illustrated in the next example.

EXAMPLE 2.15
Assume that the table Baseball_World_Series_Result has already been created.
Add the corresponding constraints to make the attribute 'Year' the single
primary key of this table. The structure of the table is as follows:

Attribute	Data Type
Year	Date
American_League_Team	Varchar2(30)
National_League_Team	Varchar2(30)
Winner_Manager	Varchar2(25)
Losing_Manager	Varchar2(25)
Most_Valuable_Player	Varchar2(25)
Games_Played	Char(1)

The command to make the attribute Year the PK of this table is as
follows:

```
ALTER TABLE Baseball_World_Series_Result
ADD PRIMARY KEY (year);
```

EXAMPLE 2.16
Consider the structure of the table Summer_Olympics_Games shown below, and
define a composite primary key for this table with the attributes Year and
Country.

Attribute	Data Type
Country_Name	Varchar2(25)
Year	Date
Gold	Number(3)
Silver	Number(3)
Bronze	Number(3)

The ALTER TABLE command to create the required composite key may look
something like this:

```
ALTER TABLE Summer_Olympics_Games ADD
PRIMARY KEY (Country_Name, year);
```

Since the key of this table is a composite key of two attributes, both of these attributes need to be mentioned in the clause PRIMARY KEY.

2.7 Using CHECK Constraints to Restrict a Column's Input Values

In all previous examples, we have assumed that the data used to populate the tables has been of the proper size, range, and data type. However, this is not always the case, because the user can make mistakes while entering data. For example, while taking an order from a customer, a data entry operator may enter an order that exceeds the credit amount allowed for a particular customer. In cases like this, it is better to detect these errors while inputting the data. To avoid entering incorrect values into a table, we can impose a **CHECK** constraint on the attributes of a table. Although it is possible to add CHECK constraints to a table after the table has been populated, it is better to define these types of constraints *before* populating the table. This way, we can detect input errors as early as possible. The following examples illustrate the use of the CHECK constraints.

EXAMPLE 2.17
Assume that we are creating a Mailing_List table for customers who live in one of the following zip code areas: 22801, 22802, 22803, and 22804. To avoid entering an incorrect zip code, we can create a CHECK constraint in the Mailing_List table as follows:

```
CREATE TABLE Mailing_list(
  First_name    Varchar2(25),
  Last_name     Varchar2(25),
  Address       Varchar2(25),
  City          Varchar2(25),
  Zip_code Varchar2(5) CHECK( zip_code IN ('22801',
  '22802', '22803', '22804')));
```

Notice that in this case, we have made use of a CHECK constraint to restrict the values that can be inserted into the zip_code column. The IN operator allows us to use an expression list where we can explicitly name the values that can be inserted into this column. In this particular example, we have listed the permissible input values enclosed in single quotes because the attribute zip_code is a character attribute. For additional information on the IN operator, see Chapter 3, Section 3.3.2.

EXAMPLE 2.18
Assume that we are creating a Department table where the department numbers are greater than 10 and less than 50. Write the CHECK constraint to ensure that every department number inserted into the table falls in that range.

In this case, the corresponding CREATE TABLE command may look like this:

```
CREATE TABLE department(
 Name VARCHAR2(15) CONSTRAINT department_name_nn NOT NULL,
 Location  VARCHAR2(20),
 DeptNum   NUMBER CHECK (DeptNum BETWEEN 10 and 50));
```

In this case, we have used the **BETWEEN** operator to set a range of permissible numerical values for the DeptNum attribute. For additional information on the BETWEEN operator, see Chapter 3, Section 3.3.1.

2.8 Adding Columns to an Existing Table

In some occasions, it may be necessary to add a new column to an existing table. To do this, we need to use the ADD option of the ALTER TABLE command. The syntax of this command is as follows:

ALTER TABLE table-name
ADD new-column data-type [CONSTRAINT] [constraint-type];

When adding a new column to a table, the reader should keep in mind that the initial values of each row of the new column is NULL. We can add a column with a NOT NULL constraint only to a table that contains no rows.

> **EXAMPLE 2.19**
> Add to the Department table of Example 2.18 a new column called
> Manager_LastName. Assume that this column can be up to 25 characters long.

The ALTER TABLE command to add this new column may look like this:

```
ALTER TABLE department
ADD Manager_LastName   VARCHAR2(25);
```

2.9 Modifying Columns of an Existing Table

If there is a need to change a column definition in a table already created, we can use the MODIFY option of the ALTER TABLE command. The basic syntax of this command is as follows:

ALTER TABLE table-name
MODIFY column-name   [CONSTRAINT constraint-name]
**   [constraint-type];**

The reader should keep in mind that there are some restrictions on the use of this command, since we can only change the following column characteristics: data type, size, default value, and NOT NULL column constraints. The MODIFY clause only needs the column name and the modified part, rather than the entire column definition. In summary, the limitations of the use of this command are as follows:

- It is possible to change a CHAR column to VARCHAR2 and vice versa if the column contains NULL values in all its rows.
- It is possible to change the data type and decrease the column size if all rows of the table contain NULL.
- The only constraint that can be added to a table with the MODIFY option is a NOT NULL constraint, provided that the column does not contain NULL values.
- It is always possible to increase the size of a character or the precision of a numeric column.

EXAMPLE 2.20
Increase the size of the name column of the Department table to allow entering the name of the newly created department "Operations Research and Marketing Analysis".

The corresponding ALTER TABLE command is as follows:

```
ALTER TABLE department MODIFY name VARCHAR(45);
```

2.10   Removing Constraints from a Table

To remove a given constraint from a table, we can use the DROP option of the ALTER TABLE command. The variations of this command to drop unnamed and name constraints are as follows:

To remove a PK of a given table, use the following command:

```
ALTER TABLE table-name DROP PRIMARY KEY [CASCADE];
```

To remove an unnamed UNIQUE constraint, use the following command:

```
ALTER TABLE table-name DROP
UNIQUE ( column [,column [,column...]]..) [CASCADE];
```

To remove a named constraint, use the following command:

```
ALTER TABLE table-name DROP CONSTRAINT constraint-name [CASCADE];
```

In all these commands, the clause CASCADE removes any constraint that depends on the dropped integrity constraint. Without the use of this clause, we cannot drop a UNIQUE or PK that is part of a referential integrity constraint without also dropping the foreign key first. In addition, notice that there is no option to remove specifically a CHECK or a NOT NULL constraint. However, there is a command to remove *any named* constraint. Therefore, if we name a CHECK or NOT NULL constraint, we can remove them using this variation of the ALTER TABLE command.

EXAMPLE 2.21
Remove the NOT NULL constraint defined on the name attribute of the Department table of Example 2.18.

The corresponding ALTER TABLE command is as follows:

```
ALTER TABLE department DROP CONSTRAINT department_name_nn;
```

Notice that in this example, we dropped the constraint name instead of specifying the particulars of the constraint. This is one of the advantages of using constraint names, since we only need to remember one particular case of the ALTER TABLE command that works for all cases.

Solved Problems

Note: Before answering the following questions run the script SG.SOL to refresh the contents of the Sporting Goods database.

2.1. Write a query to display all orders placed by the customer 204. Show the order ID, the total for each order, and when they were placed. What type of relational operator is implemented by this query? Use the s_ord table.

The query to obtain the requested information and the result that it produces are shown below. The relational operator being applied is a projection.

```
SELECT id, total, date_ordered
FROM s_ord
WHERE customer_id = '204';

ID      TOTAL DATE_ORDE
--- --------- ---------
100    601100 31-AUG-92
111      2770 09-SEP-92
2 rows selected.
```

2.2. Rewrite the previous query to display the headings Order Id, Total Ordered, and Order Date. Make sure that the totals are shown with the format *ddd,ddd.00* (where *d* stands for a digit) and the headings are split in two lines.

Since the number of characters in the character definition of the attribute id is too small for displaying the heading Order Id, we need to use the SQL*Plus COLUMN command. Likewise, we need to use a numeric format to display the totals in the requested format. The COLUMN command, the SELECT query, and its results are shown in the following:

```
COLUMN id HEADING "Ordered | Id" FORMAT A7
COLUMN total HEADING "Total | Ordered" FORMAT 999,999.00
COLUMN date_ordered HEADING "Order|Date"
SELECT id, total, date_ordered
FROM s_ord
 WHERE customer_id = '204';

Ordered     Total   Order        ◄─────   New headings.
Id          Ordered Date
------- ----------- ---------
100      601,100.00 31-AUG-92
111        2,770.00 09-SEP-92
2 rows selected.
```

2.3. Display how many different customers have placed an order in the S_ORD table. Rename the column Customers who have placed an order, and split the title in two different lines. What type of relational operation is being applied to the table to answer this query?

Before issuing this query, it is necessary to format the customer column to change its heading. The following SQL*Plus command allows us to display the column heading as required:

```
COLUMN customer_id HEADING "Customers who have|placed an
order" FORMAT A20
```

The relational operator that allows us to answer this query is the projection operator. The implementation of this operator in SQL and the resulting table are shown in the following:

```
SELECT DISTINCT customer_id
FROM s_ord;
Customers who have
placed an order
--------------------
201
202
203
204
205
206
208
209
```

```
210
211
212
213
214
13 rows selected.
```

2.4. Select all the information in the table S_REGION without writing the column names of the table.

The query and its result are as follows:

```
SELECT *
FROM s_region;
Id     NAME
------- --------------------
1       North America
2       South America
3       Africa / Middle East
4       Asia
5       Europe
6       Central America /Caribbean

6 rows selected.
```

2.5. Display the last name, salary, and commission percent for all the sales representatives of the S_EMP table. Use the heading Sales Representative instead of Last Name. Is it necessary to use the SQL*Plus COLUMN command?

The query to obtain this information and the result that it produces are shown below. No, it is not necessary to use the COLUMN command, because the width of the attribute last_name is big enough to display the column alias Sales Representative.

```
SELECT last_name AS "Sales Representative", salary,
commission_pct
FROM S_emp
WHERE title = 'Sales Representative';

Sales
Representative           SALARY COMMISSION_PCT
-------------------- --------- ---------------
Henderson                  1400            10
Gilson                     1490          12.5
Sanders                    1515            10
Dameron                    1450          17.5
4 rows selected.
```

2.6. Display the name and the region in which they are located for all departments of the Sporting Goods database. What type of relational operation allows us to obtain this information?

To retrieve this information, we need to join the S_REGION and S_DEPT tables. The common attribute is `region_id` (of S_DEPT) and `id` (of S_region). Notice the use of table aliases to simplify the query. The query and the result that it produces are as follows:

```
SELECT D.name AS "Department", R.name AS "Region"
FROM s_dept D, s_region R
WHERE D.region_id = R.id;
Department              Region
-------------------- --------------------
Finance                North America
Sales                  North America
Sales                  South America
Sales                  Africa / Middle East
Sales                  Asia
Sales                  Europe
Operations             North America
Operations             South America
Operations             Africa / Middle East
Operations             Asia
Operations             Europe
Administration         North America
12 rows selected.
```

2.7. Display the first and last name of all sales representatives and their customers.

A query to obtain this information may look like the one shown below. Notice the use of the concatenation operator, the character string, and the blank spaces to change the appearance of the resulting table. Observe also the use of table aliases to simplify the query.

```
SELECT C.name || ' is the customer of ' || E.first_name ||
' ' || E.last_name AS "Sales Reps and their customers"
FROM s_emp E, s_customer C
WHERE C.sales_rep_id = E.id
ORDER BY E.last_name;
Sales Reps and their customers
---------------------------------------------------------
Toms Sporting Goods is the customer of Andre Dameron
Athletic Attire is the customer of Andre Dameron
Athletics One is the customer of Andre Dameron
Athletics Two is the customer of Andre Dameron
Shoes for Sports is the customer of Andre Dameron
Sports,Inc is the customer of Sam Gilson
.

.
24 rows selected.
```

2.8. Show the customers that have not been assigned a sales representative.

The query that satisfies this request is the outer join as follows:

```
SELECT C.name || ' is the customer of ' || E.first_name ||
' ' || E.last_name
AS "Sales Reps and their customers"
FROM s_emp E, s_customer C
WHERE C.sales_rep_id = E.id(+)
ORDER BY E.last_name;
Sales Reps and their customers
---------------------------------------------------- -----
Toms Sporting Goods is the customer of Andre Dameron
Athletic Attire is the customer of Andre Dameron
 .


 .

Hamada Sport is the customer of Jason Sanders
Muench Sports is the customer of Jason Sanders
Tall Rock Sports is the customer of            Customer without a Sales
 .                                             Representative.
 .

25 rows selected.
```

2.9. Display the last name and salary of all the employees in the S_EMP table. Make sure that the salary is displayed in the format *999,999.00*, where each *9* stands for a digit. Order the result in increasing dollar amounts.

To display the result in the required format, it is necessary to use the SQL*Plus COLUMN command. The query and a partial result are shown below. Notice that there was no need to use the reserved keyword ASC in the WHERE clause because this is the default value.

```
COLUMN salary FORMAT 999,999.00
SELECT last_name AS "Last Name", first_name AS "First
Name", salary AS "Salary"
FROM s_emp
ORDER BY salary;
Last Name              First Name              Salary
-------------------    --------------------    ----------
Patterson              Donald                   795.00
Pearl                  Roger                    795.00
Gantos                 Eddie                    800.00
Chester                Eddie                    800.00
Bell                   Alexander                850.00
 .

 .

25 rows selected.
```

2.10. Create the table Lakes_Of_The_World according to the description shown below. Use named constraints where necessary.

Attribute	Data Type	Constraint
Name	Up to 20 characters long	Primary key
Continent	Up to 15 characters long	One of the following values: Africa, Asia, Australia, Europe, Central America, North America, South America
Area	Numeric up to 6 digits	Values between 1799 and 143,244
Length	Numeric up to 3 digits	Values between 67 and 760
Elevation	Numeric up to 4 digits	Values between −92 and 12,500

The CREATE TABLE command for this particular table may look like this:

```
CREATE TABLE Lakes_Of_The_World (
Name VARCHAR2(20) PRIMARY KEY,
Continent VARCHAR2(15) CONSTRAINT Lotw_Continent_ck
CHECK( Continent IN ( 'Africa', 'Asia', 'Australia' ,
                      'Europe', 'Central America',
                      'North America', 'South America')),
Area       Number(6) CONSTRAINT Lotw_Area_ck
               CHECK ( Area between 1799 AND 143244),
Length     Number(3) CONSTRAINT Lotw_Length_ck
               CHECK(Length between 67 AND 760),
Elevation Number(4) CONSTRAINT Lotw_Elevation_ck
               CHECK( Elevation between -92 AND
                     123500));
```

2.11. Add to the S_EMP table a new column called `Performance`. The permissible values for this column are `'Satisfactory'`, `'Excellent'`, `'Unsatisfactory'`. Verify that the column has been added correctly.

To add a new column to an existing table, we need use the ALTER TABLE command. In this particular case, the command is as follows:

```
ALTER TABLE s_emp ADD performance VARCHAR2(15) CONSTRAINT
s_emp_performance_ck CHECK (performance IN ('Satisfactory',
'Excellent', 'Unsatisfactory'));
```

2.12. Increase the size of the attribute address in the S_CUSTOMER table from 20 characters to 25 characters.

To increase the size of an attribute in this table, we need to use the ALTER TABLE command. In this particular case, this command takes the form shown below. Observe that any other constraints associated with this column remain unchanged.

```
ALTER TABLE S_customer
MODIFY address VARCHAR2(25);
```

2.13. Drop the CHECK constraint added to the S_EMP table in Solved Problem 2.11.

To remove a named constraint from a table, we need to use the ALTER TABLE command. In this opportunity, this command takes the following form:

```
ALTER TABLE S_emp DROP CONSTRAINT s_emp_performance_ck;
```

2.14. Display the last name and first name of the manager of the warehouses of table S_CUSTOMER.

To retrieve this information, we need to form the equijoin of the S_EMP and S_CUSTOMER on their common attributes. The common attributes are manager_id (S_CUSTOMER) and id (S_EMP). This equijoin and the result that it produces are as follows:

```
SELECT E.first_name || ' ' || E.last_name ||
                    ' is the manager of warehouse ' || W.id
                AS "Warehouses and their managers"
FROM S_warehouse W, S_emp E
WHERE W.manager_id = E.id;
Warehouses and their managers
-----------------------------------------------------------
Molly Brown is the manager of warehouse 101
Marta Jackson is the manager of warehouse 10501
Roberta Hawkins is the manager of warehouse 201
Ben Burns is the manager of warehouse 301
Antoinette Catskill is the manager of warehouse 401
```

2.15. You have created several tables and their respective FK constraints. However, when you try to populate the tables, you start getting referential constraint errors. Why is this?

This type of error may occur when the tables cross-reference each other. That is, there may be a table A that has an FK that references table B, and at the same time, table B has an FK that references table A. To avoid this type of error, the FKs should be created after the tables have been populated.

2.16. Write a query to display all customers and their orders. If there are customers that have not placed an order, make sure that their names are also displayed. Use the following headings: Customer Id, Name, and Order Id.

To obtain this information, we need to form an outer join between the S_CUSTOMER and S_ORD tables. This join and the result that it produces are shown below. Notice the combined use of the SQL*Plus COLUMN command and the column aliases to produce the required headings.

```
COLUMN A HEADING 'Customer Id' FORMAT A15
COLUMN B HEADING 'Order Id' FORMAT A8
SELECT S_customer.id AS "A",
        S_customer.name, S_ord.id AS "B"
FROM s_customer , s_ord
WHERE S_customer.id = S_ord.customer_id(+);
```

```
Customer Id     NAME                    Order Id
-------------   -------------------     --------
201             One Sport               97
202             Deportivo Caracas       98
203             New Delhi Sports        99
204             Ladysport               100
204             Ladysport               111
205             Kim's Sporting Goods    101
206             Sportique               102
207             Tall Rock Sports    ◄──────────  This customer has not
208             Muench Sports           103          placed an order.
208             Muench Sports           104
209             Beisbol Si!             105
210             Futbol Sonora           106
210             Futbol Sonora           112
211             Helmut's Sports         107
212             Hamada Sport            108
213             Sports Emporium         109
214             Sports Retail           110
215             Sports Russia    ◄
301             Sports,Inc
302             Toms Sporting Goods         Customers who have not
303             Athletic Attire             placed an order.
304             Athletics For All
305             Shoes for Sports
306             BJ Athletics
403             Athletics One
404             Great Athletes
405             Athletics Two
406             Athletes Attic
28 rows selected.
```

2.17. Write the Class table with the attributes shown below. The composite key of this table is formed by the attributes `Course_Code` and `Class_Section`.

Attribute	Data Type	Constraints
Course_Code	Up to 5 characters	Required. Not Null
Class_Section	Up to 4 characters	Required. Not Null
Classroom	Up to 5 characters	
Instructor	Up to 25 characters	
Max_Enrollment	Number 2 digits	Between 10 and 30

Since the primary key is a composite key, it is necessary to define the PK at the table level. The corresponding CREATE TABLE command is as follows:

```
CREATE TABLE Class
( Course_Code     VARCHAR2(5),
  Class_Section   VARCHAR2(4),
  Classroom       VARCHAR(5),
  Instructor      VARCHAR2(25),
  Max_Enrollment NUMBER(2) CONSTRAINT Class_Max_Enroll_ck
                 CHECK (Max_Enrollment BETWEEN 10 AND 30),
  CONSTRAINT Class_Code_Section_pk PRIMARY KEY(Course_Code,
                                        Class_Section));
```

2.18. Add a new column to the Class table of the previous example. Call the column Teaching Assistant; the width of this column can be up to 15 characters long.

The command that allows us to add this new column is the ALTER TABLE command. In this case, the syntax of this command is as follows:

```
ALTER TABLE class ADD Teaching_Assistant VARCHAR2(15);
```

2.19. Write the corresponding command to increase the size of the Teaching_Assistant column to VARCHAR2(25).

The command that allows us to increase the size of a column is the ALTER TABLE command. In this particular case, the syntax of this command is as follows:

```
ALTER TABLE class MODIFY Teaching_Assistant VARCHAR2(25);
```

2.20. Drop the constraint associated with the attribute Max_Enrollment in the Class table.

To drop a named constraint, it is necessary to use the ALTER TABLE command. The syntax of this command is as follows.

```
ALTER TABLE class DROP CONSTRAINT Class_Max_Enroll_ck;
```

Supplementary Problems

Note: Refresh the SG database before answering the following questions.

2.21. Find the names of the employees of the Sporting Goods company that do not have customers using an outer query.

2.22. Display the first name, last name, and salary of all employees in the S_EMP table. Make sure that every row of the result is displayed using the following format:

> The salary in U.S. dollars of Donald Patterson is 795.
> The salary in U.S. dollars of Roger Pearl is 795.

2.23. Create the table RIVERS according to the description shown below.

Attribute	Data Type	Constraint
Name	Up to 20 characters long	Unique and NOT NULL
Length	Up to 4 digits	Values between 100 and 4160
Outflow	Up to 20 characters long	Required

2.24. Add a new column called `MaxDepth` to the Rivers table. Make sure that the values of this column range from 100 to 250 feet.

2.25. Run the World_Cities script, and display the name of all the South American cities in alphabetical order.

2.26. Remove the constraint `S_ITEM_PRODUCT_ID_FK` from the table S_item.

2.27. Display the first name, last name, and department name of all employees who work for the SportingGoods company. Display the results in the following format:

> Employee Jason Sanders works for department 33.

2.28. Change the heading of the result of the query of the previous problem to read `Employees and their departments`.

2.29. Modify the previous query and change the display to read according to the following pattern:

> Employee Jason Sanders works for the Sales Department.

2.30. Display the ID of the warehouses and the regions in which they are located.

2.31. Display the product name, its ID, and quantity ordered of all items. Sort the result by product name.

2.32. For all products with a suggested wholesale price greater than $100, display the product name and their suggested wholesale price. Make sure that the prices are displayed according to the following pattern:

> World Cup Net $123.00
> Bunny Boot $150.00

Use the headings `Product Name` and `Suggested Wholesale Price`, with the latter split in two columns. Order the result in ascending values by suggested wholesale price.

2.33. Display the ID of the different warehouses and the country in which they are located. Display the results according to the following format:

> Warehouse 100 is located in Seattle, USA.

2.34. Drop the constraint `s_customer_id_pk` of the table S_CUSTOMER. What happens and why?

2.35. What can be done to remove the constraint of the previous question?

Answers to Supplementary Problems

2.21.
```
SELECT C.name || ' is the customer of ' || E.first_name ||
' ' || E.last_name
AS "Sales Reps and their customers"
FROM s_emp E, s_customer C
WHERE C.sales_rep_id(+) = E.id
ORDER BY E.last_name;
```

2.22.
```
SELECT 'The salary in U.S. dollars of ' || first_name ||
' ' || last_name || ' is ' || salary AS
"Employee Salaries"
FROM s_emp
ORDER BY salary;
```

2.23.
```
CREATE TABLE Rivers (
Name    VARCHAR2(20) PRIMARY KEY,
Length  NUMBER(4) CONSTRAINT Rivers_Length_ck
                CHECK (Length BETWEEN 100 AND 4160),
Outflow VARCHAR2(20) CONSTRAINT Rivers_Outflow_nn
                NOT NULL);
```

2.24.
```
ALTER TABLE rivers ADD MaxDepth NUMBER(3) CONSTRAINT
rivers_maxdept_ck CHECK (MaxDepth BETWEEN 100 and 250);
```

2.25.
```
SELECT city
FROM world_cities
WHERE continent = 'SOUTH AMERICA'
ORDER BY CITY;
```

2.26.
```
ALTER TABLE s_item DROP CONSTRAINT S_ITEM_PRODUCT_ID_FK;
```
2.27.
```
SELECT 'Employee '||first_name||' '||last_name||' '
       ||'works for department ' || dept_id
FROM s_emp;
```

2.28.

```
CLEAR COLUMNS
COLUMN A HEADING 'Employees and their department'
FORMAT A80
SELECT 'Employee '||first_name||' '||last_name||' '
       ||'works for department ' || dept_id AS "A"
FROM s_emp;
```

2.29.

```
COLUMN A HEADING 'Employees and their department'
FORMAT A70
SELECT 'Employee '||E.first_name||' '||E.last_name||'
'||'works for the '|| D.name || ' Department' AS "A"
FROM s_emp E, s_dept D
WHERE E.dept_id = D.id;
```

2.30.

```
SELECT W.id || ' is located in region '|| R.id AS
"Warehouses and their regions"
FROM s_warehouse W, s_region R
WHERE W.region_id = R.id;
```

2.31.

```
SELECT s_product.name, s_product.id, S_item.quantity
"ORDERED" FROM s_product, s_item
WHERE s_product.id = s_item.product_id
ORDER by s_product.name;
```

2.32.

```
COLUMN Price HEADING "Suggested|Wholesale Price"
FORMAT $999,999.00
SELECT P.name AS "Product Name", P.suggested_whlsl_price AS
"Price"
FROM s_product P
WHERE P.suggested_whlsl_price >100
ORDER BY P.suggested_whlsl_price;
```

2.33.

```
COLUMN A HEADING 'Warehouses and their locations'
FORMAT A60
SELECT 'Warehouse ' ||W.id || ' is located in ' || W.city
|| ', ' || W.country AS "A"
FROM s_warehouse W;
```

2.34. This constraint cannot be dropped because the column ID is referenced by a foreign key in some other table of the database.

2.35.

```
ALTER TABLE s_customer DROP CONSTRAINT s_customer_id_pk CASCADE;
```

CHAPTER 3

Boolean Operators and Pattern Matching

3.1 Boolean Operators and Their Use in Compound Clauses

The WHERE clause of the SELECT statement allows the retrieval of tuples according to the value of a specified column. Sometimes, however, you want to retrieve tuples using the values of more than one column. For example, in a payroll table you might want to see the names of everyone making a certain hourly rate who had been with the company for over 10 years. In a billing table you might want the names of everyone who lives in a certain zip code who was late in paying a bill. Boolean operators are available for creating a compound condition in the WHERE clause of a SQL statement. A *compound condition* is one that contains two or more Boolean operators. These operators are AND, OR, and NOT. Table 3-1 shows a subset of the customer table S_CUSTOMER that will be used in the following sections.

Table 3-1. Customer table.

ID	NAME	ZIP_CODE	CREDIT_RA	SAL
301	Sports, Inc	22809	EXCELLENT	12
302	Toms Sporting Goods	22809	POOR	14
303	Athletic Attire	22808	GOOD	14
304	Athletics For All	22808	EXCELLENT	12
305	Shoes for Sports	22809	EXCELLENT	14
306	BJ Athletics	22810	POOR	12
403	Athletics One	17601	GOOD	14
404	Great Athletes	17602	EXCELLENT	12
405	Athletics Two	17602	EXCELLENT	14
406	Athletes Attic	17601	POOR	12

3.1.1 THE AND OPERATOR

The AND operator is used to connect two Boolean conditions in the WHERE clause of a SELECT statement. When the SQL statement is executed, only those rows that satisfy both conditions are retrieved. The syntax for using AND with two Boolean conditions looks like this:

```
SELECT column_list
FROM tablename
WHERE condition_1 AND condition_2;
```

EXAMPLE 3.1
Write an SQL query to list the names of all the customers in the S_CUSTOMER table who have EXCELLENT credit ratings and are in the zip code 22809.

```
SELECT name
FROM s_customer
WHERE credit_rating = 'EXCELLENT'
AND zip_code = '22809';
```

The resulting table would list Sports, Inc. and Shoes for Sports. Even though there are three stores with excellent credit ratings, only two are in the zip code 22809.

EXAMPLE 3.2
Write an SQL query to list the names of all the customers in the S_CUSTOMER table who have EXCELLENT credit ratings and work with sales rep 12.

```
SELECT name
FROM s_customer
WHERE credit_rating = 'EXCELLENT'
AND sales_rep_id = '12';
```

Three different stores would be listed—Great Athletes, Athletics for All and Sports, Inc—because they meet both conditions of the compound Boolean statement.

Any number of clauses can be connected with ANDs. All of the conditions must be true in order for a row to be included in the resulting table. The AND condition is *commutative*. This means that the condition WHERE condition_1 AND condition_2 is equivalent to the condition WHERE condition_2 AND condition_1.

EXAMPLE 3.3
Write an SQL query to list the names of all the customers in the S_CUSTOMER table who have EXCELLENT credit ratings, are in zip code 22809, and deal with sales rep 12.

```
SELECT name
FROM s_customer
WHERE credit_rating = 'EXCELLENT'
AND zip_code = '22809'
AND sales_rep_id = '12';
```

This time, only Sports, Inc meets all three criteria.

3.1.2 THE OR OPERATOR

The OR operator is also used to connect two Boolean conditions in the WHERE clause of a SELECT statement. The rows that are retrieved are those that satisfy either or both conditions. The syntax for using OR with two Boolean conditions looks like this:

```
SELECT column_list
FROM table_name
WHERE condition_1 OR condition_2;
```

Like the AND condition, the OR condition is commutative.

EXAMPLE 3.4
Write an SQL query to list the names of all the customers in the S_CUSTOMER table who have EXCELLENT or GOOD credit ratings.

```
SELECT name
FROM s_customer
WHERE credit_rating = 'EXCELLENT'
OR credit_rating = 'GOOD';
```

Five stores have EXCELLENT credit ratings, and two stores are GOOD. Therefore, seven names will be listed in the resulting table.

EXAMPLE 3.5
Write an SQL query to list the names, credit ratings, and sales rep of all the customers in the S_CUSTOMER table who have EXCELLENT credit ratings or deal with sales rep 12.

```
SELECT name, credit_rating, sales_rep_id
FROM s_customer
WHERE credit_rating = 'EXCELLENT'
OR sales_rep_id = '12';
```

The resulting table is shown below. Two stores match only the EXCELLENT credit rating. Two match only the sales rep 12 criterion. Notice that even though other stores meet both criteria, they are still only listed once in the output. The OR operator is *inclusive*. That is, it will choose the tuples that match any one criterion or all the criteria.

```
NAME                    CREDIT_RA SA
--------------------    ---------- --
Sports,Inc              EXCELLENT 12
Athletics For All       EXCELLENT 12
Shoes for Sports        EXCELLENT 14
BJ Athletics            POOR      12
Great Athletes          EXCELLENT 12
Athletics Two           EXCELLENT 14
Athletes Attic          POOR      12
```

Once again, any number of OR conditions may be used. The order in which the conditions are listed does not matter.

EXAMPLE 3.6

Write an SQL query to list the names, credit ratings, zip codes, and sales rep of all the customers in the S_CUSTOMER table who have EXCELLENT credit ratings, or a zip code of 22809 or deal with sales rep 12.

```
SELECT name,credit_rating,zip_code,sales_rep_id
FROM s_customer
WHERE credit_rating = 'EXCELLENT'
OR zip_code = '22809'
OR sales_rep_id = '12';
```

The only stores not listed in the resulting table would be Athletic Attire and Athlete One, because they do not meet any of the conditions. Notice that Athletic Attire has the following values: the credit rating is GOOD, the zip code is 22808, and the sales rep is 14.

3.1.3   THE NOT OPERATOR

Usually the WHERE clause tells you which tuples to include in the resulting table. Sometimes, however, you want to specify the tuples to exclude. The NOT operator is used to specify the column values that are used to exclude the record from display. The AND and the OR may be used to connect two or more conditions. They are binary operators. The NOT acts only on one condition. It is a unary operator. The syntax for using NOT with a WHERE condition looks like this:

```
SELECT column_list
FROM table_name
WHERE NOT condition;
```

EXAMPLE 3.7

Write an SQL query to list the names, zip codes, and sales reps of all the customers in the S_CUSTOMER table who are NOT in the 22808 zip code area.

```
SELECT name, zip_code, sales_rep_id
FROM s_customer
WHERE NOT zip_code = '22808';
NAME                    ZIP_CODE          SAL
-------------------- ---------------- ---
Sports,Inc              22809              12
Toms Sporting Goods     22809              14
Shoes for Sports        22809              14
BJ Athletics            22810              12
Athletics One           17601              14
Great Athletes          17602              12
Athletics Two           17602              14
Athletes Attic          17601              12
```

Notice the placement of the NOT, immediately before the attribute or column in the condition. This placement is awkward when reading it in English. It would sound better to place it like this:

```
                    WHERE zip_code NOT = '22808';
```

However, it is invalid to place the NOT operator immediately adjacent to the equal-to relational operator (=). If we do this, the RDBMS will generate an error message. If that sequence is desired, it would be better to use the not-equal-to relational operator (<>), explained in Chapter 1. The following two conditions are interchangeable and will produce the same output:

```
WHERE NOT zip_code = '22808';
WHERE zip_code <> '22808';
```

As indicated before, the NOT only acts upon one condition. If two item values are to be excluded, the NOT must be repeated.

EXAMPLE 3.8
Write an SQL query to list the names, zip codes, and sales reps of all the customers in the S_CUSTOMER table who are NOT in the 22808 zip code area and also NOT dealing with sales rep 14.

```
SELECT name, zip_code, sales_rep_id
FROM s_customer
WHERE NOT zip_code = '22808'
AND NOT sales_rep_id = '14';
NAME                    ZIP_CODE          SAL
-------------------- ---------------- ---
Sports,Inc              22809              12
BJ Athletics            22810              12
Great Athletes          17602              12
Athletes Attic          17601              12
```

Notice the combination of the NOT and the AND' operators. The WHERE clause

```
WHERE NOT zip_code = '22808' AND sales_rep_id = '14';
```

would produce very different results, as shown below. The NOT is a unary operator and must be repeated with each condition unless parentheses are used.

```
NAME                    ZIP_CODE          SAL
--------------------    ---------------   ---
Toms Sporting Goods     22809             14
Shoes for Sports        22809             14
Athletics One           17601             14
Athletics Two           17602             14
```

When using Boolean operators, it is helpful to examine some equivalent ways of expressing the same conditions. Table 3-2 demonstrates alternate ways of expressing the same condition using combinations of the operators AND, OR, NOT, and parentheses. These conditions are also known as the *D'Morgan's Laws*.

Table 3-2.　Logical equivalencies.

a. NOT (p AND q)	is the same as	NOT p OR NOT q
b. NOT (p OR q)	is the same as	NOT p AND NOT q
c. NOT (NOT p)	is the same as	p

For example, examine the query in Example 3.8. The WHERE condition looked like this:

```
WHERE NOT zip_code = '22808'AND NOT sales_rep_id = '14';
```

According statement a in Table 3-2, the WHERE condition can be restated in this way and produce identical results:

```
SELECT name, zip_code, sales_rep_id
FROM s_customer
WHERE NOT (zip_code = '22808' OR sales_rep_id = '14');
```

Statement b from Table 3-2 will be illustrated in Example 3.9. Be careful about using NOT with OR. If the NOT is used with OR in a condition with no parentheses, often the entire table is listed because nothing is excluded.

EXAMPLE 3.9
What will print using the following SELECT statement?

```
SELECT name, zip_code
FROM s_customer
WHERE NOT zip_code = '22809'
OR NOT zip_code = '22808';
```

The entire table would be printed because the tuples with the zip code 22809 meet the condition NOT = 22808 and tuples with other zip codes meet the condition NOT = 22809. The tuple with any other zip code meets both conditions, so the entire table would be displayed. The following alternate form would produce identical results:

```
SELECT name, zip_code
FROM s_customer
WHERE NOT (zip_code = '22809'AND zip_code = '22808');
```

3.1.4   ORDER OF PRECEDENCE FOR COMPOUND CONDITIONS

The three Boolean operators may be combined in any compound condition of the WHERE statement as long as the operators are carefully placed. The order of precedence is similar to other programming languages. This order of precedence for evaluation and the truth tables for the Boolean operators is shown in Table 3-3. This order can be modified through the use of parentheses. Carefully examine the examples below. The formation of correct compound clauses does not always mirror the English expression of the problem.

Table 3-3.   Order of precedence for Boolean operators.

OPERATOR	DEFINITION	DESCRIPTION	ORDER
( )		Everything inside parentheses evaluated.	Evaluated first
NOT p	NOT p F T T F	Changes the value of p to the opposite.	Evaluate second
p AND q	p AND q T T T T F F F F T F F F	Both conditions p and q must be true.	Evaluate third
p OR q	p OR q T T T T T F F T T F F F	Either condition p or q or both may be true.	Evaluate last

EXAMPLE 3.10
Suppose you want to retrieve the customers who have excellent credit ratings from the 22808 and 22809 zip code areas. A first way of writing the query is below. What is the resulting table?

```
SELECT name, zip_code, credit_rating
FROM s_customer
WHERE zip_code = '22809'
OR zip_code = '22808'
AND credit_rating = 'EXCELLENT';
NAME                    ZIP_CODE        CREDIT_RA
--------------------    --------------- ---------
Sports, Inc             22809           EXCELLENT
Toms Sporting Goods     22809           POOR
Athletics For All       22808           EXCELLENT
Shoes for Sports        22809           EXCELLENT
```

The output does not meet the requirements because the AND is evaluated first. All the rows with zip codes of 22808 with an excellent credit rating are included. However, the OR is then evaluated, listing every tuple with 22809 zip code. In order to retrieve the desired tuples, the OR should be evaluated first. To force this order, use parentheses to retrieve all information in the two zip codes. Then the AND is evaluated to select the desired tuples. The correct statement to produce the table without Toms Sporting Goods would look like this:

```
SELECT name, zip_code, credit_rating
FROM s_customer
WHERE (zip_code = '22809'OR zip_code = '22808')
AND credit_rating = 'EXCELLENT';
```

EXAMPLE 3.11
Write an SQL statement to list the name, credit rating, and sales representatives of the customers who either do not use the sales representative 12 whatever their credit rating or do not have an EXCELLENT credit rating whoever their sales representative is.

a. A first attempt to answer the question looks like this:

```
SELECT name, credit_rating, sales_rep_id
FROM s_customer
WHERE NOT sales_rep_id = '12'
OR credit_rating = 'EXCELLENT';
NAME                    CREDIT_RA SAL
--------------------    --------- ---
Sports, Inc             EXCELLENT 12
Toms Sporting Goods     POOR      14
Athletic Attire         GOOD      14
```

```
Athletics For All      EXCELLENT 12
Shoes for Sports       EXCELLENT 14
Athletics One          GOOD      14
Great Athletes         EXCELLENT 12
Athletics Two          EXCELLENT 14
```

This query, however, lists those with EXCELLENT credit ratings instead of those without. In order for the NOT to apply to both parts of the condition, it is necessary to use parentheses.

b. A second attempt, similar to the one above, is shown below. Notice the resulting table is very different from the first table, but it still does not fulfill the specifications.

```
SELECT name, credit_rating, sales_rep_id
FROM s_customer
WHERE NOT (sales_rep_id = '12'
OR credit_rating = 'EXCELLENT');
NAME                   CREDIT_RA SAL
---------------------- --------- ---
Toms Sporting Goods    POOR      14
Athletic Attire        GOOD      14
Athletics One          GOOD      14
```

This table lists those customers who do not use representative 12 and do not have an EXCELLENT credit rating. But it misses those without an EXCELLENT rating who use 12 and those who don't use 12 with any credit rating.

c. The original specification asked to list those who do not use the sales representative 12 whatever their credit rating or those who do not have an EXCELLENT credit rating whoever their sales representative is. It should include any customers who use representative 12 and have a POOR or GOOD rating. This third try fulfills the requirements.

```
SELECT name, credit_rating, sales_rep_id
FROM s_customer
WHERE NOT sales_rep_id = '12'
OR NOT credit_rating = 'EXCELLENT';
NAME                   CREDIT_RA SAL
---------------------- --------- ---
Toms Sporting Goods    POOR      14
Athletic Attire        GOOD      14
Shoes for Sports       EXCELLENT 14
BJ Athletics           POOR      12
Athletics One          GOOD      14
Athletics Two          EXCELLENT 14
Athletes Attic         POOR      12
```

EXAMPLE 3.12
Write an SQL query to print the name, zip code and credit rating of the entire list except those in zip code 22809 with an EXCELLENT credit rating.

In order to construct this query, first establish the group to exclude (zip_code = '22809' AND credit_rating = 'EXCELLENT') and then put a NOT in front of the condition.

```
SELECT name, zip_code, credit_rating
FROM s_customer
WHERE NOT(zip_code = '22809' AND credit_rating = 'EXCELLENT');
NAME                    ZIP_CODE         CREDIT_RA
------------------- --------------- ---------
Toms Sporting Goods     22809            POOR
Athletic Attire         22808            GOOD
Athletics For All       22808            EXCELLENT
BJ Athletics            22810            POOR
Athletics One           17601            GOOD
Great Athletes          17602            EXCELLENT
Athletics Two           17602            EXCELLENT
Athletes Attic          17601            POOR
```

Notice not all those in zip code 22809 have been excluded and not all those with excellent credit ratings have been excluded. Great care must be taken when designing any complex condition.

3.2 Pattern Matching—the LIKE Statement and Wildcard Characters

All the previous examples retrieved tuples based upon the exact value of a column or columns. Sometimes you don't know the exact value, or you want to retrieve tuples with similar values. The LIKE operator is used to match specific patterns. For example, you might want to retrieve the tuples for everyone whose name begins with J or for all those who live on a St rather than a Rd or Blvd. SQL provides a pattern-matching mechanism for character columns. The LIKE operator works only with character string columns. Compound conditions can also be constructed combining the NOT, AND, and OR with LIKE. The syntax looks like this:

```
SELECT column_list
FROM table_name
WHERE column_name LIKE 'pattern';
```

The pattern contained within the single quotation marks makes use of wildcard characters percent (%) and underline (_). Table 3-4 contains the subset of the customer table with more information that will be used as an example in the following sections.

Table 3-4. Expanded customer table.

ID	NAME	ADDRESS	CITY	ST	ZIP_COD	PHONE
301	Sports, Inc	72 High St	Harrisonburg	VA	22809	540-123-4567
302	Toms Sporting Goods	6741 Main St	Harrisonburg	VA	22809	540-987-6543
303	Athletic Attire	54 Market St	Harrisonburg	VA	22808	540-123-6789
304	Athletics For All	286 Main St	Harrisonburg	VA	22808	540-987-1234
305	Shoes for Sports	538 High St	Harrisonburg	VA	22809	540-123-9876
306	BJ Athletics	632 Water St	Harrisonburg	VA	22810	540-987-9999
403	Athletics One	912 Columbia Rd	Lancaster	PA	17601	717-234 6786
404	Great Athletes	121 Litiz Pike	Lancaster	PA	17602	717-987-2341
405	Athletics Two	435 High Rd	Lancaster	PA	17602	717-987-9875
406	Athletes Attic	101 Greenfield Rd	Lancaster	PA	17601	717-234-9888

3.2.1 PERCENT SIGN (%)

The percent sign is used as a wildcard character that can represent a string of zero or more characters. For example, the pattern `'S%'` would represent any column value beginning with uppercase S of any length, including the single letter S. The pattern `'%s'` represents any column value ending with the lowercase s. The value must end in s and contain no trailing blank letters. The pattern `'%s%'` would test for any words containing the lower case s in any location. Remember that patterns inside the quotation marks are case-sensitive.

EXAMPLE 3.13
Write an SQL query to list the name, address, city and state of any customers whose names begin with words like *Athlete* or *Athletics*. List them alphabetically.

```
SELECT name, address, city, state
FROM s_customer
WHERE name LIKE 'Athl%'
ORDER BY name;
NAME                ADDRESS             CITY            STATE
----------------    ----------------    ------------    -----
Athletes Attic      101 Greenfield Rd   Lancaster       PA
Athletic Attire     54 Market St        Harrisonburg    VA
Athletics For All   286 Main St         Harrisonburg    VA
Athletics One       912 Columbia Rd     Lancaster       PA
Athletics Two       435 High Rd         Lancaster       PA
```

EXAMPLE 3.14
Write an SQL query to list the name, address, city, and state of any customers who live on *streets*, not *roads*. List them in order alphabetically.

```
SELECT name, address, city, state
FROM s_customer
WHERE address LIKE '%St'
ORDER BY name;
NAME                 ADDRESS            CITY             STATE
----------------     ---------------    --------------   -----
Athletic Attire      54 Market St       Harrisonburg     VA
Athletics For All    286 Main St        Harrisonburg     VA
BJ Athletics         632 Water St       Harrisonburg     VA
Shoes for Sports     538 High St        Harrisonburg     VA
Sports, Inc          72 High St         Harrisonburg     VA
Toms Sporting Goods  6741 Main St       Harrisonburg     VA
```

EXAMPLE 3.15

Write an SQL query to list the name, address, city, and state of any customers who do NOT live on *streets*. Don't specify an order.

```
SELECT name, address, city, state
FROM s_customer
WHERE address NOT LIKE '%St';
NAME                 ADDRESS            CITY             STATE
----------------     ---------------    --------------   -----
Athletics One        912 Columbia Rd    Lancaster        PA
Great Athletes       121 Litiz Pike     Lancaster        PA
Athletics Two        435 High Rd        Lancaster        PA
Athletes Attic       101 Greenfield Rd  Lancaster        PA
```

Notice the location of the word NOT. When used with LIKE, it is placed in the normal English sequence.

EXAMPLE 3.16

Write an SQL query to list the name, address, city, and state of any customers who live on `High`, whether it is a street or road.

```
SELECT name, address, city, state
FROM s_customer
WHERE address LIKE '%High%';
NAME                 ADDRESS            CITY             STATE
----------------     ---------------    --------------   -----
Sports, Inc          72 High St         Harrisonburg     VA
Shoes for Sports     538 High St        Harrisonburg     VA
Athletics Two        435 High Rd        Lancaster        PA
```

The pattern matched any record with `High` in the address.

3.2.2   UNDERLINE CHARACTER (_)

The underline character is used to represent *exactly one* character. Use it with character columns where you know the exact length and need a wildcard for a specific number of characters.

EXAMPLE 3.17

Write an SQL query to list the name and phone number of any customers who are in the United States 540 area code. Phone numbers are always the same length, with three-digit area code, the group of three digits, the exchange, and finally, the last four digits in this format: *xxx-xxx-xxxx*. Because you know the exact length of the column, you can use one underline character to represent each of the other digits of the phone number.

```
SELECT name, phone
FROM s_customer
WHERE phone LIKE '540-___-____';
NAME                     PHONE
--------------------     -----------
Sports,Inc               540-123-4567
Toms Sporting Goods      540-987-6543
Athletic Attire          540-123-6789
Athletics For All        540-987-1234
Shoes for Sports         540-123-9876
BJ Athletics             540-987-9999
```

Note that in this example you could also use the pattern '540%'. It would produce the same results. Sometimes, however, the length of the string you are checking makes a difference.

EXAMPLE 3.18

Assume that there are two related franchises, Athletics One and Athletics Two. Write an SQL query to list the name and phone number of only these two customers.

```
SELECT name, phone
FROM s_customer
WHERE name LIKE 'Athletics ___';
```

The pattern contains the word *Athletics* followed by a space and three underline characters. This query would produce the desired result. In this case, if you had used 'Athletics%', you would have also retrieved the phone number of the customer Athletics for All.

EXAMPLE 3.19

Write an SQL query to list the name and phone number of any customers who have a 987 exchange (middle three digits), whatever their area code. Because you know the exact length of the phone numbers (3 digits-3 digits-4 digits), you

can use one underline character to represent each of the other digits of the
phone number.

```
SELECT name, phone
FROM s_customer
WHERE phone LIKE '___-987-____';
NAME                    PHONE
--------------------    ------------
Toms Sporting Goods     540-987-6543
Athletics For All       540-987-1234
BJ Athletics            540-987-9999
Great Athletes          717-987-2341
Athletics Two           717-987-9875
```

The resulting table above demonstrates that this query using underline
characters retrieves the correct tuples. If you had tried `'%987%'` instead, it
would have produced the table below, which lists other tuples. It matched the *987*
anywhere in the column, not in the exact placement required.

```
NAME                    PHONE
--------------------    ------------
Toms Sporting Goods     540-987-6543
Athletics For All       540-987-1234
Shoes for Sports        540-123-9876
BJ Athletics            540-987-9999
Great Athletes          717-987-2341
Athletics Two           717-987-9875
```

The percent sign works well for matching any group of characters, and the
underline character matches any one character. However, trying to match a
percent sign or an underline character itself can create a problem. In order to
indicate that you really want to match the sign, use the escape character, usually
\, before the symbol in the query. Although helpful, this does not work in many
implementations of SQL.

3.3　Matching Values in a List or a Range of Values

The LIKE condition is used to match specific patterns. Sometimes you want to
select rows based upon the values of a certain range or values in a specific list.
BETWEEN and IN are the operators to use for these functions. Usually the
Boolean operators AND or OR can be used to duplicate the queries using
BETWEEN and IN. However, using BETWEEN and IN can sometimes be more
convenient.

3.3.1   THE BETWEEN OPERATOR

Use BETWEEN to identify a range of acceptable values. To indicate a range, both a low value and a high value must be specified, and the lower value must be specified first. The range of values to be selected includes the low value, the high value, and everything between. The syntax looks like this:

```
SELECT column_list
FROM table_name
WHERE column_name BETWEEN lowvalue AND highvalue;
```

> **EXAMPLE 3.20**
> Write an SQL query to list the ID, name, and phone number of any customers whose ID falls between 303 and 306.

```
SELECT id, name, phone
FROM s_customer
WHERE id BETWEEN '303' AND '306';
```

The query retrieves any tuples with id of 303, 304, 305, and 306. The resulting chart looks like this:

```
ID   NAME                PHONE
---  ------------------  ----------------
303  Athletic Attire     540-123-6789
304  Athletics For All   540-987-1234
305  Shoes for Sports    540-123-9876
306  BJ Athletics        540-987-9999
```

Another way to obtain a similar result is shown below:

```
SELECT id, name, phone
FROM s_customer
WHERE id >= '303' AND id <= '306';
```

Notice that using the BETWEEN makes the specification more clear.

The BETWEEN operator can be used with numeric or string columns. The following example illustrates another string column.

> **EXAMPLE 3.21**
> Write an SQL query to list the ID, name, and phone number of any customers whose name begins with letters of the alphabet between A and G.

a. A first attempt to design a query looks like this:

```
SELECT id, name, phone
FROM s_customer
WHERE name BETWEEN 'A' AND 'G';
ID   NAME               PHONE
---  -----------------  ------------
303  Athletic Attire    540-123-6789
304  Athletics For All  540-987-1234
306  BJ Athletics       540-987-9999
403  Athletics One      717-234-6786
405  Athletics Two      717-987-9875
406  Athletes Attic     717-234-9888
```

b. Notice that the store Great Athletes is not included in the resulting table. The reason for this is that the high value indicated was `'G'`, which allows for no letters to follow the `'G'`. In order to include Great Athletes in the chart, use `'H'` as the high value. If any store's actual name was "H", it would be included, but that is unlikely. The correct query should look like this:

```
SELECT id, name, phone
FROM s_customer
WHERE name BETWEEN 'A' AND 'H';
```

EXAMPLE 3.22

Write an SQL query to list the ID, name, and phone number of any customers whose ID is not between *302* and *306*. The use of the Boolean NOT excludes the tuples with ID's of *302*, *306*, and everything between.

```
SELECT id, name, phone
FROM s_customer
WHERE id NOT BETWEEN '302' AND '306';
ID   NAME               PHONE
---  -----------------  ------------
301  Sports,Inc         540-123-4567
403  Athletics One      717-234-6786
404  Great Athletes     717-987-2341
405  Athletics Two      717-987-9875
406  Athletes Attic     717-234-9888
```

3.3.2   THE IN OPERATOR

Use the IN operator to choose a row based upon values in a particular list of any length. The list is specified in parentheses, with the individual list items separated by commas. The syntax looks like this:

```
SELECT column_list
FROM table_name
WHERE column_name IN (value_1, value_2, ... value_n);
```

This query will retrieve the rows that have any of the specified values in that column. It usually helps readability to list the list items in sequence, but this is not required. The items may be numeric or character string. Each item in a list of character strings must be enclosed in single quotes.

EXAMPLE 3.23
Write an SQL query to list the ID, name, and phone number of the customers whose ID is *303*, *305*, *403*, and *406*.

```
SELECT id, name, phone
FROM s_customer
WHERE id IN ('303', '305', '403', '406');
```

Only the tuples for Athletic Attire, Shoes for Sports, Athletics One, and Athletes Attic are chosen.

EXAMPLE 3.24
Write an SQL query to list the ID, name, and phone number of the customers whose ID is not *303*, *305*, *403*, and *406*. The addition of the NOT operator reverses the query.

```
SELECT id, name, phone
FROM s_customer
WHERE id NOT IN ('303', '403', '305', '406');
```

Only the tuples for Athletic Attire, Shoes for Sports, Athletics One, and Athletes Attic are not chosen. The values in parentheses may be written in any order.

EXAMPLE 3.25
Write an SQL query to list the name and credit rating for the customers who have an EXCELLENT or POOR credit rating.

```
SELECT name, credit_rating
FROM s_customer
WHERE credit_rating IN ('EXCELLENT', 'POOR');
```

The resulting table would list all in those two categories.

Solved Problems

Note: Before answering the following questions, rerun the SG script to refresh the database. Also, use this subset of the employee table S_EMP for these questions.

ID	LAST_NAME	FIRST_NAME	MAN	TITLE	DEP	SALARY
1	Martin	Carmen		President	50	4500
2	Smith	Doris	1	VP, Operations	41	2450
3	Norton	Michael	1	VP, Sales	31	2400
4	Quentin	Mark	1	VP, Finance	10	2450
5	Roper	Joseph	1	VP, Administration	50	2550
6	Brown	Molly	2	Warehouse Manager	41	1600
7	Hawkins	Roberta	2	Warehouse Manager	42	1650
8	Burns	Ben	2	Warehouse Manager	43	1500
9	Catskill	Antoinette	2	Warehouse Manager	44	1700
10	Jackson	Marta	2	Warehouse Manager	45	1507
11	Henderson	Colin	3	Sales Representative	31	1400
12	Gilson	Sam	3	Sales Representative	32	1490
13	Sanders	Jason	3	Sales Representative	33	1515
14	Dameron	Andre	3	Sales Representative	35	1450
15	Hardwick	Elaine	6	Stock Clerk	41	1400
16	Brown	George	6	Stock Clerk	41	940
17	Washington	Thomas	7	Stock Clerk	42	1200
18	Patterson	Donald	7	Stock Clerk	42	795
19	Bell	Alexander	8	Stock Clerk	43	850
20	Gantos	Eddie	9	Stock Clerk	44	800
21	Stephenson	Blaine	10	Stock Clerk	45	860
22	Chester	Eddie	9	Stock Clerk	44	800
23	Pearl	Roger	9	Stock Clerk	34	795
24	Dancer	Bonnie	7	Stock Clerk	45	860
25	Schmitt	Sandra	8	Stock Clerk	45	1100

3.1. Write an SQL query and show the resulting table to list the last name, first name, department ID, and salary of the employees in department 41 whose salary is greater than $1000.

```
SELECT last_name, first_name, dept_id, salary
FROM s_emp
WHERE dept_id = '41'AND salary > 1000;
LAST_NAME        FIRST_NAME        DEP    SALARY
---------------  ----------------  ------ ------
Smith            Doris             41     2450
Brown            Molly             41     1600
Hardwick         Elaine            41     1400
```

George Brown is in department 41, but he makes under $1000, so he is not listed in the table. Remember that when using AND, both conditions must be true.

3.2. Write an SQL query and show the resulting table to list the last name, first name, department, ID, and salary of all the warehouse managers of departments 42 through 44 whose salary is greater than $1600.

```
SELECT last_name, first_name, dept_id, salary
FROM s_emp
WHERE title = 'Warehouse Manager'
AND dept_id >= '42'
AND dept_id <= '44'
AND salary > 1600;
LAST_NAME          FIRST_NAME          DEP    SALARY
--------------     ----------------    -----  ------
Hawkins            Roberta             42     1650
Catskill           Antoinette          44     1700
```

Remember that string values are case-sensitive. The value of title in the quotation marks must be the correct case. The condition title='WAREHOUSE MANAGER' would have produced an empty table. Also, in order to retrieve all the departments between 42 and 44, the department ID must be greater than or equal to 42 *and* less than or equal to 44. The warehouse manager of department 43 who makes less than $1600 is not listed in the table.

3.3. Write an SQL query and show the resulting table to list the last name, first name, and department ID of all the employees in departments 31 and 41.

```
SELECT last_name, first_name, dept_id
FROM s_emp
WHERE dept_id = '31'
OR dept_id = '41';
LAST_NAME          FIRST_NAME          DEP
--------------     ----------------    ---
Smith              Doris               41
Norton             Michael             31
Brown              Molly               41
Henderson          Colin               31
Hardwick           Elaine              41
Brown              George              41
```

Notice that the specifications said *departments 31 and 41*. However, in this query we could not use the AND because the department ID is never both. Instead, we can use the OR to list the people whether their department is 31 or 41.

3.4. Write an SQL query and show the resulting table to list the last name, first name, title, and manager ID of all the employees whose manager IDs are 1, 2, or NULL. Order the results alphabetically by title, last name, and first name. Remember, you can order by as many attributes as desired.

```
SELECT title, last_name, first_name, manager_id
FROM s_emp
WHERE manager_id is NULL
OR manager_id = '1'
OR manager_id = '2'
ORDER BY title, last_name, first_name;
```

TITLE	LAST_NAME	FIRST_NAME	MAN
President	Martin	Carmen	
VP, Administration	Roper	Joseph	1
VP, Finance	Quentin	Mark	1
VP, Operations	Smith	Doris	1
VP, Sales	Norton	Michael	1
Warehouse Manager	Brown	Molly	2
Warehouse Manager	Burns	Ben	2
Warehouse Manager	Catskill	Antoinette	2
Warehouse Manager	Hawkins	Roberta	2
Warehouse Manager	Jackson	Marta	2

To retrieve a manager ID with a NULL value, use manager_id IS NULL, instead of manager_id = NULL. Remember, the equal sign is not the same as the IS.

3.5. Write an SQL query and show the resulting table to list the last name, first name, department ID and salary of all employees who do not make over $1200.

```
SELECT last_name, first_name, dept_id, salary
FROM s_emp
WHERE NOT salary > 1200;
```

LAST_NAME	FIRST_NAME	DEP	SALARY
Brown	George	41	940
Washington	Thomas	42	1200
Patterson	Donald	42	795
Bell	Alexander	43	850
Gantos	Eddie	44	800
Stephenson	Blaine	45	860
Chester	Eddie	44	800
Pearl	Roger	34	795
Dancer	Bonnie	45	860
Schmitt	Sandra	45	1100

The condition in the WHERE clause could also have been written WHERE salary <= 1200. If the specifications had said "salary of all employees who do not make $1200 or higher," the condition would have been written WHERE NOT salary >= 1200. In that case, Thomas Washington would not have been included in the resulting table. Also notice that no commas are used in numeric values within the query.

3.6. Write an SQL query and show the resulting table to list the last name, first name, department ID, and salary of all the employees making over $2000 who are not in departments 31 or 41.

```
SELECT last_name, first_name, dept_id, salary
FROM s_emp
WHERE salary > 2000
AND NOT dept_id = '31'
AND NOT dept_id = '41';
LAST_NAME            FIRST_NAME         DEP     SALARY
--------------       ----------------   -------  ------
Martin               Carmen             50      4500
Quentin              Mark               10      2450
Roper                Joseph             50      2550
```

Remember the correct placement of the NOT before the column name. Also, the specifications said "not in department 31 or 41." That means NOT department 31 AND NOT department 41. Be careful in the wording of the conditions.

3.7. Write an SQL query and show the resulting table to list the last name, first name, title, and department ID of those in department 41 who are either a stock clerk or a warehouse manager.

```
SELECT last_name, first_name, title, dept_id
FROM s_emp
WHERE dept_id = '41'
AND (title = 'Stock Clerk' OR title = 'Warehouse Manager');
LAST_NAME            FIRST_NAME         TITLE               DEP
--------------       ----------------   -----------------   ---
Brown                Molly              Warehouse Manager   41
Hardwick             Elaine             Stock Clerk         41
Brown                George             Stock Clerk         41
```

The OR operator is evaluated first. Doris Smith is not included because she meets neither of the title requirements. Remember, without the parentheses, the AND would have been evaluated first, and the requirement of department 41 would not have applied to the warehouse managers. The incorrect table would have looked like this:

```
LAST_NAME            FIRST_NAME         TITLE               DEP
--------------       ----------------   -----------------   ---
Brown                Molly              Warehouse Manager   41
Hawkins              Roberta            Warehouse Manager   42
Burns                Ben                Warehouse Manager   43
Catskill             Antoinette         Warehouse Manager   44
Jackson              Marta              Warehouse Manager   45
Hardwick             Elaine             Stock Clerk         41
Brown                George             Stock Clerk         41
```

3.8. Write an SQL query and show the resulting table to list the last name, first name, title, department ID, and salary of those whose salary is over $1500 and who are not warehouse managers or in department 50.

```
SELECT last_name, first_name, title, dept_id, salary
FROM s_emp
WHERE salary > 1500
AND NOT (title='Warehouse Manager' OR dept_id = '50');
LAST_NAME       FIRST_NAME    TITLE                DEP  SALARY
-----------     -----------   ------------------   ---  ------
Smith           Doris         VP, Operations       41   2450
Norton          Michael       VP, Sales            31   2400
Quentin         Mark          VP, Finance          10   2450
Sanders         Jason         Sales Representative 33   1515
```

3.9. Write an SQL query and show the resulting table to list the last name and first name of all employees whose last names begin with the letter *B*. List them alphabetically by last name and first name.

```
SELECT last_name, first_name
FROM s_emp
WHERE last_name LIKE 'B%'
ORDER BY last_name, first_name;
LAST_NAME               FIRST_NAME
-------------------     -------------------
Bell                    Alexander
Brown                   George
Brown                   Molly
Burns                   Ben
```

Notice that the last names are in alphabetical order, and the two with the same last name also have the first names listed in alphabetical order.

3.10. Write an SQL query and show the resulting table to list the last name, first name, and title of the employees whose last names end in the letters *son*. List them alphabetically by last name.

```
SELECT last_name, first_name, title
FROM s_emp
WHERE last_name LIKE '%son'
ORDER BY last_name;
LAST_NAME         FIRST_NAME        TITLE
--------------    --------------    --------------------
Gilson            Sam               Sales Representative
Henderson         Colin             Sales Representative
Jackson           Marta             Warehouse Manager
Patterson         Donald            Stock Clerk
Stephenson        Blaine            Stock Clerk
```

3.11. Write an SQL query and show the resulting table to list the first name and last name of the employees whose first names contain the letter *m*.

```
SELECT first_name, last_name
FROM s_emp
WHERE first_name LIKE '%m%';
FIRST_NAME            LAST_NAME
-------------------- --------------------
Carmen                Martin
Sam                   Gilson
Thomas                Washington
```

The resulting table does *not* list Mark or Molly or anyone else whose name has an uppercase *M*. In order to include both letters, use OR in the condition, as shown below. This statement would retrieve the tuples of everyone with either an upper- or lowercase *m*.

```
SELECT first_name, last_name
FROM s_emp
WHERE first_name LIKE '%m%' OR first_name LIKE '%M%';
```

3.12. Write an SQL query and show the resulting table to list the first name and last name of the employees whose first name ends in *e* and who have exactly six letters in the first name.

```
SELECT first_name, last_name
FROM s_emp
WHERE first_name LIKE '_____e';
FIRST_NAME            LAST_NAME
-------------------- --------------------
Elaine                Hardwick
George                Brown
Blaine                Stephenson
Bonnie                Dancer
```

Notice that names like "Eddie" are not included because the requirement is exactly six characters.

3.13. Write an SQL query and show the resulting table to list the first name and last name of the employees whose first name begins with *M* and contains exactly five letters.

```
SELECT first_name, last_name
FROM s_emp
WHERE first_name LIKE 'M____';
FIRST_NAME            LAST_NAME
-------------------- --------------------
Molly                 Brown
Marta                 Jackson
```

Again, Mark and Michael were not selected because the condition retrieved only names exactly five characters long.

3.14. The underline character can be used to match the exact length of the string with no specified characters. Write an SQL query and show the resulting table to list the first name and last name of any employee whose first and last names both have exactly `five` characters.

```
SELECT first_name, last_name
FROM s_emp
WHERE first_name LIKE '_____' AND last_name LIKE '_____';
FIRST_NAME               LAST_NAME
-------------------      --------------------
Doris                    Smith
Molly                    Brown
Roger                    Pearl
```

3.15. Write an SQL query and show the resulting table to list the first name, last name, and title of any employees with *no space* character in the title.

```
SELECT first_name, last_name, title
FROM s_emp
WHERE title NOT LIKE '% %';
```

The only record listed will be that of the President, Carmen Martin, because the title is only one word and therefore has no spaces in it.

3.16. Write an SQL query and show the resulting table to list the first name, last name, and salary of those employees whose salary is between $1000 and $1500.

```
SELECT first_name, last_name, salary
FROM s_emp
WHERE salary BETWEEN 1000 AND 1500;
FIRST_NAME               LAST_NAME               SALARY
-------------------      --------------------    ---------
Ben                      Burns                   1500
Colin                    Henderson               1400
Sam                      Gilson                  1490
Andre                    Dameron                 1450
Elaine                   Hardwick                1400
Thomas                   Washington              1200
Sandra                   Schmitt                 1100
```

Notice that Ben Burns is included because his salary is exactly $1500. Remember that neither a comma (i.e., 1,500) nor the dollar sign is used in SQL queries. To format the result in that way, see Chapter 4.

3.17. Write an SQL query and show the resulting table to list the ID, first name, last name, and user ID of those employees whose user ID starts with letters *p* through *s*.

```
SELECT id, first_name, last_name, userid
FROM s_emp
WHERE userid BETWEEN 'p' AND 't';
ID  FIRST_NAME          LAST_NAME            USERID
--- ------------------- -------------------- --------
18  Donald              Patterson            patterdv
23  Roger               Pearl                pearlrg
4   Mark                Quentin              quentiml
5   Joseph              Roper                roperjm
13  Jason               Sanders              sanderjk
25  Sandra              Schmitt              schmitss
2   Doris               Smith                smithdj
21  Blaine              Stephenson           stephebs
```

Remember, in order to include all the user IDs beginning with *s*, the string `'t'` must be used as the upper limit.

3.18. Write an SQL query and show the resulting table to list the ID, first name, and last name of the employees whose ID numbers are 13, 15, 17, and 10. (Remember, the list values in the parentheses can be in any sequence.)

```
SELECT id, first_name, last_name
FROM s_emp
WHERE id IN ('13', '15', '17', '10');
ID  FIRST_NAME          LAST_NAME
--- ------------------- --------------------
10  Marta               Jackson
17  Thomas              Washington
15  Elaine              Hardwick
13  Jason               Sanders
```

The ORDER BY clause could be used to display the output in order of ID.

3.19. Write an SQL query and show the resulting table to list the ID, first name, last name, and title of the employees whose last names are Brown, Burns, Washington, and Jackson. List them in alphabetical order.

```
SELECT id, first_name, last_name, title
FROM s_emp
WHERE last_name IN ('Brown', 'Burns', 'Washington', 'Jackson')
ORDER BY last_name;
ID  FIRST_NAME  LAST_NAME            TITLE
--- ----------- -------------------- ------------------
6   Molly       Brown                Warehouse Manager
16  George      Brown                Stock Clerk
8   Ben         Burns                Warehouse Manager
10  Marta       Jackson              Warehouse Manager
17  Thomas      Washington           Stock Clerk
```

3.20. Write an SQL query and show the resulting table to list last and first names of the vice presidents, along with their department ID and the name of their department.

```
SELECT s_emp.last_name, s_emp.dept_id, s_dept.name
FROM s_emp, s_dept
WHERE s_emp.dept_id = s_dept.id AND title LIKE 'VP%';
LAST_NAME             DEP NAME
--------------------  --- --------------------
Smith                 41  Operations
Norton                31  Sales
Quentin               10  Finance
Roper                 50  Administration
```

Notice that this query requires data from two different tables. Therefore, the table name must precede each field name for clarity.

3.21. Write an SQL query and show the resulting table to list the customer name and the last name of the sales representative for all sales representatives whose last name begins with *H*.

```
SELECT s_customer.name, s_emp.last_name
FROM s_emp, s_customer
WHERE s_emp.id = s_customer.sales_rep_id
AND s_emp.last_name LIKE 'H%';
NAME                  LAST_NAME
--------------------  ---------------
New Delhi Sports      Henderson
Ladysport             Henderson
Kim's Sporting Goods  Henderson
Beisbol Si!           Henderson
Helmut's Sports       Henderson
Sports Emporium       Henderson
Sports Retail         Henderson
Sports Russia         Henderson
```

The query requests information from both the employee and the customer table.

3.22. Write an SQL query and show the resulting table to show the customer name, the region name, the sales representative's last name, and the country for all customers with a POOR credit rating. (*Hint*: This time you need to query three different tables.)

```
SELECT s_customer.name "CUSTOMER", s_region.name "REGION",
       s_emp.last_name "SALES REP", s_customer.country "COUNTRY"
FROM s_customer, s_region, s_emp
WHERE s_customer.sales_rep_id = s_emp.id
AND s_customer.region_id = s_region.id
AND s_customer.credit_rating = 'POOR';
CUSTOMER            REGION          SALES REP    COUNTRY
------------------  --------------  ----------   -----------
Toms Sporting Goods North America   Dameron      US
BJ Athletics        North America   Gilson       US
Athletes Attic      North America   Gilson       US
Sports Retail       North America   Henderson    US
Sports Russia       Europe          Henderson    Russia
```

Supplementary Problems

Note: Before answering the following questions, rerun the SG script to refresh the database. Also, use this order table S_ORD for the Supplementary Problems 3.23 through 3.36.

```
ID   DATE_ORDE DATE_SHIP SAL   TOTAL PAYMEN
---  --------- --------- ---   ------- ------
100  31-AUG-92 10-SEP-92 11     601100 CREDIT
101  31-AUG-92 15-SEP-92 14     8056.6 CREDIT
102  01-SEP-92 08-SEP-92 15       8335 CREDIT
103  02-SEP-92 22-SEP-92 15        377 CASH
104  03-SEP-92 23-SEP-92 15      32430 CREDIT
105  04-SEP-92 18-SEP-92 11    2722.24 CREDIT
106  07-SEP-92 15-SEP-92 12      15634 CREDIT
107  07-SEP-92 21-SEP-92 15     142171 CREDIT
108  07-SEP-92 10-SEP-92 13     149570 CREDIT
109  08-SEP-92 28-SEP-92 11    1020935 CREDIT
110  09-SEP-92 21-SEP-92 11    1539.13 CASH
111  09-SEP-92 21-SEP-92 11       2770 CASH
97   28-AUG-92 17-SEP-92 12      84000 CREDIT
98   31-AUG-92 10-SEP-92 14        595 CASH
99   31-AUG-92 18-SEP-92 14       7707 CREDIT
112  31-AUG-92 10-SEP-92 12        550 CREDIT
```

3.23. Write an SQL query and show the resulting table to list the order number, date ordered, sales representative, and order total for the orders from sales representative, 14 on August 31, 1992.

3.24. Write an SQL query and show the resulting table to list the order number, date ordered, sales representative, and order total for the orders from sales representative 14 on August 31, 1992, where the total is greater than $6000.

3.25. Write an SQL query and show the resulting table to list the order number, date ordered, sales representative, and payment type for the orders on August 31, 1992, or the orders where the payment type was cash.

3.26. Write an SQL query and show the resulting table to list the order number, date ordered, sales representative, and order total for all credit orders not ordered on August 31, 1992:

3.27. Write an SQL query and show the resulting table to list the order number, date ordered, sales representative, and order total for all orders not ordered on August 31, 1992.

3.28. Write an SQL query and show the resulting table to list the order number, date ordered, sales representative and order total the orders ordered from sales representative 12 on August 31, 1992, or September 1, 1992.

3.29. Write an SQL query and show the resulting table to list the order number, date ordered, and date shipped for the orders made before the end of August or shipped before September 10.

3.30. Write an SQL query and show the resulting table to list the order number, date shipped, and payment type for all orders except those shipped after September 15 that were credit orders. List the table in the order of when they were shipped.

3.31. Write an SQL query and show the resulting table to list the order number, date ordered, date shipped, and order total for those orders for more than $6000 that were either not ordered after August 31 or shipped before September 10.

3.32. Write an SQL query and show the resulting table to list the order number, date ordered, date shipped, and order total for those orders that were ordered in August.

3.33. Write an SQL query and show the resulting table to list the order number, date ordered, sales representative, and order total for those orders whose total was between $6000 and $8000.

3.34. Write an SQL query and show the resulting table to list the order number, date ordered, and date shipped for all the orders that were ordered during the month of September 1992.

3.35. Write an SQL query and show the resulting table to list the order number, customer number, and date ordered for customers 204, 206, 201, and 202. List the resulting table in order of customer number.

3.36. Write an SQL query and show the resulting table to list the customer name, customer ID, and payment type for all items ordered. Display them in order of customer ID. Don't display any customer twice. (*Hint*: This query requires two different tables.)

Use this subset of the table WORLD_CITIES for the Supplementary Problems 3.37 through 3.42.

CITY	COUNTRY	CONTINENT
ATHENS	GREECE	EUROPE
ATLANTA	UNITED STATES	NORTH AMERICA
DALLAS	UNITED STATES	NORTH AMERICA
NASHVILLE	UNITED STATES	NORTH AMERICA
VICTORIA	CANADA	NORTH AMERICA
PETERBOROUGH	CANADA	NORTH AMERICA
VANCOUVER	CANADA	NORTH AMERICA
TOLEDO	UNITED STATES	NORTH AMERICA
WARSAW	POLAND	EUROPE
LIMA	PERU	SOUTH AMERICA
RIO DE JANEIRO	BRAZIL	SOUTH AMERICA
SANTIAGO	CHILE	SOUTH AMERICA
BOGOTA	COLOMBIA	SOUTH AMERICA
BUENOS AIRES	ARGENTINA	SOUTH AMERICA
QUITO	ECUADOR	SOUTH AMERICA
CARACAS	VENEZUELA	SOUTH AMERICA
MADRAS	INDIA	ASIA
NEW DELHI	INDIA	ASIA
BOMBAY	INDIA	ASIA
MANCHESTER	ENGLAND	EUROPE
LONDON	ENGLAND	EUROPE
MOSCOW	RUSSIA	EUROPE

```
PARIS            FRANCE             EUROPE
SHENYANG         CHINA              ASIA
CAIRO            EGYPT              AFRICA
TRIPOLI          LIBYA              AFRICA
BEIJING          CHINA              ASIA
ROME             ITALY              EUROPE
TOKYO            JAPAN              ASIA
SYDNEY           AUSTRALIA          AUSTRALIA
SPARTA           GREECE             EUROPE
MADRID           SPAIN              EUROPE
```

3.37. Write an SQL query and show the resulting table to list the city and country for all the cities that begin with the letter *S*.

3.38. Write an SQL query and show the resulting table to list the city and country for all the cities that end with the letter *O*.

3.39. Write an SQL query and show the resulting table to list the city and country for all the cities that begin with *M* and have exactly `six` letters in them.

3.40. Write an SQL query and show the resulting table to list the city and country for all the cities that contain an *A* as the *second* letter.

3.41. Write an SQL query and show the resulting table to list the city and country for all the cities that are not in North or South America and that do not contain `six` letters.

3.42. Write an SQL query and show the resulting table to list the city, country, and continent for all the cities in Africa, Australia, and Asia.

Answers to Supplementary Problems

3.23.
```
SELECT id, date_ordered, sales_rep_id, total
FROM s_ord
WHERE sales_rep_id = '14'
AND date_ordered = '31-AUG-92';
ID   DATE_ORDE SAL   TOTAL
---  --------- ---   ------
101 31-AUG-92 14   8056.6
98  31-AUG-92 14     595
99  31-AUG-92 14    7707
```

3.24.
```
SELECT id, date_ordered, sales_rep_id, total
FROM s_ord
WHERE sales_rep_id = '14'
AND date_ordered = '31-AUG-92'
```

```
AND total > 6000;
ID  DATE_ORDE SAL   TOTAL
--- --------- ---   ------
101 31-AUG-92 14    8056.6
99  31-AUG-92 14      7707
```

3.25.

```
SELECT id, date_ordered, sales_rep_id, payment_type
FROM s_ord
WHERE date_ordered = '31-AUG-92'
OR payment_type = 'CASH';
ID  DATE_ORDE SAL PAYMEN
--- --------- --- ------
100 31-AUG-92 11  CREDIT
101 31-AUG-92 14  CREDIT
103 02-SEP-92 15  CASH
110 09-SEP-92 11  CASH
111 09-SEP-92 11  CASH
98  31-AUG-92 14  CASH
99  31-AUG-92 14  CREDIT
112 31-AUG-92 12  CREDIT
```

3.26.

```
SELECT id, date_ordered, sales_rep_id, payment_type
FROM s_ord
WHERE NOT date_ordered = '31-AUG-92';
ID  DATE_ORDE SAL PAYMEN
--- --------- --- ------
102 01-SEP-92 15  CREDIT
103 02-SEP-92 15  CASH
104 03-SEP-92 15  CREDIT
105 04-SEP-92 11  CREDIT
106 07-SEP-92 12  CREDIT
107 07-SEP-92 15  CREDIT
108 07-SEP-92 13  CREDIT
109 08-SEP-92 11  CREDIT
110 09-SEP-92 11  CASH
111 09-SEP-92 11  CASH
97  28-AUG-92 12  CREDIT
```

3.27.

```
SELECT id, date_ordered, sales_rep_id, payment_type
FROM s_ord
WHERE NOT date_ordered = '31-AUG-92'
AND payment_type = 'CREDIT';
ID  DATE_ORDE SAL PAYMEN
--- --------- --- ------
102 01-SEP-92 15  CREDIT
104 03-SEP-92 15  CREDIT
```

```
105 04-SEP-92 11   CREDIT
106 07-SEP-92 12   CREDIT
107 07-SEP-92 15   CREDIT
108 07-SEP-92 13   CREDIT
109 08-SEP-92 11   CREDIT
97  28-AUG-92 12   CREDIT
```

3.28.

```
SELECT id, date_ordered, sales_rep_id, total
FROM s_ord
WHERE sales_rep_id = '12'
AND (date_ordered = '31-AUG-92' OR date_ordered = '01-SEP-92');
ID  DATE_ORDE SAL  TOTAL
--- --------- --- ---------
112 31-AUG-92 12   550
```

3.29.

```
SELECT id, date_ordered, date_shipped
FROM s_ord
WHERE date_ordered <= '31-AUG-92'
OR date_shipped <= '10-SEP-92';
ID  DATE_ORDE DATE_SHIP
--- --------- ---------
100 31-AUG-92 10-SEP-92
101 31-AUG-92 15-SEP-92
102 01-SEP-92 08-SEP-92
108 07-SEP-92 10-SEP-92
97  28-AUG-92 17-SEP-92
98  31-AUG-92 10-SEP-92
99  31-AUG-92 18-SEP-92
112 31-AUG-92 10-SEP-92
```

3.30.

```
SELECT id, date_shipped, payment_type
FROM s_ord
WHERE NOT (date_shipped > '15-SEP-92'
AND payment_type = 'CREDIT')
ORDER BY date_shipped;
ID  DATE_SHIP PAYMEN
--- --------- ------
102 08-SEP-92 CREDIT
100 10-SEP-92 CREDIT
108 10-SEP-92 CREDIT
112 10-SEP-92 CREDIT
98  10-SEP-92 CASH
101 15-SEP-92 CREDIT
106 15-SEP-92 CREDIT
110 21-SEP-92 CASH
111 21-SEP-92 CASH
103 22-SEP-92 CASH
```

3.31.

```
SELECT id, date_ordered, date_shipped, total
FROM s_ord
WHERE total > 6000
AND (NOT date_ordered > '31-AUG-92'
OR NOT date_shipped < '10-SEP-92');
ID  DATE_ORDE DATE_SHIP    TOTAL
--- --------- ---------  -------
100 31-AUG-92 10-SEP-92   601100
101 31-AUG-92 15-SEP-92   8056.6
104 03-SEP-92 23-SEP-92    32430
106 07-SEP-92 15-SEP-92    15634
107 07-SEP-92 21-SEP-92   142171
108 07-SEP-92 10-SEP-92   149570
109 08-SEP-92 28-SEP-92  1020935
97  28-AUG-92 17-SEP-92    84000
99  31-AUG-92 18-SEP-92     7707
```

3.32.

```
SELECT id, date_ordered, date_shipped, total
FROM s_ord
WHERE date_ordered LIKE '%AUG%';
```

Or since the date column is a fixed length, the following would produce the same results:

```
SELECT id, date_ordered, date_shipped, total
FROM s_ord
WHERE date_ordered LIKE '___AUG___';
ID  DATE_ORDE DATE_SHIP    TOTAL
--- --------- ---------   ------
100 31-AUG-92 10-SEP-92   601100
101 31-AUG-92 15-SEP-92   8056.6
97  28-AUG-92 17-SEP-92    84000
98  31-AUG-92 10-SEP-92      595
99  31-AUG-92 18-SEP-92     7707
112 31-AUG-92 10-SEP-92      550
```

3.33.

```
SELECT id, date_ordered, sales_rep_id, total
FROM s_ord
WHERE total BETWEEN 6000 AND 8000;
ID  DATE_ORDE SAL   TOTAL
--- --------- ---   ------
99  31-AUG-92 14     7707
```

3.34.

```
SELECT id, date_ordered, date_shipped
FROM s_ord
WHERE date_ordered BETWEEN '01-SEP-92' AND '30-SEP-92';
```

```
ID  DATE_ORDE DATE_SHIP
--- --------- ---------
102 01-SEP-92 08-SEP-92
103 02-SEP-92 22-SEP-92
104 03-SEP-92 23-SEP-92
105 04-SEP-92 18-SEP-92
106 07-SEP-92 15-SEP-92
107 07-SEP-92 21-SEP-92
108 07-SEP-92 10-SEP-92
109 08-SEP-92 28-SEP-92
110 09-SEP-92 21-SEP-92
111 09-SEP-92 21-SEP-92
```

3.35.

```
SELECT id, customer_id, date_ordered
FROM s_ord
WHERE customer_id IN (204, 206, 201, 202)
ORDER BY customer_id;
ID  CUS DATE_ORDE
--- --- ---------
97  201 28-AUG-92
98  202 31-AUG-92
100 204 31-AUG-92
111 204 09-SEP-92
102 206 01-SEP-92
```

3.36.

```
SELECT DISTINCT s_customer.name, s_customer.id,
    s_ord.payment_type "ORDERS"
FROM s_customer, s_ord
WHERE s_customer.id = s_ord.customer_id
ORDER BY s_customer.id;
NAME                    ID  ORDERS
--------------------    --- ------
One Sport               201 CREDIT
Deportivo Caracas       202 CASH
New Delhi Sports        203 CREDIT
Ladysport               204 CASH
Ladysport               204 CREDIT
Kim's Sporting Goods    205 CREDIT
Sportique               206 CREDIT
Muench Sports           208 CASH
Muench Sports           208 CREDIT
Beisbol Si!             209 CREDIT
Futbol Sonora           210 CREDIT
Helmut's Sports         211 CREDIT
Hamada Sport            212 CREDIT
Sports Emporium         213 CREDIT
Sports Retail           214 CASH
```

3.37.

```
SELECT city, country
FROM world_cities
WHERE city LIKE 'S%';
CITY                               COUNTRY
-------------------------   -------------------------
SANTIAGO                           CHILE
SHENYANG                           CHINA
SYDNEY                             AUSTRALIA
SPARTA                             GREECE
```

3.38.

```
SELECT city, country
FROM world_cities
WHERE city LIKE '%O';
CITY                               COUNTRY
-------------------------   --------------
TOLEDO                             UNITED STATES
RIO DE JANEIRO                     BRAZIL
SANTIAGO                           CHILE
QUITO                              ECUADOR
CAIRO                              EGYPT
TOKYO                              JAPAN
```

3.39.

```
SELECT city, country
FROM world_cities
WHERE city LIKE 'M_____';
CITY                               COUNTRY
-------------------------   -------------------------
MADRAS                             INDIA
MOSCOW                             RUSSIA
MADRID                             SPAIN
```

3.40.

```
SELECT city, country
FROM world_cities
WHERE city LIKE '_A%';
CITY                               COUNTRY
-------------------------   -------------------------
DALLAS                             UNITED STATES
NASHVILLE                          UNITED STATES
VANCOUVER                          CANADA
WARSAW                             POLAND
SANTIAGO                           CHILE
CARACAS                            VENEZUELA
MADRAS                             INDIA
MANCHESTER                         ENGLAND
PARIS                              FRANCE
CAIRO                              EGYPT
MADRID                             SPAIN
```

3.41.

```
SELECT city, country
FROM world_cities
WHERE city NOT LIKE '_____' AND
      continent NOT IN ('NORTH AMERICA', 'SOUTH AMERICA');
CITY                       COUNTRY
------------------------   ------------------------
NEW DELHI                  INDIA
MANCHESTER                 ENGLAND
PARIS                      FRANCE
SHENYANG                   CHINA
CAIRO                      EGYPT
TRIPOLI                    LIBYA
BEIJING                    CHINA
ROME                       ITALY
TOKYO                      JAPAN
```

3.42.

```
SELECT city, country, continent
FROM world_cities
WHERE continent IN ('ASIA', 'AFRICA', 'AUSTRALIA');
CITY                       COUNTRY                 CONTINENT
------------------------   ----------------------  -----------
MADRAS                     INDIA                   ASIA
NEW DELHI                  INDIA                   ASIA
BOMBAY                     INDIA                   ASIA
SHENYANG                   CHINA                   ASIA
CAIRO                      EGYPT                   AFRICA
TRIPOLI                    LIBYA                   AFRICA
BEIJING                    CHINA                   ASIA
TOKYO                      JAPAN                   ASIA
SYDNEY                     AUSTRALIA               AUSTRALIA
```

CHAPTER 4

Arithmetic Operations and Built-In Functions

4.1   Arithmetic Operations

As we indicated in Chapter 1, SQL is a database language for the retrieval of information. It was not designed for complex mathematical processes. However, it is sometimes desirable to perform simple arithmetic with numeric or character columns of the table. The new columns that are the result of the calculations do not become permanent fields of the table. They are for display purposes only.

The arithmetic operators supported by SQL and their order of precedence are shown in Table 4-1. The precedence follows standard arithmetic order, with multiplication and division performed before addition and subtraction. As is standard in most programming languages, operators of the same precedence are evaluated from left to right. Parentheses can always be used to change the order of evaluation or simply for clarity.

Table 4-1.   Order of precedence of arithmetic operators.

Operator	Description	Order of Precedence
( )	Parentheses	Evaluated first
* /	Multiplication and division	Evaluated next
+ −	Addition and subtraction	Evaluated last

Calculations are often used for keeping track of inventory. Table 4-2 shows a subset of an inventory table S_INVENTORY that will be used in the following sections.

Table 4-2.   Inventory table.

PRODUCT	WAREHOU	AMOUNT_IN_STOCK	REORDER_POINT	MAX_IN_STOCK	RESTOCK_D
20106	101	993	625	1000	
20108	101	700	700	1225	
20510	101	1389	850	1400	
20512	101	850	850	1450	
30421	101	1822	1800	3150	
40422	101	0	350	600	08-FEB-93
20106	201	220	150	260	
20108	201	166	150	260	
20510	201	175	100	175	
20512	201	162	100	175	
30421	201	102	80	140	
30433	201	130	130	230	

The following examples demonstrate the use of arithmetic operations in SQL queries.

EXAMPLE 4.1
The warehouse manager of warehouse 101 does not want to count the inventory and thinks it would be easier to order an additional 100 of each stock item. Write an SQL query to show what is currently in stock and what would be in stock if warehouse 101 ordered an additional 100 items of everything in stock.

```
SELECT product_id, amount_in_stock, amount_in_stock+100
FROM s_inventory
WHERE warehouse_id='101';
```

PRODUCT	AMOUNT_IN_STOCK	AMOUNT_IN_STOCK+100
20106	993	1093
20108	700	800
20510	1389	1489
20512	850	950
30421	1822	1922
40422	0	100

Notice in the resulting table that the new column is named AMOUNT_IN_STOCK+100, not very original, but descriptive. Remember that the new column does not exist in the table. It is a pseudocolumn. It is possible to give that column a new name in the resulting table by specifying an alias for this pseudocolumn.

EXAMPLE 4.2
The warehouse manager doesn't want anyone to notice the extra stock. He would like to know if ordering 100 of everything would take the inventory above the maximum amount as specified by management. Write an SQL query to answer his question.

```
SELECT product_id, max_in_stock-(amount_in_stock+100) "RESULT"
FROM s_inventory
WHERE warehouse_id = '101';
PRODUCT    RESULT
-------  ----------
20106         -93
20108         425
20510         -89
20512         500
30421        1228
40422         500
```

Notice that two column names (max_in_stock and amount_in_stock) are used in the calculation. Any number of columns can be used. The manager can see from the resulting table that two items, 20106 and 20510, will be taken over the maximum allowed if this order is placed.

EXAMPLE 4.3

The warehouse manager in warehouse 201 predicts there is about to be a run on products 20106 and 20108. She is afraid that the inventory of those items will be cut in half. Write an SQL query to show how many of those items will be left if she is right.

```
SELECT product_id, amount_in_stock, amount_in_stock /2
FROM s_inventory
WHERE warehouse_id = '201'
AND (product_id = '20106' OR product_id = '20108');
PRODUCT  AMOUNT_IN_STOCK  AMOUNT_IN_STOCK/2
-------  ---------------- ------------------
20106                220                110
20108                166                 83
```

EXAMPLE 4.4

Given the information in the table from Example 4.3 that shows how many of those items would be left, the manager needs to know if this is below the reorder point, and by how much. Write an SQL query to answer this question. Call the new column "ORDER".

```
SELECT product_id, amount_in_stock, reorder_point,
     reorder_point - (amount_in_stock/2) "ORDER"
FROM s_inventory
WHERE warehouse_id = '201' AND
(product_id = '20106' OR product_id = '20108');
PRODUCT  AMOUNT_IN_STOCK  REORDER_POINT      ORDER
-------  ---------------- -------------- ---------
20106                220            150         40
20108                166            150         67
```

Now the manager knows that she should order 40 of item 20106 and 67 of item 20108. Parentheses were used for clarity. However, because of the order of precedence, the outcome would not be affected if they were ignored in this example. The next example demonstrates an instance when the parentheses are required for correct output.

EXAMPLE 4.5

The manager of warehouse 201 decides to order 100 of items 20106 and 20108. Following the order, if half of the new number of each item is sold, how many items will be left? Will they still be above the reorder point? Write an SQL query to answer this question.

```
SELECT product_id, amount_in_stock, (amount_in_stock + 100)/2,
     reorder_point
FROM s_inventory
WHERE warehouse_id = '201' AND
(product_id = '20106' OR product_id = '20108');
PRODUCT AMOUNT_IN_STOCK (AMOUNT_IN_STOCK+100)/2 REORDER_POINT
------- --------------- ----------------------- -------------
20106               220                     160           150
20108               166                     133           150
```

If the statement had been written without parentheses, `amount_in_stock + 100/2`, it would have only added 50 to the amount in stock and produced the values 270 and 216. It is a good idea to use parentheses in every case for clarity, whether this is essential for correct calculations or not.

4.2   Built-In Functions

The SQL language provides a number of built-in functions for manipulating data. There are several different kinds of built-in functions. Table 4-3 shows the categories and where they are explained in this book.

Table 4-3.   **Types of built-in functions.**

Operate on:	Explained in:
Individual numeric values in a single row	Section 4.3
Individual character values in a single row	Section 4.4
Groups of entire columns or rows	Chapter 5
Date and time values	Chapter 6

The processing of SQL functions is described in Figure 4-1 below. Each function has a name, usually descriptive of its task, and receives one or more arguments. The argument is often a column name, but it also might be a variable

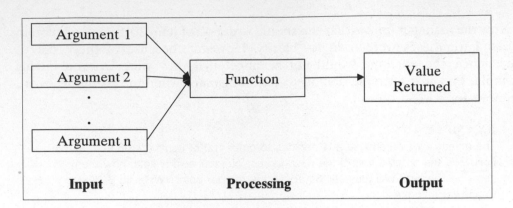

Figure 4-1.   SQL function processing.

value, a constant, or an expression. The output of some functions actually change the values in each column, while others report information about them.

Built-in functions are called using this syntax:

function_name(column or expression [, argument 2, …])

The number of arguments depends upon the function. The first argument is usually a column name or some calculated expression using a column name.

4.3   Built-In Functions—Individual Numeric

This section describes several common functions that operate on single numeric values. Table 4-4 lists a few of the most commonly used functions, each of which is explained below. Other functions used in scientific calculations, such as cosine, sine, tangent, and others, are not explained here but are available if needed.

Table 4-4.   Individual numeric value functions.

Function	Input Argument	Value Returned
ABS(m)	m = value	Absolute value of m
MOD(m, n)	m = value n = divisor	Remainder of m divided by n
POWER(m, n)	m = value n = exponent	m raised to the nth power
ROUND(m [,n])	m = value n = number of decimal places (optional)	m rounded to the nth decimal place—n defaults to 0
TRUNC(m [,n])	m = value n = number of decimal places (optional)	m truncated to the nth decimal place—n defaults to 0

Individual numeric functions usually manipulate the data in a particular column. They act on each row and return one result per row. This result may be a new value to be inserted in the column, or it may be information about the value in that column.

4.3.1   THE ABS(*m*) FUNCTION

The absolute value of a number is equal to its numeric value, ignoring a positive or negative sign. This is often used to find the difference between numbers when it does not matter if the value is above or below the target.

EXAMPLE 4.6

For each item in stock, write an SQL query to display the difference between the amount in stock and the reorder point and the absolute value of that difference.

```
SELECT product_id, warehouse_id,
     (amount_in_stock - reorder_point)"DIFFERENCE",
     ABS(amount_in_stock - reorder_point)
FROM s_inventory;
PRODUCT WAREHOU DIFFERENCE ABS(AMOUNT_IN_STOCK-REORDER_POINT)
------- ------- ---------- ----------------------------------
20106   101           368                                 368
20108   101             0                                   0
20510   101           539                                 539
20512   101             0                                   0
30421   101            22                                  22
40422   101          -350                                 350
20106   201            70                                  70
20108   201            16                                  16
20510   201            75                                  75
20512   201            62                                  62
30421   201            22                                  22
30433   201             0                                   0
```

The value resulting from the ABS( ) function gives no indication of whether the amount in stock is above or below the reorder point, just how far away it is. Notice that the column heading again contains the entire expression, including the function name. Usually it is better to use a more descriptive column name in the display through the use of an alias, as shown for the "DIFFERENCE" column.

4.3.2 THE MOD(*m,n*) FUNCTION

This function returns the remainder of dividing *m* by *n*. For example, function MOD(26, 3) returns a value of 2, as shown in the following:

$$
\begin{array}{r}
8 \leftarrow \text{quotient} \\
3\overline{)26} \\
\underline{24} \\
2 \leftarrow \text{remainder}
\end{array}
$$

Remember that *m* is called the dividend and *n* is the divisor.

> **EXAMPLE 4.7**
> Write an SQL query to display the remainder if the amount of each item in stock is divided by 9.

```
SELECT product_id, warehouse_id, amount_in_stock,
MOD(amount_in_stock, 9)
FROM s_inventory;
PRODUCT   WAREHOU AMOUNT_IN_STOCK MOD(AMOUNT_IN_STOCK,9)
-------   ------- --------------- ----------------------
20106     101                 993                      3
20108     101                 700                      7
20510     101                1389                      3
20512     101                 850                      4
30421     101                1822                      4
40422     101                   0                      0
20106     201                 220                      4
20108     201                 166                      4
20510     201                 175                      4
20512     201                 162                      0
30421     201                 102                      3
30433     201                 130                      4
```

4.3.3 THE POWER(*m,n*) FUNCTION

The POWER(*m,n*) function returns the result of raising the first argument to the power indicated by the second argument. The second argument should be an integer.

> **EXAMPLE 4.8**
> Write an SQL query to return the amount in stock squared. For each item, display the amount in stock and its square.

```
SELECT amount_in_stock, POWER(amount_in_stock, 2)
FROM s_inventory;
AMOUNT_IN_STOCK  POWER(AMOUNT_IN_STOCK,2)
---------------  ------------------------
            993                    986049
            700                    490000
           1389                   1929321
            850                    722500
           1822                   3319684
              0                         0
            220                     48400
            166                     27556
            175                     30625
            162                     26244
            102                     10404
            130                     16900
```

4.3.4   THE ROUND(*m [,n]*) FUNCTION

The ROUND(*m [,n]*) function is often used to round the results of calculation to a particular decimal point. If no argument is given specifying the decimal place, the default is 0, which will round the value to the closest integer. The value can also be rounded to the nearest 10 or 100 by using a negative 1 or negative 2, respectively. These examples are illustrated below.

EXAMPLE 4.9
Divide the amount in stock of each item by 9. Display the result rounded to the nearest integer.

```
SELECT amount_in_stock/9, ROUND(amount_in_stock/9)
FROM s_inventory;
AMOUNT_IN_STOCK/9 ROUND(AMOUNT_IN_STOCK/9)
----------------- ------------------------
        110.33333                      110
        77.777778                       78
        154.33333                      154
        94.444444                       94
        202.44444                      202
                0                        0
        24.444444                       24
        18.444444                       18
        19.444444                       19
               18                       18
        11.333333                       11
        14.444444                       14
```

Notice that since no decimal place was specified, the default was 0. This function could have been called as `ROUND(amount_in_stock/9, 0)`, and the results would have been the same.

EXAMPLE 4.10

Once again, divide the amount in stock of each item by 9. Display the result rounded to the tenth and also the nearest hundredth.

```
SELECT amount_in_stock/9, ROUND(amount_in_stock/9,1) "TO TENTH",
     ROUND(amount_in_stock/9,2) "TO HUNDREDTH"
FROM s_inventory;
```

AMOUNT_IN_STOCK/9	TO TENTH	TO HUNDREDTH
110.33333	110.3	110.33
77.777778	77.8	77.78
154.33333	154.3	154.33
94.444444	94.4	94.44
202.44444	202.4	202.44
0	0	0
24.444444	24.4	24.44
18.444444	18.4	18.44
19.444444	19.4	19.44
18	18	18
11.333333	11.3	11.33
14.444444	14.4	14.44

EXAMPLE 4.11

Once again, divide the amount in stock of each item by 9. This time, display the result rounded to the nearest ten and also the nearest hundred with no decimal places.

```
SELECT amount_in_stock/9, ROUND(amount_in_stock/9,-1) "TO TENS",
     ROUND(amount_in_stock/9,-2) "TO HUNDREDS"
FROM s_inventory;
```

AMOUNT_IN_STOCK/9	TO TENS	TO HUNDREDS
110.33333	110	100
77.777778	80	100
154.33333	150	200
94.444444	90	100
202.44444	200	200
0	0	0
24.444444	20	0
18.444444	20	0
19.444444	20	0
18	20	0
11.333333	10	0
14.444444	10	0

Notice that when a value such as 20 is rounded to the nearest hundred, it is 0. Also, 51 rounded to the nearest hundred would be 100.

Rounding performed on negative numbers performs in a similar manner. The built-in table DUAL is used to illustrate rounding negative numbers.

EXAMPLE 4.12
Consider the two numbers −55.55 and −44.44. Show how the ROUND( ) function performs by rounding these numbers to the nearest ten, integer, and tenth. Use two SELECT statements.

```
SELECT ROUND(-55.55, -1), ROUND(-55.55, 0), ROUND(-55.55, 1)
FROM DUAL;
ROUND(-55.55,-1) ROUND(-55.55,0) ROUND(-55.55,1)
---------------- --------------- ---------------
            -60              -56            -55.6


SELECT ROUND(-44.44, -1), ROUND(-44.44, 0), ROUND(-44.44, 1)
FROM DUAL;
ROUND(-44.44,-1) ROUND(-44.44,0) ROUND(-44.44,1)
---------------- --------------- ---------------
            -40              -44            -44.4
```

4.3.5   THE TRUNC($m,[n]$) FUNCTION

The TRUNC($m,[n]$) function is used to truncate the results of a calculation to a particular decimal point. If no argument is given specifying the decimal place (n), the default is 0, which will truncate the value to the closest integer number less than or equal to m. All decimal values are ignored. A value such as 99.99 would be truncated to 99. The value can also be truncated to the nearest ten or hundred by using a negative 1 or negative 2. These examples are illustrated below.

EXAMPLE 4.13
Divide the amount in stock of each item by 9. Display the result truncated to the nearest integer.

```
SELECT amount_in_stock/9, TRUNC(amount_in_stock/9)
FROM s_inventory;
AMOUNT_IN_STOCK/9 TRUNC(AMOUNT_IN_STOCK/9)
----------------- ------------------------
        110.33333                      110
        77.777778                       77
        154.33333                      154
        94.444444                       94
        202.44444                      202
                0                        0
        24.444444                       24
```

```
18.444444                      18
19.444444                      19
       18                      18
11.333333                      11
14.444444                      14
```

Compare these results to those from Example 4.9 above. Notice that decimal values over 0.5 are rounded, such as 77.777778 rounded to 78 but truncated to 77. Decimal values less than 0.5, such as 110.33333, are the same rounded and truncated.

EXAMPLE 4.14
Once again, divide the amount in stock of each item by 9. Display the result truncated to the tenth and also the nearest hundredth.

```
SELECT amount_in_stock/9, TRUNC(amount_in_stock/9,1) "TO TENTH",
    TRUNC(amount_in_stock/9,2) "TO HUNDREDTH"
FROM s_inventory;
AMOUNT_IN_STOCK/9   TO TENTH   TO HUNDREDTH
-----------------   --------   ------------
       110.33333      110.3         110.33
       77.777778       77.7          77.77
       154.33333      154.3         154.33
       94.444444       94.4          94.44
       202.44444      202.4         202.44
               0          0              0
       24.444444       24.4          24.44
       18.444444       18.4          18.44
       19.444444       19.4          19.44
              18         18             18
       11.333333       11.3          11.33
       14.444444       14.4          14.44
```

EXAMPLE 4.15
Once again, divide the amount in stock of each item by 9. This time, display the result truncated to the ten and also the nearest hundred with no decimal places.

```
SELECT amount_in_stock/9, TRUNC(amount_in_stock/9,-1) "TO TENS",
    TRUNC(amount_in_stock/9,-2) "TO HUNDREDS"
FROM s_inventory;
AMOUNT_IN_STOCK/9   TO TENS   TO HUNDREDS
-----------------   -------   -----------
       110.33333       110          100
       77.777778        70            0
       154.33333       150          100
       94.444444        90            0
       202.44444       200          200
               0         0            0
       24.444444        20            0
       18.444444        10            0
```

```
19.444444          10              0
        18          10              0
11.333333          10              0
14.444444          10              0
```

Again compare the results to Example 4.11 to see the difference between rounding and truncating. It is important to choose the correct function for the desired result.

4.3.6 NESTING THE FUNCTIONS

Nesting functions means using the result of one function as the argument of another. The built-in functions can be nested in the same expression. Sometimes such nesting is critical to obtain the desired results.

EXAMPLE 4.16
Write an SQL query to display the remainder of the amount in stock divided by 81 rounded to the nearest ten for each item.

```
SELECT amount_in_stock, MOD(amount_in_stock,81) "MOD 81",
    ROUND(MOD(amount_in_stock,81),-1) "ROUNDED"
FROM s_inventory;
AMOUNT_IN_STOCK      MOD 81      ROUNDED
---------------- ---------- ----------
             993          21          20
             700          52          50
            1389          12          10
             850          40          40
            1822          40          40
               0           0           0
             220          58          60
             166           4           0
             175          13          10
             162           0           0
             102          21          20
             130          49          50
```

In this example, the results of the MOD( ) function became the first argument to the ROUND( ) function. If the statement had been reversed

```
MOD (ROUND (amount_in_stock,81),-1) "ROUNDED"
```

the results would have been very different and incorrect. When nesting functions, be very careful to determine which function should be evaluated first.

Table 4-5. Individual character value functions.

Case Conversion		
Function	**Input Argument**	**Value Returned**
INITCAP(*st*)	*st* = character string value	Returns *st* with first letter of each word changed to uppercase. All other letters are in lowercase.
LOWER(*st*)	*st* = character string value	Returns *st* with all letters changed to lowercase.
UPPER(*st*)	*st* = character string value	Returns *st* with all letters changed to upper case.
Character Manipulation		
Function	**Input Argument**	**Value Returned**
CONCAT(*st1, st2*)	*st1* = character string value *st2* = character string value	Returns *st* with *st2* concatenated to the end of *st1*—operator "‖" can also be used.
LPAD(*st1, n [,st2]*)	*st1* = character string value *n* = integer value *st2* = character string value	Returns *st* right-justified and padded left with sequence of characters in *st2* up to length *n*; *st2* defaults to spaces.
RPAD(*st1, n [,st2]*)	*st1* = character string value *n* = integer value *st2* = character string value	Returns *st1* left-justified and padded right with sequence of characters in *st2* up to length *n*; *st2* defaults to spaces.
LTRIM(*st[,set]*)	*st* = character string value *set* = set of characters	Returns *st1* with characters removed up to the first character not in set; defaults to space.
RTRIM(*st[,set]*)	*st* = character string value *set* = set of characters	Returns *st* with final characters removed after the last character not in set; defaults to space.
REPLACE(*st, search_st [,replace_st]*)	*st* = character string value *search_st* = target string *replace_st* = replacement string	Returns a *st* with every occurrence of *search_st* in *st1* replaced by *replace_st*; default removes *search_st*.
SUBSTR(*st, m [,n]*)	*st* = character string value *m* = beginning position *n* = number of characters	Returns a substring from *st*, beginning in position *m* and *n* characters long; default returns to end of *st*.
Information Return		
Function	**Input Argument**	**Value Returned**
LENGTH(*st*)	*st* = character string value	Numeric; returns the number of characters in *st*.
INSTR(*st1, st2 [,m[,n]]*)	*st1* = character string value *st2* = character string value *m* = beginning position *n* = occurrence of st2 in st1	Numeric, returns the position of the *nth* occurrence of *st2* in *st1*, beginning at position *m*, both *m* and *n* default to 1.

4.4 Built-In Functions—Character

Several common functions are available that operate on single values made up of one or more characters. These values are often called *strings*. Table 4-5 lists a few of the most commonly used functions, each of which is explained below. Other functions are available if needed. Functions that operate on character strings can convert the case of one or more alphabet letters, manipulate the string in some way, or return information about the string.

Table 4-6 shows a subset of a customer table S_CUSTOMER that will be used in the following sections.

Table 4-6. Subset of S_CUSTOMER.

```
NAME                 ADDRESS              CITY                 STATE
-------------------  -------------------  -------------------  ------
Sports,Inc           72 High St           Harrisonburg         VA
Toms Sporting Goods  6741 Main St         Harrisonburg         VA
Athletic Attire      54 Market St         Harrisonburg         VA
Athletics For All    286 Main St          Harrisonburg         VA
Shoes for Sports     538 High St          Harrisonburg         VA
BJ Athletics         632 Water St         Harrisonburg         VA
Athletics One        912 Columbia Rd      Lancaster            PA
Great Athletes       121 Litiz Pike       Lancaster            PA
Athletics Two        435 High Rd          Lancaster            PA
Athletes Attic       101 Greenfield Rd    Lancaster            PA
```

4.4.1 THE CASE CONVERSION FUNCTIONS

The first group of functions is essential for database retrieval when case is unknown. Often the person who entered the data may not have consistently followed a convention of all caps or all lowercase letters. Some columns may contain mixed-case data. These functions may also be used to format the data in a desired fashion through the use of the SELECT statement.

INITCAP(*st*) is a function that takes a string value and returns it with only the initial character capitalized and the rest lowercase. The string itself within the database is not changed.

> **EXAMPLE 4.17**
> If a name string is "THOMAS" or "thomas" or any other mixture of case, it can be returned as "Thomas" using this function. Use the built-in table DUAL to demonstrate the SQL query.

```
SELECT INITCAP('THOMAS'), INITCAP('thomas')
FROM DUAL;
INITCA INITCA
------ ------
Thomas Thomas
```

UPPER(*st*) and LOWER(*st*) can be used to retrieve character string data and display in all caps or all lowercase letters.

EXAMPLE 4.18

Write an SQL query on the S_CUSTOMER table that displays the customer name three ways: (1) as represented in the table, (2) in all caps, and (3) in all lowercase letters.

```
SELECT name, UPPER(name), LOWER(name)
FROM s_customer;
NAME                    UPPER(NAME)            LOWER(NAME)
-------------------     -------------------    -------------------
Sports,Inc              SPORTS,INC             sports,inc
Toms Sporting Goods     TOMS SPORTING GOODS    toms sporting goods
Athletic Attire         ATHLETIC ATTIRE        athletic attire
Athletics For All       ATHLETICS FOR ALL      athletics for all
Shoes for Sports        SHOES FOR SPORTS       shoes for sports
BJ Athletics            BJ ATHLETICS           bj athletics
Athletics One           ATHLETICS ONE          athletics one
Great Athletes          GREAT ATHLETES         great athletes
Athletics Two           ATHLETICS TWO          athletics two
Athletes Attic          ATHLETES ATTIC         athletes attic
```

4.4.2 THE CONCATENATING FUNCTION

Character strings can be combined through the use of the CONCAT(*st1, st2*) function. The function returns a new string containing both strings. CONCAT(*st1, st2*) can hook only two strings together.

EXAMPLE 4.19

Use the built-in table DUAL to concatenate the following first and last names together: `'Thomas'`, `'Jefferson'` and `'Benjamin'`, `'Franklin'`.

```
SELECT CONCAT('Thomas','Jefferson') "FIRST",
     CONCAT('Benjamin','Franklin') "SECOND"
FROM DUAL;
FIRST           SECOND
--------------- ----------------
ThomasJefferson BenjaminFranklin
```

Notice that there is no space between the words. The strings are reproduced exactly. If a space is required, it would have to be present in one of the strings. Since this is not likely in the table, there is a concatenation operator (| |) available to connect as many strings contained in single quotes as desired. Concatenating a series of character strings, the previous example could be written in this way:

```
SELECT 'Thomas' || ' ' || 'Jefferson' "FIRST",
       'Benjamin' || ' ' || 'Franklin' "SECOND"
FROM DUAL;
FIRST             SECOND
----------------  -----------------
Thomas Jefferson  Benjamin Franklin
```

EXAMPLE 4.20

Write an SQL query that will print the names of the customers in one column
and their cities and states together in another column.

```
SELECT name, city || ', ' || state
FROM s_customer;
NAME                  CITY||','||STATE
------------------    ------------------
Sports,Inc            Harrisonburg, VA
Toms Sporting Goods   Harrisonburg, VA
Athletic Attire       Harrisonburg, VA
Athletics For All     Harrisonburg, VA
Shoes for Sports      Harrisonburg, VA
BJ Athletics          Harrisonburg, VA
Athletics One         Lancaster, PA
Great Athletes        Lancaster, PA
Athletics Two         Lancaster, PA
Athletes Attic        Lancaster, PA
```

The concatenation operator can also be used to format the output into any
desired fashion, even complete sentences. Each string is contained in single
quotes. Column names are not.

EXAMPLE 4.21

Write an SQL query that will print the following sentence for each row of the
S_CUSTOMER table: The store <name> is located in <city, state>.

```
SELECT 'The store ' || name || ' is located in ' ||
     city || ', ' || state ||'.'
FROM s_customer;
'THESTORE'||NAME||'ISLOCATEDIN'||CITY||','||STATE||'.'
-----------------------------------------------------------
The store Sports,Inc is located in Harrisonburg, VA.
The store Toms Sporting Goods is located in Harrisonburg, VA.
The store Athletic Attire is located in Harrisonburg, VA.
The store Athletics For All is located in Harrisonburg, VA.
The store Shoes for Sports is located in Harrisonburg, VA.
The store BJ Athletics is located in Harrisonburg, VA.
The store Athletics One is located in Lancaster, PA.
The store Great Athletes is located in Lancaster, PA.
The store Athletics Two is located in Lancaster, PA.
The store Athletes Attic is located in Lancaster, PA.
```

4.4.3   THE PADDING AND TRIMMING FUNCTIONS

The functions LPAD(*st1*, *n* [,*st2*]) and RPAD(*st1*, *n* [,*st2*]) provide a way to concatenate a second series of a number of characters to the left or to the right of the original string. The length argument to the function tells the exact length of the resulting string, including the original string. If the second string is omitted, the string is padded with spaces.

EXAMPLE 4.22

Write an SQL query to pad the left of the customer name with spaces up to a column width of 25 and then pad the right with asterisks up to a length of 15.

```
SELECT LPAD(name,25), RPAD(name,15, '*')
FROM s_customer;
LPAD(NAME,25)                RPAD(NAME,15,'*
-------------------------- ---------------
              Sports,Inc Sports,Inc*****
       Toms Sporting Goods Toms Sporting G
          Athletic Attire Athletic Attire
         Athletics For All Athletics For A
          Shoes for Sports Shoes for Sport
               BJ Athletics BJ Athletics***
             Athletics One Athletics One**
            Great Athletes Great Athletes*
             Athletics Two Athletics Two**
             Athletes Attic Athletes Attic*
```

Notice that when the second string is omitted, spaces are used. The resulting chart also demonstrates that if the specified width is too small for the string, it will be truncated from the right to fit. The padding string can be more than one character, as demonstrated below.

EXAMPLE 4.23

Write an SQL query to display the names of the customers, padded to the right with a series of three periods and a space up to a width of 30. In the second column, display the credit rating.

```
SELECT RPAD(name, 30, '... '), credit_rating
FROM s_customer;
RPAD(NAME,30,'...') CREDIT_RA
------------------------------- ---------
Sports,Inc. . . . . . . . . . . . .      EXCELLENT
Toms Sporting Goods. . . . . . . .      POOR
Athletic Attire. . . . . . . . . . . .      GOOD
Athletics For All. . . . . . . . .      EXCELLENT
Shoes for Sports. . . . . . . . . .      EXCELLENT
BJ Athletics. . . . . . . . . . . .      POOR
```

```
Athletics One. . . . . . . . . . .    GOOD
Great Athletes. . . . . . . . . . .   EXCELLENT
Athletics Two. . . . . . . . . . .    EXCELLENT
Athletes Attic. . . . . . . . . .     POOR
```

The trimming functions, RTRIM(*st[,set]*) and LTRIM(*st[,set]*) trim off any unwanted characters from the ends of the string. The arguments to these functions are the column name or string to be trimmed and the set of characters to remove. If no set of characters is included, any spaces are trimmed. It is dangerous to assume that the person entering the data did not accidentally include spaces before or after any string. Any set of desired characters may be removed with the same LTRIM( ) or RTRIM( ) function. The trimming functions are particularly helpful when finding the actual length of a string, as shown below in Section 4.4.6.

EXAMPLE 4.24
Write an SQL query to trim any periods and the words *St* and *Rd* from the end of each address in the customer table.

```
SELECT name, RTRIM(address,'. St Rd')
FROM s_customer;
NAME                     RTRIM(ADDRESS,'.STRD
-------------------      --------------------
Sports,Inc               72 High
Toms Sporting Goods      6741 Main
Athletic Attire          54 Marke
Athletics For All        286 Main
Shoes for Sports         538 High
BJ Athletics             632 Water
Athletics One            912 Columbia
Great Athletes           121 Litiz Pike
Athletics Two            435 High
Athletes Attic           101 Greenfiel
```

A careful examination of the resulting table shows that not only were *St* and *Rd* removed, but any *s*, *t*, *r*, or *d* at the end of the street names were also removed (e.g., Marke is listed instead of *Market*). SQL treats the characters in the set as individual characters, not separate words. Therefore, use the trimming functions with care, and specify only the exact characters that you want to be trimmed.

4.4.4   THE REPLACING FUNCTION

The REPLACE(*st, search_st [,replace_st]*) function is similar to the "search and replace" found in most word processor programs. Every instance in the given string of the target character or characters is replaced by the replacement character or characters. Once again, use this function with care.

EXAMPLE 4.25

Write an SQL query to display the names of the customers with every letter `'a'` replaced by an asterisk.

a. The first attempt at the query might look like this:

```
SELECT name, REPLACE(name,'a','*')
FROM s_customer;
NAME                    REPLACE(NAME,'A','*'
--------------------    --------------------
Sports,Inc              Sports,Inc
Toms Sporting Goods     Toms Sporting Goods
Athletic Attire         Athletic Attire
Athletics For All       Athletics For All
Shoes for Sports        Shoes for Sports
BJ Athletics            BJ Athletics
Athletics One           Athletics One
Great Athletes          Gre*t Athletes
Athletics Two           Athletics Two
Athletes Attic          Athletes Attic
```

The examination of the resulting table shows that only lowercase *a*'s were replaced. Characters within a string are case-sensitive. In order to correct this problem, use the case conversion function, either UPPER('A') or LOWER('a').

b. The second query tried is closer to the desired results:

```
SELECT name, REPLACE(LOWER(name),'a','*')
FROM s_customer;
NAME                    REPLACE(LOWER(NAME),
--------------------    --------------------
Sports,Inc              sports,inc
Toms Sporting Goods     toms sporting goods
Athletic Attire         *thletic *ttire
Athletics For All       *thletics for *ll
Shoes for Sports        shoes for sports
BJ Athletics            bj *thletics
Athletics One           *thletics one
Great Athletes          gre*t *thletes
Athletics Two           *thletics two
Athletes Attic          *thletes *ttic
```

All the *a*'s, both upper- and lowercase, are removed. However, all the other names are displayed in all lowercase.

c. Once again, another function can be combined with this to try and find the desired results. The next version of the query looks like this:

```
SELECT name, INITCAP(REPLACE(LOWER(name),'a','*'))
FROM s_customer;
NAME                        INITCAP(REPLACE(LOWE
--------------------        --------------------
Sports,Inc                  Sports,Inc
Toms Sporting Goods         Toms Sporting Goods
Athletic Attire             *Thletic *Ttire
Athletics For All           *Thletics For *Ll
Shoes for Sports            Shoes For Sports
BJ Athletics                Bj *Thletics
Athletics One               *Thletics One
Great Athletes              Gre*T *Thletes
Athletics Two               *Thletics Two
Athletes Attic              *Thletes *Ttic
```

The resulting table still does not meet the original specifications. If all the data is entered into a table in all one case, this kind of problem can be eliminated. Since that is not always possible, a variety of queries must be tried to see which is the most acceptable. Sequences of characters can also be replaced.

EXAMPLE 4.26

Write an SQL query to find all the sequence of characters `Athl` and replace them with the sequence `Asc`. This query will only work on the exact case of these letters.

```
SELECT name, REPLACE(name, 'Athl','Asc')
FROM s_customer;
NAME                        REPLACE(NAME,'ATHL','ASC')
--------------------        --------------------------------
Sports,Inc                  Sports,Inc
Toms Sporting Goods         Toms Sporting Goods
Athletic Attire             Ascetic Attire
Athletics For All           Ascetics For All
Shoes for Sports            Shoes for Sports
BJ Athletics                BJ Ascetics
Athletics One               Ascetics One
Great Athletes              Great Ascetes
Athletics Two               Ascetics Two
Athletes Attic              Ascetes Attic
```

4.4.5   THE SUBSTRING FUNCTION

The SUBSTR (*st, m [,n]*) function will return the string of characters found in the string argument, beginning at position *m* and continuing for *n* number of characters. If the length *n* is not specified, it will return all the letters to the end of the string. This function can be demonstrated using the built-in table DUAL.

EXAMPLE 4.27

Write an SQL query to display 9 characters from `'ARCHIBALD BEARISOL'`, beginning with character 6. Display the rest of the characters beginning with position 11. Display the first four characters and the characters 5, 6, and 7 from the word `'ALEXANDER'`.

```
SELECT    SUBSTR('ARCHIBALD BEARISOL',6,9),
          SUBSTR('ARCHIBALD BEARISOL',11),
          SUBSTR ('ALEXANDER',1,4), SUBSTR ('ALEXANDER',5,3)
FROM DUAL;
SUBSTR('A  SUBSTR('   SUBS   SUB
---------  --------   ----   ---
BALD BEAR  BEARISOL   ALEX   AND
```

Examine the resulting table carefully. It demonstrates that a space is considered a character and must be counted when extracting substrings.

4.4.6   FUNCTIONS RETURNING INTEGERS

The last two character functions we will consider both return integers. Once again, it is important to remember that all characters in a string are counted, including spaces, periods, commas, and so forth. LENGTH(*st*) returns the exact number of characters in the string. INSTR(*st1, st2 [,m[,n]]*) returns the position of the *n*th occurrence of the second string in the first, beginning at position *m*. Both *m* and *n* default to 1 if not included.

EXAMPLE 4.28

Write an SQL query to return the exact number of characters in the names of the customers. To be sure no trailing spaces are included, use the RTRIM( ) function to remove any that exist.

```
SELECT name, LENGTH(RTRIM(name))
FROM s_customer;
NAME                       LENGTH(RTRIM(NAME))
-------------------        -------------------
Sports,Inc                          10
Toms Sporting Goods                 19
Athletic Attire                     15
Athletics For All                   17
Shoes for Sports                    16
BJ Athletics                        12
```

```
Athletics One                    13
Great Athletes                   14
Athletics Two                    13
Athletes Attic                   14
```

EXAMPLE 4.29

Many of the customer names have more than one word. Use the INSTR( ) function to return the position of the first space in each name. Also return the position of the second space in each name, in case there are more than two words. The first query attempt looks like this:

```
SELECT name, INSTR(name,' '), INSTR(name,' ',1,2)
FROM s_customer;
NAME                     INSTR(NAME,'') INSTR(NAME,'',1,2)
------------------------ -------------- ------------------
Sports,Inc                      0                 0
Toms Sporting Goods             5                14
Athletic Attire                 9                 0
Athletics For All              10                14
Shoes for Sports                6                10
BJ Athletics                    3                 0
Athletics One                  10                 0
Great Athletes                  6                 0
Athletics Two                  10                 0
Athletes Attic                  9                 0
```

A close examination of the resulting chart reveals an interesting fact. When the first customer name was entered, no space was typed between the comma and the I. If a space is desired there, this function would help to identify the problem, and then it could be corrected using the UPDATE statement. (See Chapter 1.)

EXAMPLE 4.30

Assume there is a table called PRESIDENT that contains a name column including the last name, a comma, a space, and then the first name, as in Jefferson, Thomas and Lincoln, Abraham. Write an SQL query that will display a column displaying the first name and the last name, separated by a space with no commas, as in Thomas Jefferson.

Use a variety of functions to accomplish this task. You need to perform three steps:

a. Find the position of the comma.
b. Extract the last name and first name.
c. Concatenate the last name at the end of the first name.

Each step is described below.

a. Use the INSTR ( ) function to find the position of the comma. The following query demonstrates this:

```
SELECT name, INSTR(name, ',')
FROM president;
NAME                                   INSTR(NAME,',')
------------------------               ---------------
Jefferson, Thomas                      10
Lincoln, Abraham                       8
```

b. Extract the first name and the last name by using the function LENGTH ( ) along with SUBSTR ( ). The first name begins at the second position *after* the comma. The last name ends at the position immediately *before* the comma.

```
SELECT name, SUBSTR(name, INSTR(name, ',')+2) "First",
           SUBSTR(name, 1, INSTR(name, ',')-1) "Second"
FROM president;
NAME                        First                     Second
------------------------    ----------------------    ----------
Jefferson, Thomas           Thomas                    Jefferson
Lincoln, Abraham            Abraham                   Lincoln
```

c. The previous query produced the two strings for the first name and the last name. Now all that remains is to concatenate the two together into one string, with a space between:

```
SELECT name, SUBSTR(name, INSTR(name, ',')+2) || ' ' ||
           SUBSTR(name, 1, INSTR(name, ',')-1) "Reverse"
FROM president;
NAME                        Reverse
------------------------    ------------------------------------
Jefferson, Thomas           Thomas Jefferson
Lincoln, Abraham            Abraham Lincoln
```

4.5 Important Conversion Functions

The built-in functions are designed to operate specifically on numeric or character data. This can sometimes cause problems. Sometimes certain rows might contain NULL values that complicate the working of the function. Possibly we might want to use a numeric function on a column that has been designed to contain string data, or we might want to use a character function on a column that has been designed to contain numeric data. The data would have to be converted before the function can be used. Table 4-7 shows several common functions that can be used for manipulation and conversion of numeric and character data. Others are available if needed.

Table 4-7.   Some utility functions.

Function	Input Argument	Value Returned
NVL(*m, n*)	*m* = numeric or string value *n* = substitute value	*n* if *m* is NULL; otherwise returns *m*.
TO_CHAR(*m[,fmt]*)	*m* = numeric value *fmt* = format for string	*m* converted from a number to a character string in the designated format; default for *fmt* is a value exactly wide enough to hold all significant digits.
TO_NUMBER(*st[,fmt]*)	*st* = character string value *fmt* = format for number	*st*, which is a character value containing a number in the designated string format; default is a string the size needed for the entire number.

4.5.1   USING OPERATIONS OR FUNCTIONS ON NULL VALUES

Recall that in SQL a particular value may be NULL, or empty with no value at all. NULL represents an unknown value, which is not the same as zero. Since a zero is not automatically substituted for NULL, performing any operations on an unknown value, or NULL, will have NULL as a result.

EXAMPLE 4.31

Suppose you have a table called MULT (shown below) that contains two columns of numbers, some of which might be NULL. Write an SQL query to show the result of multiplying the two numbers together.

```
    FIRST     SECOND
--------- ---------
      987         2
       22
                 35
        5         4
```

```
SELECT first, second, first * second "RESULT"
FROM mult;
    FIRST    SECOND    RESULT
--------- --------- ---------
      987         2      1974
       22
                 35
        5         4        20
```

Notice the empty spots in the result column. It was impossible to multiply something by a number that is unknown. The result of multiplying NULL values produces a NULL result. Often you do not want this to happen. The NVL(m, n) function is available to convert the NULL value to a default value that you determine for the purposes of calculations. The NVL( ) function can also be used on character strings when necessary. The return value is always the same as the datatype of the value sent to the function.

EXAMPLE 4.32

Write an SQL query to show the result of multiplying the two numbers in table MULT together. This time, substitute 1 if there is a NULL value. Zero could be substituted, but it would always produce a zero result.

```
SELECT first, second, NVL(first, 1) * NVL(second, 1)
FROM mult;
    FIRST    SECOND NVL(FIRST,1)*NVL(SECOND,1)
--------- --------- --------------------------
      987         2                       1974
       22                                   22
                 35                          35
        5         4                          20
```

EXAMPLE 4.33

Suppose you are accessing a table of names called NAMES (shown below) that might have the first or last names unavailable. Write an SQL query to print the table, substituting the word 'UNKNOWN' if there is a NULL in either column.

```
FIRSTNAME                        LASTNAME
------------------------- ----------------
THOMAS                           JEFFERSON
                                 SOCRATES

SELECT NVL(firstname, 'UNKNOWN'), NVL(lastname, 'UNKNOWN')
FROM names;
NVL(FIRSTNAME,'UNKNOWN')  NVL(LASTNAME,'UNKNOWN')
------------------------- -------------------------
THOMAS                           JEFFERSON
UNKNOWN                          SOCRATES
```

4.5.2   CONVERTING BETWEEN STRINGS AND NUMBERS

The two conversion functions explained here are TO_CHAR($m[,fmt]$) and TO_NUMBER($st[,fmt]$). The function TO_DATE($st[,fmt]$) is similar and will be explained in Chapter 6. Basically, their tasks are obvious. TO_CHAR( ) takes in a number and changes it into a string value in a specific format if specified. Any string functions can then be used to manipulate the value. TO_NUMBER( ) takes in a string and changes it to a number value in a specific format if specified. Now the number value can be manipulated by numeric functions or used in arithmetic operations. Usually the formatting is default, creating a number or string just the correct size for the incoming value.

EXAMPLE 4.34

Write an SQL query to perform some calculations on numbers stored as strings. In order to perform arithmetic calculations, you need to change them to numbers. This example will use the built-in table DUAL to demonstrate.

```
SELECT TO_NUMBER('123.45') + TO_NUMBER('234.56')
FROM DUAL;
TO_NUMBER('123.45')+TO_NUMBER('234.56')
----------------------------------------
                                  358.01
```

EXAMPLE 4.35

Write an SQL query to display social security numbers. In a particular table, the social security numbers are kept as a 9-digit number (987654321). However in the display, you want to show them in the customary 3-2-4 digit format (987-65-4321). To accomplish this, you need to perform three tasks:

a. Change the value into a string
b. Separate it into three pieces of the correct length
c. Concatenate the three sections with hyphens in between

The built-in table DUAL will be used for this example. However, any name of a column with number values could be substituted for the (987654321).

a. Change the value into a string using the function TO_CHAR( ):

```
SELECT TO_CHAR(987654321)
FROM DUAL;
TO_CHAR(9
---------
987654321
```

The resulting value does not look any different, but it can now be manipulated with string functions.

b. Separate it into three pieces of the correct length. Use the result as input to the SUBSTR( ) function:

```
SELECT SUBSTR(TO_CHAR(987654321), 1, 3) "3",
       SUBSTR(TO_CHAR(987654321), 4, 2) "2",
       SUBSTR(TO_CHAR(987654321), 6) "4"
FROM DUAL;
3   2   4
--- -- ----
987 65 4321
```

c. Finally concatenate the three sections with hyphens in between:

```
SELECT SUBSTR(TO_CHAR(987654321), 1, 3) || '-'||
       SUBSTR(TO_CHAR(987654321), 4, 2) ||'-'||
       SUBSTR(TO_CHAR(987654321), 6) "SS Number"
FROM DUAL;
SS Number
----------
987-65-4321
```

Changing a number to a string is a little more complicated if you want to control the formatting. Table 4-8 shows the formats that can be used in the TO_CHAR( ) function to display the number in specific ways. The format argument to the function is like a template that should be followed with a 9 representing each digit of the number.

Table 4-8. Formats for TO_CHAR( ) function.

Symbol	Explanation
9	Each 9 represents one digit in the result.
0	Represents a leading zero to be displayed.
$	Floating dollar sign; printed to left of number.
L	Any local floating currency symbol.
.	Prints the decimal point.
,	Prints the comma to represent thousands.

EXAMPLE 4.36
Use the built-in table DUAL to display the numbers 123, 54321, and 9874321 as dollar values with commas for readability. Allow values up to a million.

```
SELECT TO_CHAR(123,'$9,999,999'),
   TO_CHAR(54321,'$9,999,999'),
   TO_CHAR(9874321, '$9,999,999')
FROM DUAL;
TO_CHAR(123 TO_CHAR(543 TO_CHAR(987
----------- ----------- -----------
       $123     $54,321  $9,874,321
```

From the resulting table, it is easy to see that the formatting template is followed. The dollar sign is placed directly to the left of the number, and commas are placed in the proper spots.

EXAMPLE 4.37

Display the same numbers above as currency, this time forcing decimal places to be displayed.

```
SELECT TO_CHAR(123,'$9,999,999.99'),
    TO_CHAR(54321,'$9,999,999.99'),
    TO_CHAR(9874321, '$9,999,999.99')
FROM DUAL;
TO_CHAR(123,'$ TO_CHAR(54321,    TO_CHAR(987432
-------------- ---------------- ---------------
      $123.00        $54,321.00  $9,874,321.00
```

EXAMPLE 4.38

Display these numbers using only three decimal places and placing commas for readability: 1234.12345, 0.4567, 1.1. Numbers will be less than a million.

```
SELECT TO_CHAR(1234.12345, '999,999.999'),
    TO_CHAR(0.4567,'999,999.999'),
    TO_CHAR(1.1, '999,999.999')
FROM DUAL;
TO_CHAR(1234 TO_CHAR(0.45 TO_CHAR(1.1,
------------ ------------ ------------
   1,234.123         .457        1.100
```

Notice that commas are inserted properly. If there are not enough digits in the number, zeros are added to make the specified number of decimal places. If there are too many digits to the right, the number is rounded to allow the specified number of digits to be displayed on the right of the decimal point.

Solved Problems

Note: The DUAL table is a built-in table that can be used to display the results of calculations on constant values. This table will be used for some of the problems below. Also, before answering the following questions, rerun the SG script to refresh the database. Use the employee table S_EMP for these questions.

ID	LAST_NAME	FIRST_NAME	MAN	TITLE	DEP	SALARY
1	Martin	Carmen		President	50	4500
2	Smith	Doris	1	VP, Operations	41	2450
3	Norton	Michael	1	VP, Sales	31	2400
4	Quentin	Mark	1	VP, Finance	10	2450

5	Roper	Joseph	1	VP, Administration	50	2550
6	Brown	Molly	2	Warehouse Manager	41	1600
7	Hawkins	Roberta	2	Warehouse Manager	42	1650
8	Burns	Ben	2	Warehouse Manager	43	1500
9	Catskill	Antoinette	2	Warehouse Manager	44	1700
10	Jackson	Marta	2	Warehouse Manager	45	1507
11	Henderson	Colin	3	Sales Representative	31	1400
12	Gilson	Sam	3	Sales Representative	32	1490
13	Sanders	Jason	3	Sales Representative	33	1515
14	Dameron	Andre	3	Sales Representative	35	1450
15	Hardwick	Elaine	6	Stock Clerk	41	1400
16	Brown	George	6	Stock Clerk	41	940
17	Washington	Thomas	7	Stock Clerk	42	1200
18	Patterson	Donald	7	Stock Clerk	42	795
19	Bell	Alexander	8	Stock Clerk	43	850
20	Gantos	Eddie	9	Stock Clerk	44	800
21	Stephenson	Blaine	10	Stock Clerk	45	860
22	Chester	Eddie	9	Stock Clerk	44	800
23	Pearl	Roger	9	Stock Clerk	34	795
24	Dancer	Bonnie	7	Stock Clerk	45	860
25	Schmitt	Sandra	8	Stock Clerk	45	1100

4.1. The salaries in the list are monthly. Write an SQL query and show the resulting table of salaries if all the warehouse managers were given a $250 per month raise.

```
SELECT last_name, first_name, salary, salary + 250
FROM s_emp
WHERE title = 'Warehouse Manager';
LAST_NAME            FIRST_NAME                     SALARY SALARY+250
----------------     --------------------           ---------- ----------
Brown                Molly                             1600       1850
Hawkins              Roberta                           1650       1900
Burns                Ben                               1500       1750
Catskill             Antoinette                        1700       1950
Jackson              Marta                             1507       1757
```

4.2. Write an SQL query and show the resulting table to display the amount each warehouse manager currently makes in a year, and how much each one would make in a year with the $250 per month raise. Name the new columns appropriately.

```
SELECT last_name, first_name, salary * 12 "CURRENT YEARLY",
(salary + 250) * 12 "NEW YEARLY"
FROM s_emp
WHERE title = 'Warehouse Manager';
LAST_NAME            FIRST_NAME                CURRENT YEARLY  NEW YEARLY
---------------      ------------------        --------------  ----------
Brown                Molly                          19200         22200
Hawkins              Roberta                        19800         22800
```

```
Burns           Ben                         18000       21000
Catskill        Antoinette                  20400       23400
Jackson         Marta                       18084       21084
```

4.3. What would be the resulting table from this SQL query? Explain the results.

```
SELECT last_name,first_name,
((((salary + 250) * 12)-salary * 12)/(salary * 12)* 100)
FROM s_emp
WHERE title = 'Warehouse Manager';
```

The resulting table shows the percentage of raise each warehouse manager would get based on the yearly salary. Marta Jackson gets the largest percentage of increase, or a 16.6% raise. Antoinette Catskill gets the smallest percentage of increase, or a 14.7% raise.

```
LAST_NAME    FIRST_NAME    ((((SALARY+250)*12)-SALARY*12)/(SALARY*12)*100)
----------   -----------   -----------------------------------------------
Brown        Molly                                              15.625
Hawkins      Roberta                                            15.151515
Burns        Ben                                                16.666667
Catskill     Antoinette                                         14.705882
Jackson      Marta                                              16.58925
```

4.4. What would be the resulting table from this SQL query? Explain the results.

```
SELECT last_name,first_name, salary * 12 ,
(salary * 12) + (salary * 12 * .2)
FROM s_emp
WHERE title like 'VP%';
```

The resulting table shows the current yearly salary of the vice presidents, and the projected yearly salary if they were all given a 20% raise.

```
LAST_NAME    FIRST_NAME       SALARY*12 (SALARY*12)+(SALARY*12*.2)
----------   --------------   --------- ---------------------------
Smith        Doris            29400                         35280
Norton       Michael          28800                         34560
Quentin      Mark             29400                         35280
Roper        Joseph           30600                         36720
```

4.5. Write an SQL query to display the absolute value of the following numbers:

$$345.2, -222, 0, -1.$$

```
SELECT ABS(345.2), ABS(-222), ABS(0), ABS(-1)
FROM DUAL;
ABS(345.2) ABS(-222)    ABS(0)    ABS(-1)
---------- ---------  ---------  ---------
     345.2       222          0          1
```

4.6. What would be the resulting table from this SQL query? Explain the results.

```
SELECT last_name, first_name, ROUND(salary, -2)
FROM s_emp;
```

LAST_NAME	FIRST_NAME	ROUND(SALARY,-2)
Martin	Carmen	4500
Smith	Doris	2500
Norton	Michael	2400
Quentin	Mark	2500
Roper	Joseph	2600
Brown	Molly	1600
Hawkins	Roberta	1700
Burns	Ben	1500
Catskill	Antoinette	1700
Jackson	Marta	1500
Henderson	Colin	1400
Gilson	Sam	1500
Sanders	Jason	1500
Dameron	Andre	1500
Hardwick	Elaine	1400
Brown	George	900
Washington	Thomas	1200
Patterson	Donald	800
Bell	Alexander	900
Gantos	Eddie	800
Stephenson	Blaine	900
Chester	Eddie	800
Pearl	Roger	800
Dancer	Bonnie	900
Schmitt	Sandra	1100

The table displays all the employee's salaries rounded to the nearest $100.

4.7 Use the TRYNUM table below for this problem.

FIRST	SECOND	THIRD
987	987	987
987.222	987	987.23
98.5	99	98.5
98765	98765	98765
23.987	24	23.99
.00003	0	0
100.9	101	100.9
.00005	0	0
1.9	2	1.9
10.1	10	10

Write the SQL query to display the column FIRST from TRYNUM rounded to the nearest tenth, hundredth, and thousandth.

```
SELECT first, ROUND(first, 1), ROUND(first,2), ROUND(first,3)
FROM trynum;
    FIRST ROUND(FIRST,1)  ROUND(FIRST,2)  ROUND(FIRST,3)
--------- -------------  --------------  --------------
      987           987             987             987
  987.222         987.2          987.22         987.222
     98.5          98.5            98.5            98.5
    98765         98765           98765           98765
   23.987            24           23.99          23.987
   .00003             0               0               0
    100.9         100.9           100.9           100.9
   .00005             0               0               0
      1.9           1.9             1.9             1.9
     10.1          10.1            10.1            10.1
```

4.8. Use the TRYNUM table for this problem. Write the SQL query to display the column FIRST from this table rounded to the nearest integer, the nearest 10 and 100.

```
SELECT first, ROUND(first), ROUND(first, -1), ROUND(first, -2)
FROM trynum;
FIRST ROUND(FIRST) ROUND(FIRST,-1) ROUND(FIRST,-2)
--------- ------------ --------------- ---------------
      987          987             990            1000
  987.222          987             990            1000
     98.5           99             100             100
    98765        98765           98770           98800
   23.987           24              20               0
   .00003            0               0               0
    100.9          101             100             100
   .00005            0               0               0
      1.9            2               0               0
     10.1           10              10               0
```

4.9. Use the TRYNUM table for this problem. What would be the resulting table from this SQL query? Explain the results.

```
SELECT second, TRUNC(second/ 25), MOD(second,25)
FROM trynum;
   SECOND TRUNC(SECOND/25)  MOD(SECOND,25)
--------- ----------------  --------------
      987               39              12
      987               39              12
       99                3              24
    98765             3950              15
       24                0              24
        0                0               0
      101                4               1
        0                0               0
        2                0               2
       10                0              10
```

This query displays for each row in the table the value of the column SECOND and the results when it is divided by 25. Column 2 shows the integer quotient, and Column 3 shows the remainder.

4.10. Write an SQL query that will display the number 5 and its power to 2, 3, and 4.

```
SELECT POWER(5,1), POWER(5,2), POWER(5,3), POWER(5,4)
FROM DUAL;
POWER(5,1) POWER(5,2) POWER(5,3) POWER(5,4)
---------- ---------- ---------- ----------
         5         25        125        625
```

4.11. What would be the resulting table from this SQL query? Explain the results.

```
SELECT id, salary, ROUND(salary + salary*.15, -1)
FROM s_emp
WHERE title LIKE 'VP%';
 ID     SALARY ROUND(SALARY+SALARY*.15,-1)
--- ---------- ---------------------------
  2       2450                        2820
  3       2400                        2760
  4       2450                        2820
  5       2550                        2930
```

This table shows what the monthly salaries of all the vice presidents would be if they got a 15% raise. The new monthly salary is rounded to the nearest $10.

4.12. Use the TRYNUM table for this question. Write an SQL query to display each value of THIRD and the remainder if the integer portion only is divided by 32.

```
SELECT third, MOD(TRUNC(third), 32)
FROM trynum;
    THIRD MOD(TRUNC(THIRD),32)
--------- --------------------
      987                   27
   987.23                   27
     98.5                    2
    98765                   13
    23.99                   23
        0                    0
    100.9                    4
        0                    0
      1.9                    1
       10                   10
```

4.13. Write an SQL query to find a daily salary for the stock clerks in the table S_EMP. Assume a 30-day month. Round off the daily salary to the nearest cent. Name the column "DAILY PAY".

```
SELECT last_name, first_name, ROUND(salary/30,2) "DAILY PAY"
FROM s_emp
WHERE title = 'Stock Clerk';
LAST_NAME            FIRST_NAME             DAILY PAY
----------------     --------------------   ---------
Hardwick             Elaine                     46.67
Brown                George                     31.33
Washington           Thomas                        40
Patterson            Donald                      26.5
Bell                 Alexander                  28.33
Gantos               Eddie                      26.67
Stephenson           Blaine                     28.67
Chester              Eddie                      26.67
Pearl                Roger                       26.5
Dancer               Bonnie                     28.67
Schmitt              Sandra                     36.67
```

4.14. Write an SQL query to display the first names and last names in all capital letters and the titles in all lowercase for all the vice presidents.

```
SELECT UPPER(first_name), UPPER(last_name), LOWER(title)
FROM s_emp
WHERE title LIKE 'VP%';
UPPER(FIRST_NAME)     UPPER(LAST_NAME)      LOWER(TITLE)
--------------------  --------------------  ---------------------
DORIS                 SMITH                 vp, operations
MICHAEL               NORTON                vp, sales
MARK                  QUENTIN               vp, finance
JOSEPH                ROPER                 vp, administration
```

4.15. Write an SQL query to display this line of text with all first characters capitalized: 'happy birthday to you!' Use the built-in table DUAL.

```
SELECT INITCAP('happy birthday to you!')
FROM DUAL;
INITCAP('HAPPYBIRTHDAY
----------------------
Happy Birthday To You!
```

Remember that the INITCAP( ) function operates on every separate word within the target string.

4.16. Write an SQL query that will create *one* column called "EMPLOYEES" that shows the following sentence:

"The employee <id> firstinitial <last_name> is the <title>."

```
SELECT 'The employee ' || id || ' ' || SUBSTR(first_name,1,1)
       || ' '|| last_name ||
       ' is the '|| title "EMPLOYEES"
```

```
FROM s_emp;
EMPLOYEES
--------------------------------------------------------------------
The employee 1 C Martin is the President
The employee 2 D Smith is the VP, Operations
The employee 3 M Norton is the VP, Sales
The employee 4 M Quentin is the VP, Finance
The employee 5 J Roper is the VP, Administration
The employee 6 M Brown is the Warehouse Manager
The employee 7 R Hawkins is the Warehouse Manager
The employee 8 B Burns is the Warehouse Manager
The employee 9 A Catskill is the Warehouse Manager
The employee 10 M Jackson is the Warehouse Manager
The employee 11 C Henderson is the Sales Representative
The employee 12 S Gilson is the Sales Representative
The employee 13 J Sanders is the Sales Representative
The employee 14 A Dameron is the Sales Representative
The employee 15 E Hardwick is the Stock Clerk
The employee 16 G Brown is the Stock Clerk
The employee 17 T Washington is the Stock Clerk
The employee 18 D Patterson is the Stock Clerk
The employee 19 A Bell is the Stock Clerk
The employee 20 E Gantos is the Stock Clerk
The employee 21 B Stephenson is the Stock Clerk
The employee 22 E Chester is the Stock Clerk
The employee 23 R Pearl is the Stock Clerk
The employee 24 B Dancer is the Stock Clerk
The employee 25 S Schmitt is the Stock Clerk
```

4.17. What would be the resulting table from this SQL query? Explain the results.

```
SELECT LPAD(last_name,20),SUBSTR(first_name,1,1),
    TO_CHAR(salary,'$9,999.99')
FROM s_emp
WHERE title = 'Stock Clerk';
```

The query will display the last name, right-justified in 20 spaces, the first initial of the first name, and then the formatted salary for all the stock clerks. The format of the salary will include the dollar sign and two decimal places. The resulting table looks like this:

```
LPAD(LAST_NAME,20)    S TO_CHAR(SA
-------------------- - ----------
           Hardwick E  $1,400.00
              Brown G    $940.00
         Washington T  $1,200.00
          Patterson D    $795.00
               Bell A    $850.00
             Gantos E    $800.00
         Stephenson B    $860.00
            Chester E    $800.00
              Pearl R    $795.00
             Dancer B    $860.00
            Schmitt S  $1,100.00
```

4.18. Write an SQL query to print the same chart as Problem 4.17, except in this case, pad the left of the salary column with asterisks up to 15 characters.

```
SELECT LPAD(last_name,20),SUBSTR(first_name,1,1),
      LPAD(TO_CHAR(salary,'$9,999.99'),15,'*')
FROM s_emp
WHERE title = 'Stock Clerk';
LPAD(LAST_NAME,20)    S LPAD(TO_CHAR(SA
-------------------- - ----------------
          Hardwick E ***** $1,400.00
             Brown G *****   $940.00
        Washington T ***** $1,200.00
         Patterson D *****   $795.00
              Bell A *****   $850.00
            Gantos E *****   $800.00
         Stephenson B *****   $860.00
           Chester E *****   $800.00
             Pearl R *****   $795.00
            Dancer B *****   $860.00
           Schmitt S ***** $1,100.00
```

Notice that there are only `five` asterisks in each row. When you pad a column that was converted from number to character, the padding only extends up to one character before the format specified. In this case, the format $9,999.99 is `nine` characters. One space is allowed to the left, and then the other five spaces contain the asterisks.

4.19. Write an SQL query to display the titles of the vice presidents. Replace every instance of VP with the title `'Vice President'`. Name the column `"VICE PRESIDENT TITLES"`.

```
SELECT REPLACE(title, 'VP', 'Vice President') "VICE PRESIDENT TITLES"
FROM s_emp
WHERE title LIKE 'VP%';
VICE PRESIDENT TITLES
--------------------------------------------------
Vice President, Operations
Vice President, Sales
Vice President, Finance
Vice President, Administration
```

4.20. What would be the resulting table from this SQL query? Explain the results.

```
SELECT last_name, first_name
FROM s_emp
WHERE LENGTH(last_name) = 5 AND LENGTH(first_name) = 5;
```

The resulting table shows that this query prints the names of everyone who has exactly `five` characters in their first and their last names.

```
LAST_NAME            FIRST_NAME
-------------------- --------------------
Smith                Doris
Brown                Molly
Pearl                Roger
```

4.21. Someone created a table called PEOPLE below. It has one column holding a title, a first name, and a last name

```
P_NAME
------------------------
Mr. John Doe
Mrs. Susan Blake
```

Write an SQL query that takes this column and creates three separate columns called "TITLE", "FIRST", and "LAST".

- To solve this problem, you need to find the first space to locate the title and the beginning of the first name: INSTR(p_name, ' ')
- Then you need to find the second space to locate the end of the first name and the beginning of the last name: INSTR(p_name, ' ',1,2)
- Finally, use the SUBSTR() function to print each column.

```
SELECT SUBSTR(p_name, 1, INSTR(p_name, ' ')) "TITLE",
SUBSTR(p_name, INSTR(p_name, ' ')+1, INSTR(p_name, ' ',2))"FIRST",
SUBSTR(p_name, INSTR(p_name, ' ',1,2)+1)"SECOND"
FROM people;
```

The resulting chart demonstrates that this query works as desired:

```
TITLE                FIRST                SECOND
-------------------- -------------------- --------------------
Mr.                  John                 Doe
Mrs.                 Susan                Blake
```

4.22. Write an SQL query that will print the ID, the first name, and the last name of the employees with odd-numbered IDs. Remember that the IDs are stored as character data. Convert them to numbers, and then find the odd numbers using the MOD function. (If a number MOD 2 is exactly 1, it is odd.) These functions will be in the WHERE clause of the statement.

```
SELECT id, first_name, last_name
FROM s_emp
WHERE MOD(TO_NUMBER(id),2) = 1;
ID  FIRST_NAME           LAST_NAME
--- -------------------- --------------------
1   Carmen               Martin
3   Michael              Norton
5   Joseph               Roper
7   Roberta              Hawkins
9   Antoinette           Catskill
```

```
11   Colin                Henderson
13   Jason                Sanders
15   Elaine               Hardwick
17   Thomas               Washington
19   Alexander            Bell
21   Blaine               Stephenson
23   Roger                Pearl
25   Sandra               Schmitt
```

4.23. Someone created a small table for a drugstore. A different tax rate is assessed on different items. However, any medicine has only 2.5% tax, but that is not included in the table. Here is the table:

```
ITEM                     COST      TAX
----------------------- --------- ---------
bandages                 1.52      .05
aspirin                  2.55
candy                     .79      .06
antacid                  2.34
```

Write an SQL query that will print the total cost of these items including tax. If no tax percent is listed, then 2.5% is assumed. Round it to the nearest cent.

```
SELECT item, cost, NVL(tax,0.025),
     ROUND(cost + cost * NVL(tax,0.025),2) "TOTAL"
FROM store;
ITEM                     COST NVL(TAX,0.025)    TOTAL
----------------------- --------- --------------- ---------
bandages                 1.52             .05      1.6
aspirin                  2.55            .025      2.61
candy                     .79             .06      .84
antacid                  2.34            .025      2.4
```

4.24 Repeat the preceding problem, but display any money fields with a dollar sign. Include a zero if there are no dollars.

```
SELECT item, TO_CHAR(cost,'$0.99'), TO_CHAR(NVL(tax,0.025),'$0.99'),
    TO_CHAR(ROUND(cost + cost * NVL(tax,0.025),2),'$0.99') "TOTAL"
FROM store;
ITEM                TO_CHA TO_CHA TOTAL
------------------- ------ ------ ------
bandages            $1.52  $0.05  $1.60
aspirin             $2.55  $0.03  $2.61
candy               $0.79  $0.06  $0.84
antacid             $2.34  $0.03  $2.40
```

Solved Problems

Note: Rerun the SG script to refresh the database. Use the order table S_ORD for these problems.

```
CUS  DATE_ORDE DATE_SHIP SAL      TOTAL PAYMEN
---  --------- --------- ---  --------- ------
100  31-AUG-92 10-SEP-92 11      601100 CREDIT
101  31-AUG-92 15-SEP-92 14      8056.6 CREDIT
102  01-SEP-92 08-SEP-92 15        8335 CREDIT
103  02-SEP-92 22-SEP-92 15         377 CASH
104  03-SEP-92 23-SEP-92 15       32430 CREDIT
105  04-SEP-92 18-SEP-92 11     2722.24 CREDIT
106  07-SEP-92 15-SEP-92 12       15634 CREDIT
107  07-SEP-92 21-SEP-92 15      142171 CREDIT
108  07-SEP-92 10-SEP-92 13      149570 CREDIT
109  08-SEP-92 28-SEP-92 11     1020935 CREDIT
110  09-SEP-92 21-SEP-92 11     1539.13 CASH
111  09-SEP-92 21-SEP-92 11        2770 CASH
97   28-AUG-92 17-SEP-92 12       84000 CREDIT
98   31-AUG-92 10-SEP-92 14         595 CASH
99   31-AUG-92 18-SEP-92 14        7707 CREDIT
112  31-AUG-92 10-SEP-92 12         550 CREDIT
```

4.25. Write an SQL query to show for each order how many days elapsed between order date and shipping date.

4.26. The total amount of each order does not include tax. Write an SQL query to show the amount of order, the 5% sales tax, and the total amount paid, including tax. Name the new columns appropriately.

4.27. The company has a policy during the month of August that any order totaling over $7000 will receive a $500 discount. Write an SQL query to calculate the total, including 5% sales tax, for those orders. Name the new columns appropriately.

4.28. Rewrite the SQL query of the previous problem, rounding off the total bill to the nearest dollar.

4.29. Write an SQL query to print the total, the total truncated to the nearest $100, and the absolute value of how much each order's truncated total varies from 6000. Name the columns appropriately.

4.30. Write an SQL query to print out the first 5 powers of 10. (*Hint*: Use the DUAL table.)

4.31. Perhaps the total bills will be paid by cash, using only hundred dollar bills. Write an SQL query to determine how many hundreds will be received and how much cash will need to be paid on each order beyond the hundreds. Name the columns appropriately.

Use this subset of the table WORLD_CITIES for Problems 4.32 to 4.37.

```
CITY                    COUNTRY                 CONTINENT
-------------------     -----------------------  ------------------
ATHENS                  GREECE                  EUROPE
ATLANTA                 UNITED STATES           NORTH AMERICA
DALLAS                  UNITED STATES           NORTH AMERICA
NASHVILLE               UNITED STATES           NORTH AMERICA
VICTORIA                CANADA                  NORTH AMERICA
PETERBOROUGH            CANADA                  NORTH AMERICA
VANCOUVER               CANADA                  NORTH AMERICA
TOLEDO                  UNITED STATES           NORTH AMERICA
WARSAW                  POLAND                  EUROPE
LIMA                    PERU                    SOUTH AMERICA
RIO DE JANEIRO          BRAZIL                  SOUTH AMERICA
SANTIAGO                CHILE                   SOUTH AMERICA
BOGOTA                  COLOMBIA                SOUTH AMERICA
BUENOS AIRES            ARGENTINA               SOUTH AMERICA
QUITO                   ECUADOR                 SOUTH AMERICA
CARACAS                 VENEZUELA               SOUTH AMERICA
MADRAS                  INDIA                   ASIA
NEW DELHI               INDIA                   ASIA
BOMBAY                  INDIA                   ASIA
MANCHESTER              ENGLAND                 EUROPE
LONDON                  ENGLAND                 EUROPE
MOSCOW                  RUSSIA                  EUROPE
PARIS                   FRANCE                  EUROPE
SHENYANG                CHINA                   ASIA
CAIRO                   EGYPT                   AFRICA
TRIPOLI                 LIBYA                   AFRICA
BEIJING                 CHINA                   ASIA
ROME                    ITALY                   EUROPE
TOKYO                   JAPAN                   ASIA
SYDNEY                  AUSTRALIA               AUSTRALIA
SPARTA                  GREECE                  EUROPE
MADRID                  SPAIN                   EUROPE
```

4.32. The WORLD_CITIES table is stored in all caps. Write an SQL query to display the cities in North and South America with the first letter capitalized and everything else lower case.

4.33. Write an SQL query to display two columns. The first should be called " PLACE " and include both the city and country with initial caps, separated by a comma. The second column should be the continent in all lowercase letters. Display the cities in all the continents except North and South America.

4.34. Write an SQL query that lists the cities and countries in Europe, only trim the last three letters from the front of Europe, so only EUR is displayed.

4.35. Write an SQL query that displays the cities in Europe where the city name has all S's replaced with a dollar sign.

4.36. Write an SQL query that will print the cities and countries in North or South America. Display the continent as `"N America"` or `"S America"`. Display all columns with only beginning characters capitalized.

4.37. Write an SQL query to display all the cities and countries that have the same number of letters in the city name and the country name.

4.38. Write an SQL query to display the customer ID and the total payment from every customer with an even-numbered customer ID in the S_ORD table. List by customer number.

4.39. Repeat the previous problem, only this time, display the total payments rounded to the nearest 10 and padded with asterisks to the left up to 15 characters wide.

4.40. There is a table called ADDIT (shown below) with two columns of numbers. Some are NULL. Write an SQL query that will display the two numbers and their sums, substituting zero for any NULL values.

```
    FIRST     SECOND
--------- ---------
  4567.88     23.33
   345.34
            2554.23
   2.99876      4.34
```

 # Answers to Supplementary Problems

4.25.

```
SELECT id, date_ordered, date_shipped,
date_shipped-date_ordered
FROM s_ord;
ID  DATE_ORDE DATE_SHIP DATE_SHIPPED-DATE_ORDERED
--- --------- --------- -------------------------
100 31-AUG-92 10-SEP-92                        10
101 31-AUG-92 15-SEP-92                        15
102 01-SEP-92 08-SEP-92                         7
103 02-SEP-92 22-SEP-92                        20
104 03-SEP-92 23-SEP-92                        20
105 04-SEP-92 18-SEP-92                        14
106 07-SEP-92 15-SEP-92                         8
107 07-SEP-92 21-SEP-92                        14
108 07-SEP-92 10-SEP-92                         3
109 08-SEP-92 28-SEP-92                        20
110 09-SEP-92 21-SEP-92                        12
111 09-SEP-92 21-SEP-92                        12
97  28-AUG-92 17-SEP-92                        20
```

```
98  31-AUG-92 10-SEP-92                                  10
99  31-AUG-92 18-SEP-92                                  18
112 31-AUG-92 10-SEP-92                                  10
```

4.26.

```
SELECT id, total, total * .05 "TAX",
total + (total * .05) "TOTAL BILL"
FROM s_ord;
ID  TOTAL            TAX TOTAL BILL
--- --------- --------- ----------
100    601100     30055     631155
101    8056.6    402.83    8459.43
102      8335    416.75    8751.75
103       377     18.85     395.85
104     32430    1621.5    34051.5
105   2722.24   136.112   2858.352
106     15634     781.7    16415.7
107    142171   7108.55  149279.55
108    149570    7478.5   157048.5
109   1020935  51046.75  1071981.8
110   1539.13   76.9565  1616.0865
111      2770     138.5     2908.5
97      84000      4200      88200
98        595     29.75     624.75
99       7707    385.35    8092.35
112       550      27.5      577.5
```

4.27.

```
SELECT id,date_ordered, total- 500, (total - 500)* .05 "TAX",
(total - 500) + ((total - 500) * .05) "TOTAL BILL"
FROM s_ord
WHERE date_ordered < TO_DATE('01-SEP-1992','DD-MON-YYYY') AND
     date_ordered >= TO_DATE('01-AUG-1992','DD-MON-YYYY')
     AND total >= 7000;
ID  DATE_ORDE TOTAL-500       TAX TOTAL BILL
--- --------- --------- --------- ----------
100 31-AUG-92    600600     30030     630630
101 31-AUG-92    7556.6    377.83    7934.43
97  28-AUG-92     83500      4175      87675
99  31-AUG-92      7207    360.35    7567.35
```

For more help on comparing dates, see Chapter 6.

4.28.

```
SELECT id,date_ordered, total- 500, (total - 500)* .05 "TAX",
ROUND(((total - 500) + (total - 500) * .05)) "TOTAL BILL"
FROM s_ord
WHERE date_ordered < TO_DATE('01-SEP-1992','DD-MON-YYYY')
     AND date_ordered >= TO_DATE('01-AUG-1992','DD-MON-YYYY')
     AND total >= 7000;
```

```
ID   DATE_ORDE  TOTAL-500        TAX  TOTAL BILL
---  ---------  ---------  ---------  ----------
100  31-AUG-92     600600      30030      630630
101  31-AUG-92     7556.6     377.83        7934
97   28-AUG-92      83500       4175       87675
99   31-AUG-92       7207     360.35        7567
```

4.29.

```
SELECT total, TRUNC(total, -2), ABS(TRUNC(total, -2)- 6000)
FROM s_ord;
    TOTAL TRUNC(TOTAL,-2)  ABS(TRUNC(TOTAL,-2)-6000)
--------- ---------------  -------------------------
   601100          601100                     595100
   8056.6            8000                       2000
     8335            8300                       2300
      377             300                       5700
    32430           32400                      26400
  2722.24            2700                       3300
    15634           15600                       9600
   142171          142100                     136100
   149570          149500                     143500
  1020935         1020900                    1014900
  1539.13            1500                       4500
     2770            2700                       3300
    84000           84000                      78000
      595             500                       5500
     7707            7700                       1700
      550             500                       5500
```

4.30.

```
SELECT POWER(10,1), POWER(10,2), POWER(10,3), POWER(10,4),
POWER(10,5)
FROM DUAL;
POWER(10,1) POWER(10,2) POWER(10,3) POWER(10,4) POWER(10,5)
----------- ----------- ----------- ----------- -----------
         10         100        1000       10000      100000
```

4.31.

```
SELECT total, TRUNC(total/100) "HUNDREDS",
      MOD(total, 100) "OTHER CASH"
FROM s_ord;
    TOTAL  HUNDREDS  OTHER CASH
--------- ---------  ----------
   601100      6011           0
   8056.6        80        56.6
     8335        83          35
      377         3          77
    32430       324          30
  2722.24        27       22.24
    15634       156          34
```

```
 142171        1421          71
 149570        1495          70
1020935       10209          35
1539.13          15       39.13
   2770          27          70
  84000         840           0
    595           5          95
   7707          77           7
    550           5          50
```

4.32.

```
SELECT INITCAP(city),INITCAP(country),INITCAP(continent)
FROM world_cities
WHERE continent LIKE '%AMERICA';
INITCAP(CITY)          INITCAP(COUNTRY)        INITCAP(CONTINENT)
--------------------   --------------------   ------------------
Atlanta                United States          North America
Dallas                 United States          North America
Nashville              United States          North America
Victoria               Canada                 North America
Peterborough           Canada                 North America
Vancouver              Canada                 North America
Toledo                 United States          North America
Lima                   Peru                   South America
Rio De Janeiro         Brazil                 South America
Santiago               Chile                  South America
Bogota                 Colombia               South America
Buenos Aires           Argentina              South America
Quito                  Ecuador                South America
Caracas                Venezuela              South America
```

4.33.

```
SELECT INITCAP(city) || ', '|| INITCAP(country) "PLACE",
     LOWER(continent)
FROM world_cities
WHERE NOT continent LIKE '%AMERICA';
PLACE
                                                        LOWER(CONTINENT)
--------------------------------------------------   ------------
Athens, Greece                                       europe
Warsaw, Poland                                       europe
Madras, India                                        asia
New Delhi, India                                     asia
Bombay, India                                        asia
Manchester, England                                  europe
London, England                                      europe
Moscow, Russia                                       europe
Paris, France                                        europe
Shenyang, China                                      asia
Cairo, Egypt                                         africa
```

```
Tripoli, Libya                                     africa
Beijing, China                                     asia
Rome, Italy                                        europe
Tokyo, Japan                                       asia
Sydney, Australia                                  australia
Sparta, Greece                                     europe
Madrid, Spain                                      europe
```

4.34.

```
SELECT city, country, RTRIM(continent, 'OPE') "TRIMMED"
FROM world_cities
WHERE continent = 'EUROPE';
CITY                        COUNTRY                     TRIMMED
--------------------------  --------------------------  ---------
ATHENS                      GREECE                      EUR
WARSAW                      POLAND                      EUR
MANCHESTER                  ENGLAND                     EUR
LONDON                      ENGLAND                     EUR
MOSCOW                      RUSSIA                      EUR
PARIS                       FRANCE                      EUR
ROME                        ITALY                       EUR
SPARTA                      GREECE                      EUR
MADRID                      SPAIN                       EUR
```

4.35.

```
SELECT REPLACE(city, 'S', '$')
FROM WORLD_CITIES
WHERE continent = 'EUROPE';
REPLACE(CITY,'S','$')
--------------------------
ATHEN$
WAR$AW
MANCHE$TER
LONDON
MO$COW
PARI$
ROME
$PARTA
MADRID
```

4.36.

```
SELECT INITCAP(city), INITCAP(country) "COUNTRY",
       SUBSTR(continent, 1, 1)|| ' ' ||
       INITCAP(SUBSTR(continent, INSTR(continent, ' ')+1))
       "CONTINENT"
FROM WORLD_CITIES
WHERE continent LIKE '%AMERICA';
```

```
INITCAP(CITY)            COUNTRY                 CONTINENT
----------------------   ----------------------  ------------
Atlanta                  United States           N America
Dallas                   United States           N America
Nashville                United States           N America
Victoria                 Canada                  N America
Peterborough             Canada                  N America
Vancouver                Canada                  N America
Toledo                   United States           N America
Lima                     Peru                    S America
Rio De Janeiro           Brazil                  S America
Santiago                 Chile                   S America
Bogota                   Colombia                S America
Buenos Aires             Argentina               S America
Quito                    Ecuador                 S America
Caracas                  Venezuela               S America
```

4.37.

```
SELECT city, country, LENGTH(city)
FROM world_cities
WHERE LENGTH(city) = LENGTH(country);
CITY                     COUNTRY                 LENGTH(CITY)
----------------------   ----------------------  ------------
ATHENS                   GREECE                             6
WARSAW                   POLAND                             6
LIMA                     PERU                               4
MOSCOW                   RUSSIA                             6
CAIRO                    EGYPT                              5
TOKYO                    JAPAN                              5
SPARTA                   GREECE                             6
```

4.38.

```
SELECT customer_id, total
FROM s_ord
WHERE MOD(TO_NUMBER(customer_id),2) = 0
ORDER BY customer_id;
CUS     TOTAL
---  ---------
202       595
204    601100
204      2770
206      8335
208       377
208     32430
210     15634
210       550
212    149570
214   1539.13
```

4.39.

```
SELECT customer_id, LPAD(TO_CHAR(ROUND(total,-1),
'9,999'),15,'*')
FROM s_ord
WHERE MOD(TO_NUMBER(customer_id),2) = 0
ORDER BY customer_id;
CUS LPAD(TO_CHAR(RO
--- ---------------
202 ********    600
204 *********££££££
204 ********* 2,770
206 ********* 8,340
208 ********    380
208 *********££££££
210 *********££££££
210 ********    550
212 *********££££££
214 ********* 1,540
```

Notice that if a number is too long, it is not truncated. Digits are replaced with pound signs.

4.40.

```
SELECT NVL(first,0), NVL(second,0), NVL(first,0)+NVL(second,0)
FROM addit;
NVL(FIRST,0) NVL(SECOND,0) NVL(FIRST,0)+NVL(SECOND,0)
------------ ------------- ---------------------------
     4567.88         23.33                     4591.21
      345.34             0                      345.34
           0       2554.23                     2554.23
     2.99876          4.34                     7.33876
```

CHAPTER 5

Group Functions

5.1 Introduction to Group Functions

The previous chapter demonstrated using arithmetic operators and other built-in functions on individual values within the database. Often it is important to examine or manipulate multiple rows at once. For instance, in an employee table you might want to find the maximum salary, the average salary, or the number of sales representatives. This chapter focuses on *group functions*, sometimes called *aggregate functions*, which are those functions that operate on sets of rows to produce one result. The group functions are listed in Table 5-1.

Notice the keywords DISTINCT and ALL shown in the parameter list. The word ALL simply means that all the rows in the table should be examined. Since this is the default, this word is not usually included in the SQL query. The word DISTINCT means that duplicate values are removed from the column before the calculation. It must be included if that is what you want to do. DISTINCT will be demonstrated in the COUNT( ) section below. The STDEV( ) and VARIANCE( ) functions are not usually needed for most business applications. They will not be covered in this book but are available if required.

Rerun your SG script if necessary to restore the database. Table 5-2 shows a subset of an items-ordered information table S_ITEM that will be used in the following sections.

5.2 The SUM(n) and AVG(n) Functions

The SUM(n) and AVG(n) functions return the sum and the average, respectively, of all the values in the particular column. They ignore any NULL values.

EXAMPLE 5.1
Write an SQL query that displays the sum of all the items ordered and the average cost of the items.

Table 5-1. Group functions.

Function	Input Argument	Value Returned
AVG(*[DISTINCT\ALL]n*)	*n* = column	The average value of the column *n*.
COUNT(*[ALL]**)	none	The number of rows returned by the particular query *including* duplicates and NULLs.
COUNT(*[DISTINCT\ALL]n*)	*n* = column or expression	The number of rows where the value of the column or expression is not NULL.
MAX(*[DISTINCT\ALL]n*)	*n* = column or expression	The maximum value in the column or expression.
MIN(*[DISTINCT\ALL]n*)	*n* = column or expression	The minimum value in the column or expression.
STDEV(*[DISTINCT\ALL]n*)	*n* = column or expression	The standard deviation of the column or expression, ignoring NULL values.
SUM(*[DISTINCT\ALL]n*)	*n* = column or expression	The sum of the values in the column or expression.
VARIANCE(*[DISTINCT\ALL]n*)	*n* = column or expression	The variance of the column or expression, ignoring NULL values.

Table 5-2. Item table.

```
ORD ITEM_ID PRODUCT     PRICE  QUANTITY QUANTITY_SHIPPED
--- ------- -------  ---------  --------- ----------------
100 1       10011        135        500              500
100 2       10013        380        400              400
100 3       10021         14        500              500
100 5       30326        582        600              600
100 7       41010          8        250              250
100 6       30433         20        450              450
100 4       10023         36        400              400
101 1       30421         16         15               15
101 3       41010          8         20               20
101 5       50169       4.29         40               40
101 6       50417         80         27               27
101 7       50530         45         50               50
101 4       41100         45         35               35
101 2       40422         50         30               30
```

```
SELECT SUM(price) "SUM", AVG(price) "AVERAGE"
FROM s_item;
```

The resulting table shows that only one value is returned by each function.

```
    SUM    AVERAGE
--------- ----------
 1423.29 101.66357
```

EXAMPLE 5.2

It is possible to use these functions on a subset of the table. Write an SQL query that will display the sum and average price of the items ordered on order ID 100.

```
SELECT SUM(price) "SUM", AVG(price) "AVERAGE"
FROM s_item
WHERE ord_id = '100';
      SUM    AVERAGE
--------- ----------
     1175 167.85714
```

Another table, STATS, shown in Table 5-3, will be used in many of these examples to demonstrate how the functions work on columns with NULL values.

Table 5-3.   STATS table.

EVEN	ODD
2	1
	3
6	5
8	
10	9
	11
14	
16	15

EXAMPLE 5.3

Write an SQL query that displays the sum and the average of the even numbers in the STATS table.

```
SELECT SUM(even) "SUM", AVG(even) "AVERAGE"
FROM stats;
      SUM    AVERAGE
--------- ----------
       56 9.3333333
```

This example demonstrates that the NULL values are not assumed to be zero. They are simply ignored by both these functions.

5.3   The MAX(*n*) and MIN(*n*) Functions

The MAX(*n*) and MIN(*n*) functions return the maximum and minimum values in the specified column. These two functions can be used with any data type.

EXAMPLE 5.4
Write an SQL query that displays the highest and lowest prices for any product in the S_ITEM table.

```
SELECT MAX(price) "MAX", MIN(price) "MIN"
FROM s_item;
      MAX        MIN
--------- ---------
      582       4.29
```

By comparing the resulting table above with the original data in Table 5-2, you can see that the item with the maximum price was from order number 100 and the item with the minimum price is from order number 101. However, sometimes you want the maximum or minimum from only a specified subset of the column. The next example shows how to accomplish this.

EXAMPLE 5.5
Write an SQL query that displays the highest and lowest prices for any product in the S_ITEM table from order number 100.

```
SELECT MAX(price) "MAX", MIN(price) "MIN"
FROM s_item
WHERE ord_id = '101';
      MAX        MIN
--------- ---------
       80       4.29
```

EXAMPLE 5.6
The MAX( ) and MIN( ) functions also ignore NULL values. Write an SQL query to display the maximum and minimum values of the ODD column in the STATS table.

```
SELECT MAX(odd) "MAX", MIN(odd) "MIN"
FROM stats;
      MAX        MIN
--------- ---------
       15          1
```

Notice that the NULL values are ignored. They are not assumed to be zero or zero would have been the minimum value.

EXAMPLE 5.7
Write an SQL query to display the highest and lowest product ID.

```
SELECT MAX(product_id) "MAX", MIN(product_id) "MIN"
FROM s_item;
      MAX       MIN
--------- ---------
    50530     10011
```

The `product_id` data type of the S_ITEM table is a character string. This query demonstrates that MAX( ) and MIN( ) also work on character strings. If the values were names, such as "THOMAS" and "ALLEN", MAX( ) would return "THOMAS" because it comes after "ALLEN" in the alphabet. Be careful of using these functions on data that is mixed case. The characters are evaluated according to their ASCII values where all uppercase letters are "less than" all the lowercase letters.

5.4   The COUNT( ) Functions

The COUNT( ) functions are similar enough to be confusing. The functions return a particular number, and it is important to understand exactly what each function is counting. COUNT( ) can be used on columns with any data type.

5.4.1   THE COUNT(*) FUNCTION

The COUNT(*) function is the only function that takes the asterisk (*) as a parameter. It counts all the rows in the entire table, or a subset specified by the query, and ignores any NULL values in any column.

EXAMPLE 5.8
Write an SQL query that displays the number of rows in the table STATS.

```
SELECT COUNT(*) "NUMBER OF ROWS"
FROM stats;
NUMBER OF ROWS
--------------
             8
```

This example demonstrates that the function ignores any NULL values. The next example shows that the function will return the number of rows in the subset of the table specified by the query.

EXAMPLE 5.9
Write an SQL query that displays the number of rows in the table S_ITEM where the order ID is 100.

```
SELECT COUNT(*) "ORDER 100"
FROM s_item
WHERE ord_id = '100';
ORDER 100
---------
        7
```

5.4.2 THE COUNT(ALL *n*) AND COUNT(*n*) FUNCTIONS

These two functions are usually equivalent. They display the number of values present in the particular column *n*. You could read it as "display the count of the known values in column *n*." The ALL keyword specifies to look at all the columns when counting. Look at the next example to convince yourself that the two functions return the same value.

EXAMPLE 5.10
Write an SQL query to display the number of values in the column EVEN of the STATS table. Use both COUNT(ALL *n*) and COUNT(*n*).

```
SELECT COUNT(ALL even) "WITH ALL", COUNT(even) "WITHOUT ALL"
FROM stats;
 WITH ALL  WITHOUT ALL
--------- -----------
        6           6
```

5.4.3 THE COUNT(DISTINCT *n*) FUNCTION

The use of the keyword DISTINCT in the COUNT function returns the number of distinct values present in the particular column *n*. It can be used with any data type. Notice that there is no comma separating the keywords DISTINCT or ALL and the column name.

EXAMPLE 5.11
Write an SQL query that displays the number of total rows, product IDs and order IDs that are present in the S_ITEM table shown in Table 5-2.

```
SELECT COUNT(*) "TOTAL", COUNT(DISTINCT product_id) "PRODUCTS",
COUNT(DISTINCT ord_id) "ORDERS"
FROM s_item;
   TOTAL   PRODUCTS    ORDERS
--------- --------- ---------
      14        13         2
```

A close examination of the original table will show that the product 41010 is listed twice. The query correctly reported that there are 14 total rows with 13 different products ordered on two separate order IDs.

5.5   Combining Single-Value and Group Functions

The arithmetic operators and built-in functions operating on single values from Chapter 4 can be combined with the group functions explained in this chapter. For example, you might want to know the average amount of the order 100 in the S_ITEM table. To find the total amount of each item, you would multiply the price by the quantity, as (PRICE * QUANTITY). To find the average for the entire order 100, you would apply the AVG( ) function to the same query.

EXAMPLE 5.12
Write an SQL query that displays the average total for all the items in order 100.

```
SELECT AVG(price * quantity) "AVERAGE TOTAL OF ORDER 100"
FROM s_item
WHERE ord_id = '101';
AVERAGE TOTAL OF ORDER 100
--------------------------
                1150.9429
```

Almost any combination of the built-in functions is allowed by SQL. You can also use the arithmetic operators to manipulate the results of the group functions.

EXAMPLE 5.13
Write an SQL query that displays the range of total cost for the items in order 100. In other words, display the difference between the maximum cost and the minimum cost.

```
SELECT MAX(price*quantity)-MIN(price*quantity) "COST DIFFERENCE"
FROM s_item
WHERE ord_id = '100';
COST DIFFERENCE
---------------
         347200
```

5.6   Displaying Specific Groups

The WHERE clause chooses the individual rows to be considered by the query, and the ORDER BY displays the results sorted by a specific column. There are two group operators that perform similar tasks, but on groups not individual values: **GROUP BY** and **HAVING**. The syntax for this is as follows:

```
SELECT column_list
FROM tablename
WHERE condition_list
GROUP BY column_list HAVING condition_list;
```

5.6.1 THE GROUP BY CLAUSE

Examples 5.12 and 5.13 above showed the average cost and the range of the cost of the items in order 100. It is possible to show the average cost and the range for all the orders by using GROUP BY.

> **EXAMPLE 5.14**
> Write an SQL query that displays the average and range of total cost for the items in each order.

```
SELECT ord_id, AVG(price * quantity) "AVERAGE TOTAL OF ORDER",
    MAX(price*quantity)-MIN(price*quantity) "COST DIFFERENCE"
FROM s_item
GROUP BY ord_id;
ORD AVERAGE TOTAL OF ORDER COST DIFFERENCE
--- --------------------- ---------------
100            85871.429          347200
101            1150.9429            2090
```

Notice that in the SELECT an individual column is listed, as well as the group functions AVG( ), MAX( ), and MIN( ). Usually it is impossible to mix individual and group items in the same select statement. However, GROUP BY indicates that the individual groups are to be manipulated. For clarity, it is important to include in the display the columns that are being grouped as 100 and 101 above. The resulting chart clearly shows the totals and differences are listed for each order.

It is possible to display summary information for groups and for subgroups by including more than one column name in the GROUP BY clause. This will be demonstrated through using the subset of the PROGRAMMER table in Table 5-4.

Table 5-4. PROGRAMMER table.

EMP	LAST_NAME	HIRE_DATE	LANGUAGE	CLEARANCE
201	Campbell	01-JAN-95	VB	Secret
390	Bell	01-MAY-93	Java	Top Secret
789	Hixon	31-AUG-98	VB	Secret
134	McGurn	15-JUL-95	C++	Secret
896	Sweet	15-JUN-97	Java	Top Secret
345	Rowlett	15-NOV-99	Java	
563	Reardon	15-AUG-94	C++	Confidential

EXAMPLE 5.15
Suppose you need to know how many programmers have each kind of
clearance and how many know each kind of language. You could begin by
writing two separate queries: (a) one to display the groups of languages and (b)
one to display the groups of clearance.

a.
```
SELECT language, COUNT(*) "IN EACH LANGUAGE"
FROM programmer
GROUP BY language;
LANGUAGE          IN EACH LANGUAGE
--------------    ----------------
C++                            2
Java                           3
VB                             2
```

b.
```
SELECT clearance, COUNT(*) "IN EACH CLEARANCE"
FROM programmer
GROUP BY clearance;
CLEARANCE                      IN EACH CLEARANCE
------------------------       -----------------
Confidential                           1
Secret                                 3
Top Secret                             2
                                       1
```

Notice that the NULL clearance is considered a separate category by the
COUNT(*) function. In this example, the COUNT(*) function returns the
number of rows in each category.

c.
These two queries answered the question. Is there a way to combine them into
one table and display the languages available within each clearance? Yes. The
query would look like this:

```
SELECT language, clearance,
    COUNT(*) "IN EACH CLEARANCE"
FROM programmer
GROUP BY language, clearance;
LANGUAGE          CLEARANCE                    IN EACH CLEARANCE
--------------    ------------------------     -----------------
C++               Confidential                         1
C++               Secret                               1
Java              Top Secret                           2
Java                                                   1
VB                Secret                               2
```

5.6.2 THE HAVING CLAUSE

Just as the WHERE clause limits the number of rows to be displayed by a SELECT statement, the HAVING clause limits the number of groups to be displayed following the GROUP BY clause.

EXAMPLE 5.16
Using the information from Example 5.15, write a query to display only the languages within each clearance where there are more than one programmer.

```
SELECT language, clearance,
    COUNT(*) "IN EACH CLEARANCE"
FROM programmer
GROUP BY language, clearance
HAVING COUNT(*) > 1;
```

LANGUAGE	CLEARANCE	IN EACH CLEARANCE
Java	Top Secret	2
VB	Secret	2

The COUNT(*) function is not the only one that can be used with HAVING. Any group function can be used. It is important to recognize that WHERE is used when you are evaluating each value, and HAVING is used when you are evaluating a group function.

EXAMPLE 5.17
Write an SQL query on the S_ITEM table from Table 5-2 that will display the number of products in each order that total (price times quantity) greater than $1000. This query will use the WHERE because individual values are examined within each order.

```
SELECT ord_id, COUNT(*) "MORE THAN $1000"
FROM s_item
WHERE price*quantity > 1000
GROUP BY ord_id;
```

ORD	MORE THAN $1000
100	7
101	4

WHERE is used in this example because the value that limits the count is an individual value, or the result of price times quantity. Use HAVING when the value that limits the count is the result of a group function.

EXAMPLE 5.18
Write an SQL query that displays the number of products for the orders with an average cost of greater than $2000.

```
SELECT ord_id, AVG(price * quantity) "AVG",
     COUNT(*) "AVG MORE THAN $2000"
FROM s_item
GROUP BY ord_id
HAVING AVG(price * quantity) > 2000;
ORD       AVG AVG MORE THAN $2000
--- --------- -------------------
100 85871.429                   7
```

In this example the result of the AVG( ) function limits what the COUNT( ) function is returning. Remember that WHERE limits the displayed rows by examining individual values and HAVING limits the displayed rows by examining group function values.

Solved Problems

Note: Rerun the SG script to refresh the database before answering these quetions. Use this employee table S_EMP for the questions in this section.

ID	LAST_NAME	FIRST_NAME	MAN	TITLE	DEP	SALARY
1	Martin	Carmen		President	50	4500
2	Smith	Doris	1	VP, Operations	41	2450
3	Norton	Michael	1	VP, Sales	31	2400
4	Quentin	Mark	1	VP, Finance	10	2450
5	Roper	Joseph	1	VP, Administration	50	2550
6	Brown	Molly	2	Warehouse Manager	41	1600
7	Hawkins	Roberta	2	Warehouse Manager	42	1650
8	Burns	Ben	2	Warehouse Manager	43	1500
9	Catskill	Antoinette	2	Warehouse Manager	44	1700
10	Jackson	Marta	2	Warehouse Manager	45	1507
11	Henderson	Colin	3	Sales Representative	31	1400
12	Gilson	Sam	3	Sales Representative	32	1490
13	Sanders	Jason	3	Sales Representative	33	1515
14	Dameron	Andre	3	Sales Representative	35	1450
15	Hardwick	Elaine	6	Stock Clerk	41	1400
16	Brown	George	6	Stock Clerk	41	940
17	Washington	Thomas	7	Stock Clerk	42	1200
18	Patterson	Donald	7	Stock Clerk	42	795
19	Bell	Alexander	8	Stock Clerk	43	850
20	Gantos	Eddie	9	Stock Clerk	44	800
21	Stephenson	Blaine	10	Stock Clerk	45	860
22	Chester	Eddie	9	Stock Clerk	44	800

```
23   Pearl        Roger        9    Stock Clerk    34     795
24   Dancer       Bonnie       7    Stock Clerk    45     860
25   Schmitt      Sandra       8    Stock Clerk    45    1100
```

5.1. Write an SQL query that will display the sum and the average of the monthly salaries.

```
SELECT SUM(salary) "SUM", AVG(salary) "AVG"
FROM s_emp;
    SUM        AVG
--------- ---------
   38562    1542.48
```

5.2. Write an SQL query that displays the number of different departments represented in the table compared to the number of rows in the table.

```
SELECT COUNT(DISTINCT dept_id) "DEPTS", COUNT(*) "ROWS"
FROM s_emp;
    DEPTS      ROWS
--------- ---------
       12        25
```

5.3. Write an SQL query that displays the number of different manager IDs represented in the table compared to the number of rows in the table.

```
SELECT COUNT(DISTINCT manager_id) "MANAGER IDS",
COUNT(*) "ROWS"
FROM s_emp;
MANAGER IDS      ROWS
----------- ---------
          8        25
```

Notice in the table that the president does not have a manager ID. The NULL value is not included in the count of distinct manager IDs. That row is included, however, in the count of the total number of rows in the table.

5.4. Write an SQL query that displays the average salary of the stock clerks.

```
SELECT AVG(salary) "AVERAGE"
FROM s_emp
WHERE title = 'Stock Clerk';
  AVERAGE
---------
945.45455
```

5.5. Write an SQL query that displays the maximum and minimum salaries of the warehouse managers.

```
SELECT MAX(salary) "MAX", MIN(salary) "MIN"
FROM s_emp
WHERE title = 'Warehouse Manager';
      MAX       MIN
--------- ---------
     1700      1500
```

5.6. What is displayed by this SQL query? Explain it.

```
SELECT MAX(last_name), MIN(last_name),
     COUNT(*), COUNT(DISTINCT last_name)
FROM s_emp;
```

Recall that these functions can be used on columns with character string values. The resulting table below gives the name of the employee who comes last alphabetically, the name of the employee who comes first alphabetically, the total rows in the table, and the number of distinct last names. Notice that two employees have "Brown" as their last name.

MAX(LAST_NAME)	MIN(LAST_NAME)	COUNT(*)	COUNT(DISTINCTLAST_NAME)
Washington	Bell	25	24

5.7. Write an SQL query that will find the average of *all* the values in the odd and even columns of the STATS table in this chapter, counting a 0 for any NULL value. Compare the results to using the same functions and ignoring the NULL values.

```
SELECT AVG(NVL(odd, 0)) "AVG ODDS", AVG(odd) "IGNORING NULLS",
     AVG(NVL(even,0)) "AVG EVENS", AVG(even) "ICNORING NULLS"
FROM stats;
```

AVG ODDS	IGNORING NULLS	AVG EVENS	IGNORING NULLS
5.5	7.3333333	7	9.3333333

Usually these functions ignore the NULL values. You can use the function NVL( ) from Chapter 4 to force the group functions to consider all the values, replacing each NULL with another value.

5.8. Write an SQL query that will display the average salary of each job title except the president and vice presidents. Display the table alphabetically by title.

```
SELECT title, COUNT (*) "NUMBER", AVG(salary) "AVERAGE SALARY"
FROM s_emp
WHERE title <> 'President' AND NOT title LIKE 'VP%'
GROUP BY title
ORDER BY title;
```

TITLE	NUMBER	AVERAGE SALARY
Sales Representative	4	1463.75
Stock Clerk	11	945.45455
Warehouse Manager	5	1591.4

In this example, the WHERE clause limits which rows are examined for the GROUP BY function to group. WHERE is used because the individual value is examined. When ORDER BY is used, it is placed after the GROUP BY and HAVING clauses.

5.9. Write an SQL query that displays the average salary of each manager ID where more than one person holds that ID.

```
SELECT manager_id, COUNT (*) "NUMBER",
AVG(salary) "AVERAGE SALARY"
FROM s_emp
GROUP BY manager_id
HAVING COUNT(*) > 1;
MAN     NUMBER  AVERAGE SALARY
---  ---------  --------------
1        4           2462.5
2        5           1591.4
3        4           1463.75
6        2             1170
7        3         951.66667
8        2              975
9        3         798.33333
```

5.10. Write an SQL query that displays the average salary of each manager ID where more than one person holds that ID. Only include IDs where the average salary is greater than $1200. (*Hint*: Use the query from 5.9 and further limit the rows displayed with a compound HAVING clause.)

```
SELECT manager_id, COUNT (*) "NUMBER",
      AVG(salary) "AVERAGE SALARY"
FROM s_emp1
GROUP BY manager_id
HAVING COUNT(*) > 1 AND AVG(salary) > 1200;
MAN     NUMBER  AVERAGE SALARY
---  ---------  --------------
1        4           2462.5
2        5           1591.4
3        4           1463.75
```

5.11. Write an SQL query that displays the average salary of each manager ID by department where more than one person holds that ID. Group by manager ID within each department.

```
SELECT dept_id, manager_id, COUNT (*) "NUMBER",
      AVG(salary) "AVERAGE SALARY"
FROM s_emp
GROUP BY dept_id, manager_id
HAVING COUNT(*) > 1;
DEP MAN     NUMBER AVERAGE SALARY
---  ---  ---------  --------------
41    6        2             1170
42    7        2            997.5
44    9        2              800
```

5.12. Write an SQL query that displays the maximum and minimum salary for each job title where there is more than one person holding the title.

```
SELECT title, COUNT (*) "NUMBER", MAX(salary) "MAX SALARY",
     MIN(salary) "MIN SALARY"
FROM s_emp
GROUP BY title
HAVING COUNT(*) > 1;
TITLE                         NUMBER MAX SALARY MIN SALARY
----------------------------- ------ ---------- ----------
Sales Representative              4      1515       1400
Stock Clerk                      11      1400        795
Warehouse Manager                 5      1700       1500
```

5.13. Write an SQL query that displays the maximum and minimum salary for each department where there is more than one person in that department. Display them in order of department.

```
SELECT dept_id, MAX(salary) "MAX SALARY",
     MIN(salary) "MIN SALARY"
FROM s_emp
GROUP BY dept_id
HAVING COUNT(*) > 1
ORDER BY dept_id;
DEP MAX SALARY MIN SALARY
--- ---------- ----------
31     2400       1400
41     2450        940
42     1650        795
43     1500        850
44     1700        800
45     1507        860
50     4500       2550
```

5.14. Write an SQL query that displays the department name and ID, along with the total number of employees in that department for all departments with more than 1 employee. Display them in order of number of employees, the most first. (*Hint*: This query requests information from two different tables.)

```
SELECT s_dept.name "DEPARTMENT", s_emp.dept_id "ID",
     COUNT(s_emp.id) "EMPLOYEES"
FROM s_emp, s_dept
WHERE s_emp.dept_id = s_dept.id
GROUP BY s_emp.dept_id, s_dept.name
HAVING COUNT(s_emp.id) > 1
ORDER BY COUNT(s_emp.id) DESC;
DEPARTMENT            ID  EMPLOYEES
-------------------- --- ---------
Operations            41      4
Operations            45      4
```

```
Operations       42      3
Operations       44      3
Sales            31      2
Operations       43      2
Administration   50      2
```

5.15. Write an SQL query that shows the department name and region name of all departments along with the number of employees in each department for all departments with more than one employee. This is similar to the previous problem, except you need to query three different tables.

```
SELECT s_dept.name "DEPARTMENT", s_region.name "REGION",
      COUNT(s_dept.id) "EMPLOYEES"
FROM s_dept, s_region, s_emp
WHERE s_dept.region_id = s_region.id
AND s_emp.dept_id = s_dept.id
GROUP BY s_dept.name, s_region.name
HAVING COUNT(s_dept.id) > 1;
DEPARTMENT            REGION                      EMPLOYEES
-------------------- -------------------------- ---------
Administration       North America                      2
Operations           Africa / Middle East               2
Operations           Asia                               3
Operations           Europe                             4
Operations           North America                      4
Operations           South America                      3
Sales                North America                      2
```

5.16. Write an SQL query that displays the region ID and region name and the number of customers in that region.

```
SELECT s_region.id, s_region.name,
      COUNT(s_customer.id) "CUSTOMERS"
FROM s_region, s_customer
WHERE s_region.id = s_customer.region_id
GROUP BY s_region.id, s_region.name;
ID  NAME                         CUSTOMERS
--- -------------------------- ---------
1   North America                    13
2   South America                     3
3   Africa / Middle East              2
4   Asia                              2
5   Europe                            4
6   Central America /Caribbean        1
```

Supplementary Problems

Note: Rerun the SG script to refresh the database before answering these questions. Use the order table S_ORD for these problems.

```
CUS DATE_ORDE DATE_SHIP SAL     TOTAL PAYMEN
--- --------- --------- --- --------- ------
100 31-AUG-92 10-SEP-92 11    601100 CREDIT
101 31-AUG-92 15-SEP-92 14    8056.6 CREDIT
102 01-SEP-92 08-SEP-92 15      8335 CREDIT
103 02-SEP-92 22-SEP-92 15       377 CASH
104 03-SEP-92 23-SEP-92 15     32430 CREDIT
105 04-SEP-92 18-SEP-92 11   2722.24 CREDIT
106 07-SEP-92 15-SEP-92 12     15634 CREDIT
107 07-SEP-92 21-SEP-92 15    142171 CREDIT
108 07-SEP-92 10-SEP-92 13    149570 CREDIT
109 08-SEP-92 28-SEP-92 11   1020935 CREDIT
110 09-SEP-92 21-SEP-92 11   1539.13 CASH
111 09-SEP-92 21-SEP-92 11      2770 CASH
97  28-AUG-92 17-SEP-92 12     84000 CREDIT
98  31-AUG-92 10-SEP-92 14       595 CASH
99  31-AUG-92 18-SEP-92 14      7707 CREDIT
112 31-AUG-92 10-SEP-92 12       550 CREDIT
```

5.17. Write an SQL query that displays the total and average payments of all the credit orders.

5.18. Write an SQL query that displays the total and average payments grouped by type of payment.

5.19. Write an SQL query that will answer the question, "How many order dates are represented compared to the total number of orders?"

5.20. Write an SQL query that will answer the question, "How many customers and sales representatives are represented compared to the total number of orders?"

5.21. Write an SQL query that displays the lowest and highest payments of all the orders.

5.22. Write an SQL query to answer the question, "What is the average amount of the order for each sales representative?"

5.23. Write an SQL query to display the order dates and how many orders were on each date.

5.24. Write an SQL query to display the average order amount by payment type for each sales representative.

5.25. Write an SQL query to display the highest and lowest order for each order date where more than one order was placed.

5.26. Write an SQL query to display the average order for each order date where more than one order was placed and the average order is greater than $1000. Display them in order of average order.

5.27. Write an SQL query to display the customer name and the number of orders for each customer with more than one order. Arrange alphabetically by customer.

 # Answers to Supplementary Problems

5.17.
```
SELECT SUM(total) "SUM", AVG(total) "AVG"
FROM s_ord
WHERE payment_type = 'CREDIT';
      SUM        AVG
--------- ---------
2073210.8 172767.57
```

5.18.
```
SELECT payment_type, COUNT(*) "NUMBER",
       SUM(total) "SUM", AVG(total) "AVG"
FROM s_ord
GROUP BY payment_type;
PAYMEN    NUMBER       SUM        AVG
------ --------- --------- ---------
CASH           4   5281.13 1320.2825
CREDIT        12 2073210.8 172767.57
```

5.19.
```
SELECT COUNT(DISTINCT date_ordered) "NUM ORDER DATES",
       COUNT(*) "TOTAL"
FROM s_ord;
NUM ORDER DATES     TOTAL
--------------- ---------
              9        16
```

5.20.
```
SELECT COUNT(DISTINCT customer_id) "CUSTOMERS",
       COUNT(DISTINCT sales_rep_id) "SALES REPS",
       COUNT(*) "TOTAL"
FROM s_ord;
CUSTOMERS SALES REPS     TOTAL
--------- ---------- ---------
       13          4        16
```

5.21.
```
SELECT MAX(total) "HIGHEST", MIN(total) "LOWEST"
FROM s_ord;
  HIGHEST     LOWEST
--------- ---------
  1020935        377
```

5.22.

```
SELECT sales_rep_id, AVG(total) "AVERAGE ORDER"
FROM s_ord
GROUP BY sales_rep_id;
SAL AVERAGE ORDER
--- -------------
 11      271573.9
 12      27129.75
 13         91000
 14       39632.4
```

5.23.

```
SELECT date_ordered, COUNT(*) "NUMBER"
FROM s_ord
GROUP BY date_ordered;
DATE_ORDE    NUMBER
---------  ---------
28-AUG-92         1
31-AUG-92         5
01-SEP-92         1
02-SEP-92         1
03-SEP-92         1
04-SEP-92         1
07-SEP-92         3
08-SEP-92         1
09-SEP-92         2
```

5.24.

```
SELECT sales_rep_id, payment_type, COUNT(*) "NUMBER",
      AVG(total) "AVERAGE"
FROM s_ord
GROUP BY sales_rep_id, payment_type;
SAL PAYMEN    NUMBER    AVERAGE
--- ------ --------- ---------
 11 CASH           3 1562.0433
 11 CREDIT         3 541585.75
 12 CREDIT         4  27129.75
 13 CREDIT         2     91000
 14 CASH           1       595
 14 CREDIT         3 52644.867
```

5.25.

```
SELECT date_ordered, MAX(total) "MAX ORDER",
     MIN(total) "MIN ORDER"
FROM s_ord
GROUP BY date_ordered
HAVING COUNT(*) > 1;
DATE_ORDE MAX ORDER MIN ORDER
--------- --------- ---------
31-AUG-92    601100       550
07-SEP-92    149570     15634
09-SEP-92      2770   1539.13
```

5.26.

```
SELECT date_ordered, AVG(total) "AVERAGE ORDER"
FROM s_ord
GROUP BY date_ordered
HAVING COUNT(*) > 1 AND AVG(total) > 1000
ORDER BY AVG(total);
DATE_ORDE AVERAGE ORDER
--------- -------------
09-SEP-92      2154.565
07-SEP-92     102458.33
31-AUG-92     123601.72
```

5.27.

```
SELECT s_customer.name, COUNT(s_ord.id) "ORDERS"
FROM s_customer, s_ord
WHERE s_customer.id = s_ord.customer_id
GROUP BY s_customer.name
HAVING COUNT(s_ord.id) > 1
ORDER BY s_customer.name;
NAME                    ORDERS
-------------------- ---------
Futbol Sonora               2
Ladysport                   2
Muench Sports               2
```

CHAPTER 6

Processing Date and Time Information

6.1 Introduction to Processing Date and Time

One of the most critical jobs of a database is to keep track of dates, whether they are birth dates, holiday dates, pay dates, order dates, shipping dates, and so on. The data in the tables may span the turn of a century. In addition, international businesses must deal with a variety of time zones. Time is important, as the particular time an order is shipped might be critical. Formatting the date and time when displaying query results can make a big difference in the readability of the query or query reports. SQL provides a wide variety of methods to deal with date and time. Besides the ability to do arithmetic with dates, SQL provides a number of date functions and formatting utilities.

The sample table used throughout this chapter is a chart of pay periods for the year 2000 for a particular company. The policy is to pay twice a month, on the 16th and the 30th. If either of these dates falls on a Saturday or Sunday, the date of the check will be the Friday before the assigned pay date. The table PAY_PERIODS is shown in Table 6-1. There are two columns in this table: one for the first check date of each month and another for the second check date.

6.2 Arithmetic with Dates

Chapter 4 explained the arithmetic operators that are available in SQL. The operators available for use with dates are plus (+) and minus (–). You can do three things with these operators:

Table 6-1. **The PAY_PERIODS table.**

```
FIRST_CHE SECOND_CH
--------- ---------
14-JAN-00 28-JAN-00
16-FEB-00 29-FEB-00
16-MAR-00 30-MAR-00
14-APR-00 28-APR-00
16-MAY-00 30-MAY-00
16-JUN-00 30-JUN-00
14-JUL-00 28-JUL-00
16-AUG-00 30-AUG-00
15-SEP-00 29-SEP-00
16-OCT-00 30-OCT-00
16-NOV-00 30-NOV-00
15-DEC-00 29-DEC-00
```

- Add an interval of a number of days to a date. Results in new date
- Subtract an interval of a number of days from a date. Results in new date
- Subtract one date from another. Results in the number of days in the interval between the two dates

You have seen some date manipulation in previous chapters. Solved Problem 4.25 demonstrated subtracting one date from another. The comparison operators from Chapter 1 (>,<,>=, <=, =, <>) and the Boolean operators from Chapter 3 (AND, OR, NOT) can be used to compare dates as long as true dates are used. To compare date literals, use the TO_DATE( ) function first, as will be shown in Section 6.4. Solved Problem 4.27 showed the comparison operators used to examine dates.

Be careful when manipulating dates to focus only on the days. Because the time is stored in hours, minutes and seconds, the arithmetic operators may return unexpected values or fractions of days. See Section 6.4 to use the ROUND( ) or TRUNC( ) to solve this problem. Other examples of date arithmetic will be demonstrated here.

EXAMPLE 6.1
Write an SQL query to list the number of days between the checks, then add 7 days to the first check date of each month and subtract 7 days from the second check date of each month.

```
SELECT second_check - first_check "BETWEEN",
     first_check + 7 "AFTER", second_check - 7 "BEFORE"
FROM pay_periods;
  BETWEEN AFTER      BEFORE
--------- --------- ---------
       14 21-JAN-00 21-JAN-00
       13 23-FEB-00 22-FEB-00
       14 23-MAR-00 23-MAR-00
       14 21-APR-00 21-APR-00
       14 23-MAY-00 23-MAY-00
       14 23-JUN-00 23-JUN-00
       14 21-JUL-00 21-JUL-00
       14 23-AUG-00 23-AUG-00
       14 22-SEP-00 22-SEP-00
       14 23-OCT-00 23-OCT-00
       14 23-NOV-00 23-NOV-00
       14 22-DEC-00 22 DEC-00
```

The resulting chart shows the dates are the same because the pay dates are always 14 days apart, except for February, when the pay date is the 29th.

EXAMPLE 6.2
Write an SQL query to list the pay dates from January through June.

```
SELECT first_check, second_check
FROM pay_periods
WHERE first_check > '01-JAN-00' AND first_check < '01-JUL-00';
FIRST_CHE SECOND_CH
--------- ---------
14-JAN-00 28-JAN-00
16-FEB-00 29-FEB 00
16-MAR-00 30-MAR-00
14-APR-00 28-APR-00
16-MAY-00 30-MAY-00
16-JUN-00 30-JUN-00
```

Notice that in this query the first of January and the first of July were used as boundaries. The same result would occur if the WHERE statement used the last day of June for the second comparison.

6.3 Date Functions

A number of built-in functions are available to provide the most critical processing of dates. These functions are listed in Table 6-2. Most of them will be demonstrated in the following two sections. The NEWTIME( ), GREATEST( ), and LEAST( ) will be explained in Section 6.4, along with formatting dates and times.

Table 6-2.   Date functions.

Function	Input Argument	Value Returned
ADD_MONTHS(d,n)	d = date n = number of months	Date d plus n months.
LAST_DAY(d)	d = date	The date of the last day of the month containing d.
MONTHS_BETWEEN(d,e)	d = date e = date	The number of months by which e precedes d.
NEW_TIME(d,a,b)	d = date a = time zone (char) b = time zone (char)	The date and time in time zone b when date and time in time zone a are d.
NEXT_DAY(d, day)	d = date day = day of the week	Date of the first day (specific day of the week) after d.
SYSDATE	none	Current date and time.
GREATEST($d1$, $d2$, …dn)	$d1$..dn = list of dates	The latest of the given dates.
LEAST($d1$, $d2$, …dn)	$d1$..dn = list of dates	The earliest of the given dates.

6.3.1   THE SYSDATE FUNCTION

The built-in function SYSDATE returns the current date and time from the system clock of the particular computer where the RDBMS is currently running. The name of this function may vary from one RDBMS to another. Two other names frequently used for this function are TODAY and CURRENT DATE. No matter what the name of the function might be, they all behave in a similar manner.

EXAMPLE 6.3
List the current date. Use the DUAL table.

```
SELECT SYSDATE
FROM DUAL;
SYSDATE
---------
23-JAN-00
```

If today were the 23rd of January, 2000, the display above would occur. This command will always display the current date.

6.3.2   DAY AND MONTH FUNCTIONS

The SQL language provides several different functions for dealing with months. You can add a certain number of months to a date using ADD_MONTHS(d,n). To subtract months, use the same function, but use a negative number for n. MONTHS_BETWEEN(d,e) will display the number of months between two dates. LAST_DAY(d) will give you the date of the last day of the month specified by d. This function is necessary because of the varying number of days in each month and is particularly helpful with February. These functions can be used in any combination, as shown in the following examples.

EXAMPLE 6.4

Show the dates that are 2 months before and 2 months after the current date. Then display how many months are between the two.

```
SELECT SYSDATE, ADD_MONTHS(SYSDATE, -2) "2 MO. AGO",
     ADD_MONTHS(SYSDATE, 2) "2 MO. FROM NOW",
     MONTHS_BETWEEN(ADD_MONTHS(SYSDATE, 2),
     ADD_MONTHS(SYSDATE, -2)) "BETWEEN"
FROM DUAL;
SYSDATE    2 MO. AGO 2 MO. FRO    BETWEEN
--------- --------- --------- ---------
23-JAN-00 23 NOV-99 23-MAR-00          4
```

Notice that this version of SQL is Y2K-compliant. If the current date is January 23, 2000, the system knows that 1999 preceded 2000. However, you must be sure that any new dates are entered into the database using all four digits for the year.

EXAMPLE 6.5

As specified by our example company, the second pay date is the 30th, or the Friday before the 30th, not the last day of the month. Display the second pay date and the last day of each month in 2000 from January through June. Then display the number of days between the two.

```
SELECT second_check, LAST_DAY(second_check),
     LAST_DAY(second_check) - second_check "BETWEEN"
FROM pay_periods
WHERE second_check > '01-JAN-00' AND second_check < '01-JUL-00';
SECOND_CH LAST_DAY(    BETWEEN
--------- --------- ---------
28-JAN-00 31-JAN-00         3
29-FEB-00 29-FEB-00         0
30-MAR-00 31-MAR-00         1
28-APR-00 30-APR-00         2
30-MAY-00 31-MAY-00         1
30-JUN-00 30-JUN-00         0
```

The year 2000 is a leap year, and the chart from the previous example reflects that fact. Also, remember that the function MONTHS_BETWEEN ( ) is necessary to find the number of months between dates. The number of days between dates can be found by simply subtracting the dates.

Another useful function for finding a particular day of the week is NEXT_DAY(*d, day*). You specify the *day* of the week desired (e.g., 'Monday', 'Tuesday', etc.), and the function returns the date of the particular day that follows the date *d*. For example, you might always want to pay on a Friday or Monday. Therefore, you would use this function to find the pay dates as shown in the following example.

EXAMPLE 6.6
Display what the pay date would be if you always paid on the Friday following the date of the first check.

```
SELECT first_check, NEXT_DAY(first_check,'Friday') "FRIDAY"
FROM pay_periods;
FIRST_CHE FRIDAY
--------- ---------
14-JAN-00 21-JAN-00
16-FEB-00 18-FEB-00
16-MAR-00 17-MAR-00
14-APR-00 21-APR-00
16-MAY-00 19-MAY-00
16-JUN-00 23-JUN-00
14-JUL-00 21-JUL-00
16-AUG-00 18-AUG-00
15-SEP-00 22-SEP-00
16-OCT-00 20-OCT-00
16-NOV-00 17-NOV-00
15-DEC-00 22-DEC-00
```

6.4   Formatting Dates and Times

In order to display a date in a particular format, it must be converted into a character string. Chapter 4 demonstrated converting a value from character to number and from number to character using the functions TO_CHAR ( ) and TO_NUMBER ( ). Similar methods are used to convert dates to character and character to dates: TO_CHAR ( ) and TO_DATE ( ). Rounding and truncating the date is also possible using a form of these built-in functions. The functions that can be used to format dates are shown in Table 6-3.

Table 6-3.   Date formatting functions.

Function	Input Argument	Value Returned
TO_CHAR(*d[,fmt]*)	*d* = date value *fmt* = format for string	*d* converted from a date to a character string in the designated format—default for *fmt* is a value exactly wide enough to hold all significant digits.
TO_DATE(*st[,fmt]*)	*st* = character string value *fmt* = format for date	*st* converted from a character string to a date value—if *fmt* is omitted, string must be in default format.
ROUND(*d[,fmt]*)	*d* = date value *fmt* = format for string	*d* rounded as specified by the formatting instruction, *fmt*.
TRUNC(*d[,fmt]*)	*d* = date value *fmt* = format for string	*d* truncated as specified by the formatting instruction, *fmt*.

6.4.1   TO_DATE ( ) AND TO_CHAR ( ) FUNCTIONS AND FORMATTING

TO_CHAR(*d[,fmt]*) and TO_DATE(*st[,fmt]*) are the functions used to convert particular data back and forth between character strings and dates. Anytime you want to print the date in a nice format, it must be converted to a character string. If you want to compare date literals, they must be converted to actual dates. In both cases, the *fmt* for formatting is used to display the date and time in the desired format. The most often used formats for dates are shown in Table 6-4. If *fmt* is omitted, the default format is used, where the two-digit day comes first, followed by the three-character month abbreviation and two-digit year, all separated by hyphens and enclosed in single quotes (e.g., '01-JAN-00', '18-FEB-97').

Table 6-4.   Date formats.

Format Code	Description	Example or Range of Values
DD	Day of the month	1-31
DY	3-letter abbreviation for name of the day in uppercase	SUN, ... SAT
DAY	Complete name of the day in uppercase, padded to 9 characters	SUNDAY, ... SATURDAY
MM	Number of the month	1-12
MON	3-letter abbreviation for the name of the month in uppercase	JAN, ... DEC

Table 6-4. *(Cont.)*

MONTH	Name of the month in uppercase padded to a length of 9 characters	JANUARY, ... DECEMBER
RM	Roman numeral for the month	I, ... XII
YY or YYYY	Two-digit year or four-digit year	00, 99 or e.g. 1987, 2002, 1776
HH:MI:SS	Hours:Minutes:Seconds	e.g. 12:45:58
HH 12 or HH 24	The hour displayed in either 12- or 24-hour format	1-12 or 1-24
MI	Minutes of the hour	0-59
SS	Seconds of the minute	0-59
AM or PM	Meridian indicator	AM or PM
SP	Suffix forcing the number to be spelled out—works with any number field, e.g., YY, MM, DD, etc.	e.g., ONE, NINETEEN, TWO THOUSAND TWO
TH	Suffix meaning ordinal number to be added	e.g. 4th, 1st
FM	Prefix to MONTH or DAY or YEAR to suppress padding	MONDAY with no extra spaces at the end

A number of punctuation marks can be incorporated into the formatting string. They will be reproduced in the date that is displayed. For example, one might want the date to be displayed as January 23, 2000, instead of in the default format. A date field would be converted to string to accomplish this.

EXAMPLE 6.7
Display the first paycheck of each month as an ordinal number from January to April in the Month ddth, yyyy format.

a.
Your first attempt looks like this.

```
SELECT TO_CHAR(first_check, 'MONTH DD, YYYY')
FROM pay_periods
WHERE first_check > '01-JAN-00' AND first_check < '01-JUL-00';
TO_CHAR(FIRST_CHECK,'MONTHDD,YYYY')
--------------------------------------
JANUARY   14, 2000
FEBRUARY  16, 2000
MARCH     16, 2000
APRIL     14, 2000
MAY       16, 2000
JUNE      16, 2000
```

b.

Your resulting chart above displays each month with the name padded to nine characters. The second attempt will use the FM to suppress this padding so the date looks more natural. Also, the TH is used to make the date ordinal.

```
SELECT TO_CHAR(first_check, 'FMMONTH DDTH, YYYY')
FROM pay_periods
WHERE first_check > '01-JAN-00' AND first_check < '01-JUL-00';
TO_CHAR(FIRST_CHECK,'FMMONTHDDTH,YYYY')
---------------------------------------------
JANUARY 14TH, 2000
FEBRUARY 16TH, 2000
MARCH 16TH, 2000
APRIL 14TH, 2000
MAY 16TH, 2000
JUNE 16TH, 2000
```

As shown in Table 6-4, the month can be displayed as number, name, three-letter abbreviation, or as Roman numeral. Example 6.8 shows a variety of ways of displaying each month.

EXAMPLE 6.8
Display the months of the year in words, abbreviated words, numbers, and in Roman numerals.

```
SELECT TO_CHAR(first_check,'MONTH') "WORDS",
     TO_CHAR(first_check, 'MON') "ABBREVIATED",
     TO_CHAR(first_check, 'MM') "NUMBERS",
     TO_CHAR(first_check, 'RM') "ROMAN NUMERALS"
FROM pay_periods;
```

WORDS	ABBREVIATED	NUMBERS	ROMAN NUMERALS
JANUARY	JAN	01	I
FEBRUARY	FEB	02	II
MARCH	MAR	03	III
APRIL	APR	04	IV
MAY	MAY	05	V
JUNE	JUN	06	VI
JULY	JUL	07	VII
AUGUST	AUG	08	VIII
SEPTEMBER	SEP	09	IX
OCTOBER	OCT	10	X
NOVEMBER	NOV	11	XI
DECEMBER	DEC	12	XII

The days also can be displayed in a variety of ways. The suffix SP can be added to any numbers to spell the number out. The suffix TH can be added to show the ordinal number. Example 6.9 shows the dates of the first paycheck of January 2000 displayed in this way.

EXAMPLE 6.9

Display the first paycheck of January as words, ordinal number, number spelled out, and ordinal number spelled out.

```
SELECT TO_CHAR(first_check, 'DAY') "WORDS",
    TO_CHAR(first_check, 'DDTH') "ORDINAL",
    TO_CHAR(first_check, 'DDSP') "SPELLED OUT",
    TO_CHAR(first_check, 'DDSPTH') "ORD SPELLED OUT"
FROM pay_periods
WHERE first_check = '14-JAN-00';
WORDS       ORDINAL  SPELLED OUT    ORD SPELLED OUT
----------  -------- -------------- ------------------------

FRIDAY      14TH     FOURTEEN       FOURTEENTH
```

6.4.2 ROUND( ) AND TRUNC( ) FUNCTIONS

ROUND(*d[,fmt]*) and TRUNC(*d[,fmt]*) are functions that allow the rounding or truncating of any portion of the time item. When a date is entered in default mode, such as '02-JAN-00', the default time assumed by the system is midnight, or the beginning of that day. The SYSDATE always includes the current date and time. Therefore, later calculations regarding days sometimes result in a fraction of a day. See Example 6.10. To fix this problem, use ROUND( ) and TRUNC( ). ROUND( ) will always set the time to the closest midnight—either the current date or the day after, depending upon whether it is before or after noon. TRUNC( ), on the other hand, will always set the time to the midnight of the current date.

EXAMPLE 6.10

List the number of days between the current date (which might be January 27, 2000) and the first pay date in February.

a.
```
SELECT SYSDATE "CURRENT",
    ABS(SYSDATE - first_check) "UNTIL FIRST"
FROM pay_periods
WHERE first_check = '16-FEB-00';
CURRENT    UNTIL FIRST
--------- -----------
27-JAN-00   19.516921
```

Notice that the function returns a fraction of a day. That is because the current time is also taken into consideration by the SYSDATE function. To correct this, use ROUND( ) or TRUNC( ). If it is before noon, they will return the same number of days. Part b shows the result of the query before noon, and part c shows the result of the query after noon. After noon, the rounded time makes the number of days until payday less.

b.
```
SELECT SYSDATE "CURRENT",
    TO_CHAR(SYSDATE, 'HH:MI:SS AM') "TIME",
    ABS(ROUND(SYSDATE) - first_check) "UNTIL FIRST",
    ABS(TRUNC(SYSDATE) - first_check) "UNTIL FIRST"
FROM pay_periods
WHERE first_check = '16-FEB-00';
CURRENT   TIME                     UNTIL FIRST UNTIL FIRST
--------- ------------------------ ----------- -----------
27-JAN-00 11:40:03 AM                       20          20
```

c.
```
SELECT SYSDATE "CURRENT",
    TO_CHAR(SYSDATE, 'HH:MI:SS AM') "TIME",
    ABS(ROUND(SYSDATE) - first_check) "UNTIL FIRST",
    ABS(TRUNC(SYSDATE) - first_check) "UNTIL FIRST"
FROM pay_periods
WHERE first_check = '16-FEB-00';
CURRENT   TIME                     UNTIL FIRST UNTIL FIRST
--------- ------------------------ ----------- -----------
27-JAN-00 12:03:04 PM                       19          20
```

6.4.3 GREATEST ( ) AND LEAST ( ) FUNCTIONS

The GREATEST(*d1, d2, ...dn*) and LEAST(*d1, d2, ...dn*) functions pick the latest and earliest dates, respectively, from a given list of dates. Any number of dates may be examined. It is important, however, to be sure that a date is examined, not a character string.

EXAMPLE 6.11
Display the earliest and latest check in each month from January through June.

```
SELECT LEAST(second_check, first_check) "EARLIER",
GREATEST(second_check, first_check) "LATER"
FROM pay_periods
WHERE second_check > '01-JAN-00' AND second_check < '01-JUL-00';
EARLIER   LATER
--------- ---------
14-JAN-00 28-JAN-00
16-FEB-00 29-FEB-00
16-MAR-00 30-MAR-00
14-APR-00 28-APR-00
16-MAY-00 30-MAY-00
16-JUN-00 30-JUN-00
```

The query above worked correctly because both fields are of DATE data type. When you are working with date literals, it is not so simple, as shown in the next example.

EXAMPLE 6.12
Display the latest and earliest from these three dates: January 1, 1999; November 12, 1998; and October 19, 1997.

a.
A first attempt at this query would look like this. However, examine the output carefully.

```
SELECT GREATEST('01-Jan-99', '12-Nov-98','19-Oct-97') "LATEST",
    LEAST('01-Jan-99', '12-Nov-98','19-Oct-97') "EARLIEST"
FROM DUAL;
LATEST    EARLIEST
--------- ---------
19-Oct-97 01-Jan-99
```

It is clear that the system treated these choices as character strings, not dates. Therefore, the one beginning with '01' came first and the one beginning '19' came last. In order to compare these dates, they must be first converted into dates using the TO_DATE function.

b.
The second and correct version of this query looks like this.

```
SELECT GREATEST(TO_DATE('01-Jan-99'), TO_DATE('12-Nov-98'),
    TO_DATE('19-Oct-97')) "LATEST",
    LEAST(TO_DATE('01-Jan-99'), TO_DATE('12-Nov-98'),
    TO_DATE('19-Oct-97')) "EARLIEST"
FROM DUAL;
LATEST    EARLIEST
--------- ---------
01-JAN-99 19-OCT-97
```

Notice that now the arguments to the function are treated like dates and are correctly evaluated. This function in your version of SQL may or may not be Y2K-compatible. It is always good to test before using it.

6.4.4 NEW_TIME( ) FUNCTION

The NEW_TIME(d,a,b) function shows the date and time in time zone b when date and time in time zone a are d. Not all time zones are currently supported. Table 6-5 shows the time zones between Greenwich, England and Hawaii. Check your SQL documentation for the list of time zones supported by your current version. Example 6.12 demonstrates how to use this function.

Table 6-5. Time zones.

Time Zone	Explanation
AST/ADT	Atlantic standard/daylight time
BST/BDT	Bering standard/daylight time
CST/CDT	Central standard/daylight time
EST/EDT	Eastern standard/daylight time
GMT	Greenwich mean time
HST/HDT	Alaska-Hawaii standard/daylight time
MST/MDT	Mountain standard/daylight time
NST	Newfoundland standard time
PST/PDT	Pacific standard/daylight time
YST/YDT	YUKON standard/daylight time

EXAMPLE 6.13
Show the current time in the Eastern time zone, and then the time in England and Hawaii.

```
SELECT TO_CHAR(SYSDATE, 'HH24:MI AM') "EASTERN",
TO_CHAR(NEW_TIME(SYSDATE, 'EST','GMT'), 'HH24:MI AM') "GREENWICH",
TO_CHAR(NEW_TIME(SYSDATE, 'EST','HST'), 'HH24:MI AM') "HAWAII"
FROM DUAL;
EASTERN              GREENWICH            HAWAII
--------------       -----------------    -----------------
15:23 PM             20:23 PM             10:23 AM
```

Solved Problems

Note: Rerun the SG script to refresh the database before answering these questions. Use the employee table S_EMP for some of the questions in this section.

```
LAST_NAME        FIRST_NAME       TITLE                   START_DAT
--------------   --------------   ---------------------   ---------
Martin           Carmen           President               03-MAR-90
Smith            Doris            VP, Operations          08-MAR-90
```

Norton	Michael	VP, Sales	17-JUN-91
Quentin	Mark	VP, Finance	07-APR-90
Roper	Joseph	VP, Administration	04-MAR-90
Brown	Molly	Warehouse Manager	18-JAN-91
Hawkins	Roberta	Warehouse Manager	14-MAY-90
Burns	Ben	Warehouse Manager	07-APR-90
Catskill	Antoinette	Warehouse Manager	09-FEB-92
Jackson	Marta	Warehouse Manager	27-FEB-91
Henderson	Colin	Sales Representative	14-MAY-90
Gilson	Sam	Sales Representative	18-JAN-92
Sanders	Jason	Sales Representative	18-FEB-91
Dameron	Andre	Sales Representative	09-OCT-91
Hardwick	Elaine	Stock Clerk	07-FEB-92
Brown	George	Stock Clerk	08-MAR-90
Washington	Thomas	Stock Clerk	09-FEB-91
Patterson	Donald	Stock Clerk	06-AUG-91
Bell	Alexander	Stock Clerk	26-MAY-91
Gantos	Eddie	Stock Clerk	30-NOV-90
Stephenson	Blaine	Stock Clerk	17-MAR-91
Chester	Eddie	Stock Clerk	30-NOV-90
Pearl	Roger	Stock Clerk	17-OCT-90
Dancer	Bonnie	Stock Clerk	17-MAR-91
Schmitt	Sandra	Stock Clerk	09-MAY-91

6.1. Display the first of January, 2000, as words, ordinal number, number spelled out, and ordinal number spelled out.

```
SELECT TO_CHAR(TO_DATE('01-JAN-00'), 'DAY') "WORDS",
       TO_CHAR (TO_DATE('01-JAN-00'), 'DDTH') "ORDINAL",
       TO_CHAR(TO_DATE('01-JAN-00'), 'DDSP') "SPELLED OUT",
       TO_CHAR(TO_DATE('01-JAN-00'), 'DDSPTH') "ORD SPELLED OUT"
FROM DUAL;
WORDS        ORDINAL  SPELLED OUT  ORD SPELLED OUT
------------ -------- ------------ -------------------------
SATURDAY     01ST     ONE          FIRST
```

Notice that when you use literals in the DUAL table, they must first be changed to a date and then changed back into a character string for formatting.

6.2. Assume a new employee is hired on July 6, 1998. Write an SQL query to show the review date if there is a standard review performance after 60 days. Assume you want to review only on Fridays. Find the Friday following that review date. Remember to use the full four digits when creating the date to find the correct calendar for 1998.

```
SELECT TO_DATE('06-JUL-1998','DD-MON-YYYY') "HIRE DATE",
TO_DATE('06-JUL-1998','DD-MON-YYYY') + 60 "REVIEW DATE",
NEXT_DAY(TO_DATE('06-JUL-1998','DD-MON-YYYY') + 60, 'FRIDAY') "FRIDAY"
FROM DUAL;
HIRE DATE  REVIEW DA  FRIDAY
--------- ---------  ---------
06-JUL-98 04-SEP-98 11-SEP-98
```

6.3. One employee was hired May 14, 1990, and another employee was hired January 18, 1992. Write an SQL query to show how many months were between their hiring. Also show the number of days between.

```
SELECT MONTHS_BETWEEN('18-JAN-92', '14-MAY-90') "MONTHS",
      TO_DATE('18-JAN-92') - TO_DATE('14-MAY-90') "TOTAL DAYS"
FROM DUAL;
   MONTHS TOTAL DAYS
--------- ----------
20.129032        614
```

Notice that the MONTHS_BETWEEN( ) returns a fraction. This can be avoided by using the ROUND( ) function like this: ROUND(MONTHS_BETWEEN('18-JAN-92', '14-MAY-90')). If the ROUND( ) function is used, the total months would be 20.

6.4. A person is hired today (for our example, January 27, 2000). Write an SQL query to show the date of a review performance after 2 months. Also show the date after 60 days to compare.

```
SELECT SYSDATE "TODAY", ADD_MONTHS(SYSDATE, 2) "2 MONTHS",
      SYSDATE + 60 "60 DAYS"
FROM DUAL;
TODAY     2 MONTHS  60 DAYS
--------- --------- ---------
27-JAN-00 27-MAR-00 27-MAR-00
```

6.5. Try the same query from Problem 6.4 above, showing the resulting dates if the review is in 6 months, or 180 days.

```
SELECT SYSDATE "TODAY", ADD_MONTHS(SYSDATE, 6) "6 MONTHS",
      SYSDATE + 180 "180 DAYS"
FROM DUAL;
TODAY     6 MONTHS  180 DAYS
--------- --------- ---------
27-JAN-00 27-JUL-00 25-JUL-00
```

6.6. Write an SQL query from S_EMP to show the start date and the last day of the month that all the sales representatives were hired.

```
SELECT last_name, start_date,
      LAST_DAY(start_date) "LAST DAY OF MONTH"
FROM s_emp
WHERE title = 'Sales Representative';
LAST_NAME            START_DAT LAST DAY
-------------------- --------- ---------
Henderson            14-MAY-90 31-MAY-90
Gilson               18-JAN-92 31-JAN-92
Sanders              18-FEB-91 28-FEB-91
Dameron              09-OCT-91 31-OCT-91
```

6.7. Write an SQL query to show the date of the Monday of the week all the warehouse managers were hired.

```
SELECT last_name, start_date,
     NEXT_DAY(start_date, 'Monday') "MONDAY"
FROM s_emp
WHERE title = 'Warehouse Manager';
LAST_NAME               START_DAT MONDAY
-------------------- --------- ---------
Brown                18-JAN-91 21-JAN-91
Hawkins              14-MAY-90 21-MAY-90
Burns                07-APR-90 09-APR-90
Catskill             09-FEB-92 10-FEB-92
Jackson              27-FEB-91 04-MAR-91
```

6.8. For seniority purposes, you need to know exactly how many days between when each vice president was hired and January 1, 1997. You also want to know how many days until today (which, for example purposes, might be February 11, 2000). Write an SQL query to display this information. Remember that when doing arithmetic on literal dates, they must be changed to a date using TO_DATE( ).

```
SELECT last_name, TO_DATE('01-JAN-1997','DD-MON-YYYY')
     - start_date "START TO 1997",
     ROUND(SYSDATE) - start_date "START TO NOW"
FROM s_emp
WHERE title LIKE 'VP%';
LAST_NAME               START TO 1997 START TO NOW
-------------------- ------------- ------------
Smith                         2491         3628
Norton                        2025         3162
Quentin                       2461         3598
Roper                         2495         3632
```

6.9. Write an SQL query to display the start dates of the president in several ways: default, month and year, ordinal date, and day of the week.

```
SELECT start_date, TO_CHAR(start_date, 'MM/YY') "MM/YY",
     TO_CHAR(start_date, 'DDTH') "ORDINAL",
     TO_CHAR(start_date, 'DAY') "DAY"
FROM s_emp
WHERE title = 'President';
START_DAT MM/YY ORDINAL DAY
--------- ----- ------- ---------------------------
03-MAR-90 03/90 03RD    SATURDAY
```

6.10. Write an SQL query to display the names and starting dates for the vice presidents. Put them in a sentence format to look like "GEORGE JONES was hired 03rd of JUNE, 1996".

```
SELECT first_name || ' ' || last_name || ' was hired ' ||
       TO_CHAR(start_date,'DDTH') || ' of ' ||
       TO_CHAR(start_date,'FMMONTH') || ', ' ||
       TO_CHAR(start_date,'YYYY') "VP's"
FROM s_emp
WHERE title LIKE 'VP%';
VP's
-------------------------------------------------
Doris Smith was hired 08TH of MARCH, 1990
Michael Norton was hired 17TH of JUNE, 1991
Mark Quentin was hired 07TH of APRIL, 1990
Joseph Roper was hired 04TH of MARCH, 1990
```

6.11. Write an SQL query to show which is greatest and which is least, the sales representatives hiring date, January 1, 1992, and January 1, 1991.

a.
Your first attempt looks like this:

```
SELECT last_name,
GREATEST (start_date,
TO_DATE('01-JAN-92'),TO_DATE('01-JAN-91')) "GREATEST",
LEAST (start_date,
TO_DATE('01-JAN-92'),TO_DATE('01-JAN-91')) "LEAST"
FROM s_emp
WHERE title = 'Sales Representative';
LAST_NAME             GREATEST  LEAST
-------------------- --------- ---------
Henderson            01-JAN-92 14-MAY-90
Gilson               01-JAN-92 18-JAN-92
Sanders              01-JAN-92 18-FEB-91
Dameron              01-JAN-92 09-OCT-91
```

A close examination of the chart shows that this query failed. It shows 18-JAN-92 less than 01-JAN-92. Remember that when creating new dates in this century, you should use the entire 4 digit format.

b.
The correct query and resulting chart would look like this:

```
SELECT last_name,
GREATEST (start_date, TO_DATE('01-JAN-1992','DD-MON-YYYY'),
       TO_DATE('01-JAN-1991','DD-MON-YYYY')) "GREATEST",
       LEAST (start_date, TO_DATE('01-JAN-1992','DD-MON-YYYY'),
       TO_DATE('01-JAN-1991','DD-MON-YYYY')) "LEAST"
```

```
FROM s_emp
WHERE title = 'Sales Representative';
LAST_NAME                GREATEST   LEAST
--------------------     ---------  ---------
Henderson                01-JAN-92  14-MAY-90
Gilson                   18-JAN-92  01-JAN-91
Sanders                  01-JAN-92  01-JAN-91
Dameron                  01-JAN-92  01-JAN-91
```

6.12. Write an SQL query to display the current time in California and the Yukon. Assume the current time is in the Atlantic Standard time zone.

```
SELECT TO_CHAR(SYSDATE,'HH24:MI PM') "ATLANTIC",
  TO_CHAR(NEW_TIME(SYSDATE,'AST','PST'), 'HH24:MI AM') "CALIFORNIA",
  TO_CHAR(NEW_TIME(SYSDATE,'AST','YST'), 'HH24:MI AM') "YUKON"
FROM DUAL;
ATLANTIC   CALIFORNIA   YUKON
----------  ------------  ----------------------------------
15:22 PM   11:22 AM     10:22 AM
```

6.13. Write an SQL query to show the name and the number of months that have elapsed since each warehouse manager was hired. Order the result by the number of months, with the longest-employed employee listed first. Be sure to round the months to the nearest whole number.

```
SELECT last_name,
   ROUND(MONTHS_BETWEEN(SYSDATE, start_date)) "BETWEEN"
FROM s_emp
WHERE title = 'Warehouse Manager'
ORDER BY ROUND(MONTHS_BETWEEN(start_date, SYSDATE)) ASC;
```

The results if SYSDATE is January 27, 2000 are as follows:

```
LAST_NAME                BETWEEN
--------------------     ---------
Burns                        118
Hawkins                      116
Brown                        108
Jackson                      107
Catskill                      96
```

6.14. Show the months and days between the starting date of each stock clerk and January 1, 2000. Put the response in sentence form ordered by number of months worked.

```
SELECT first_name || ' ' || last_name ||' has been employed '||
    TRUNC(MONTHS_BETWEEN(TO_DATE('01-JAN-2000','DD-MON-YYYY'),
     start_date))|| ' months or ' ||
    TO_CHAR(TO_DATE('01-JAN-2000', 'DD-MON-YYYY')
    - start_date) ||' days.' "EMP. HISTORY AS OF 1-1-2000"
```

```
FROM s_emp
WHERE title = 'Stock Clerk'
ORDER BY ROUND(MONTHS_BETWEEN(start_date,
    TO_DATE('01-JAN-2000','DD-MON-YYYY'))) DESC;
EMP. HISTORY AS OF 1-1-2000
-------------------------------------------------------------
Elaine Hardwick has been employed 94 months or 2885 days.
Donald Patterson has been employed 100 months or 3070 days.
Alexander Bell has been employed 103 months or 3142 days.
Sandra Schmitt has been employed 103 months or 3159 days.
Blaine Stephenson has been employed 105 months or 3212 days.
Bonnie Dancer has been employed 105 months or 3212 days.
Thomas Washington has been employed 106 months or 3248 days.
Eddie Gantos has been employed 109 months or 3319 days.
Eddie Chester has been employed 109 months or 3319 days.
Roger Pearl has been employed 110 months or 3363 days.
George Brown has been employed 117 months or 3586 days.
```

Supplementary Problems

Note: Rerun the SG script to refresh the database. Use the order table S_ORD for these problems.

CUS	DATE_ORDE	DATE_SHIP	SAL	TOTAL	PAYMEN
100	31-AUG-92	10-SEP-92	11	601100	CREDIT
101	31-AUG-92	15-SEP-92	14	8056.6	CREDIT
102	01-SEP-92	08-SEP-92	15	8335	CREDIT
103	02-SEP-92	22-SEP-92	15	377	CASH
104	03-SEP-92	23-SEP-92	15	32430	CREDIT
105	04-SEP-92	18-SEP-92	11	2722.24	CREDIT
106	07-SEP-92	15-SEP-92	12	15634	CREDIT
107	07-SEP-92	21-SEP-92	15	142171	CREDIT
108	07-SEP-92	10-SEP-92	13	149570	CREDIT
109	08-SEP-92	28-SEP-92	11	1020935	CREDIT
110	09-SEP-92	21-SEP-92	11	1539.13	CASH
111	09-SEP-92	21-SEP-92	11	2770	CASH
97	28-AUG-92	17-SEP-92	12	84000	CREDIT
98	31-AUG-92	10-SEP-92	14	595	CASH
99	31-AUG-92	18-SEP-92	14	7707	CREDIT
112	31-AUG-92	10-SEP-92	12	550	CREDIT

6.15. Say that all the orders received on August 31 needed to be backordered. They will be shipped in 21 days. Write an SQL query to show the projected shipping date.

6.16. Say that the orders received on August 31 need to be backordered for 2 months. Write an SQL query to show the projected shipping date.

6.17. Write an SQL query to show the number of days between ordering and shipping for all the orders in August.

6.18. Write an SQL query to display the most complete version of the current day and time, including hours, minutes, and seconds, along with AM or PM. Display it in two ways: 12-hour and 24-hour formats.

6.19. Write an SQL query to display the distinct order dates for September spelled out two ways: with numbers and printed in full, as in `"4TH of 9TH month"` and `"fourth of September"`.

6.20. Write an SQL query to display the distinct order dates for August written in two ways: with month and year, (08/92) and as 31 August, 1992.

6.21. Write an SQL query to display the last day of the current month, the last day of 2 months previous, and the last day of the next month.

6.22. Write an SQL query to print the date of the next Friday for each distinct shipping date after the 20th of September. Be sure to use a four-digit date in the `WHERE` clause.

6.23. Write an SQL query to display the number of months between the current date and Christmas in the year 2002. Be sure to eliminate fractions of months by rounding it to the closest month.

6.24. Write an SQL query to display the current time in Chicago and Denver. Assume the current time is in Greenwich Mean Time.

6.25. Write an SQL query that will show which date is first and which date is last for each shipping date in September, comparing the shipping date to September 15th and September 20th of 1992. Be sure to use the four-digit date.

6.26. Write an SQL query that will display a sentence for each order in August specifying "The order from customer <customer_id> <date_ordered> was shipped on <date_shipped>." Be sure the period appears at the end and that the dates are written out as month day, year with no extra blanks.

 # Answers to Supplementary Problems

6.15.

```
SELECT DISTINCT date_ordered "ORIGINAL",
     date_ordered + 21 "PROJECTED"
FROM s_ord
WHERE date_ordered = TO_DATE('31-AUG-1992', 'DD-MON-YYYY');
ORIGINAL  PROJECTED
--------- ---------
31-AUG-92 21-SEP-92
```

6.16.

```
SELECT DISTINCT date_ordered "ORIGINAL",
       ADD_MONTHS(date_ordered, 2) "PROJECTED"
FROM s_ord
WHERE date_ordered = TO_DATE('31-AUG-1992', 'DD-MON-YYYY');
ORIGINAL   PROJECTED
--------- ---------
31-AUG-92 31-OCT-92
```

6.17.

```
SELECT date_ordered, date_shipped,
       date_shipped - date_ordered "BETWEEN"
FROM s_ord
WHERE TO_CHAR(date_ordered, 'MON') = 'AUG'
ORDER BY date_ordered;
DATE_ORDE DATE_SHIP   BETWEEN
--------- --------- ---------
28-AUG-92 17-SEP-92        20
31-AUG-92 10-SEP-92        10
31-AUG-92 10-SEP-92        10
31-AUG-92 10-SEP-92        10
31-AUG-92 18-SEP-92        18
31-AUG-92 15-SEP-92        15
```

6.18.

```
SELECT TO_CHAR(SYSDATE, 'fmDAY fmMONTH DD, YYYY') "DAY",
       TO_CHAR(SYSDATE, 'HH12:MI:SS AM') "12 HOUR TIME",
       TO_CHAR(SYSDATE, 'HH24:MI:SS AM') "24 HOUR TIME"
FROM DUAL;
DAY                             12 HOUR TIME  24 HOUR TIME
------------------------------- ------------  ------------------
SUNDAY JANUARY 30, 2000          1:04:37 PM   13:04:37 PM
```

6.19.

```
SELECT DISTINCT TO_CHAR(date_ordered, 'fmDDTH') || ' of ' ||
       TO_CHAR(date_ordered, 'fmMMTH') || ' MONTH' "NUMBERS",
       TO_CHAR(date_ordered, 'fmDDSPTH') || ' of ' ||
       TO_CHAR(date_ordered, 'fmMONTH') "WORDS"
FROM s_ord
WHERE TO_CHAR(date_ordered, 'MON') = 'SEP';
NUMBERS                   WORDS
------------------------- -------------------------
1ST of 9TH MONTH          FIRST of SEPTEMBER
2ND of 9TH MONTH          SECOND of SEPTEMBER
3RD of 9TH MONTH          THIRD of SEPTEMBER
4TH of 9TH MONTH          FOURTH of SEPTEMBER
7TH of 9TH MONTH          SEVENTH of SEPTEMBER
8TH of 9TH MONTH          EIGHTH of SEPTEMBER
9TH of 9TH MONTH          NINTH of SEPTEMBER
```

6.20.

```
SELECT DISTINCT TO_CHAR(date_ordered, 'MM/YY') "FIRST WAY",
       TO_CHAR(date_ordered, 'FMDD MONTH, YYYY') "SECOND WAY"
FROM s_ord
WHERE TO_CHAR(date_ordered, 'MON') = 'AUG';
FIRST WAY            SECOND WAY
------------------  -----------------------------
08/92               28 AUGUST, 1992
08/92               31 AUGUST, 1992
```

6.21. If current month is January, 2000:

```
SELECT LAST_DAY(SYSDATE) "CURRENT",
       LAST_DAY(ADD_MONTHS(SYSDATE, -2)) "2PREVIOUS",
       LAST_DAY(ADD_MONTHS(SYSDATE, 1)) "NEXT"
FROM DUAL;
CURRENT    2PREVIOUS NEXT
---------  --------- ---------
31-JAN-00 30-NOV-99 29-FEB-00
```

6.22.

```
SELECT DISTINCT date_shipped,
       NEXT_DAY(date_shipped, 'FRIDAY') "NEXT FRIDAY"
FROM s_ord
WHERE date_shipped > TO_DATE('20-SEP-1992','DD-MON-YYYY');
DATE_SHIP NEXT FRID
--------- ---------
21-SEP-92 25-SEP-92
22-SEP-92 25-SEP-92
23-SEP-92 25-SEP-92
28-SEP-92 02-OCT-92
```

6.23. If current month is January, 2000:

```
SELECT ROUND(MONTHS_BETWEEN(TO_DATE('25-DEC-02'), SYSDATE))
       "UNTIL CHRISTMAS 2002"
FROM DUAL;
UNTIL CHRISTMAS 2002
--------------------
                  35
```

6.24.

```
SELECT TO_CHAR(SYSDATE, 'HH24:MI PM') "GREENWICH",
   TO_CHAR(NEW_TIME(SYSDATE,'GMT','CST'), 'HH24:MI AM') "CHICAGO",
   TO_CHAR(NEW_TIME(SYSDATE,'GMT','MST'), 'HH24:MI AM') "DENVER"
FROM DUAL;
GREENWICH  CHICAGO       DENVER
---------- ------------- ---------------------------
15:33 PM    09:33 AM      08:33 AM
```

6.25.

```
SELECT DISTINCT date_shipped,
       LEAST(date_shipped, TO_DATE('15-SEP-1992','DD-MON-YYYY'),
       TO_DATE('20-SEP-1992', 'DD-MON-YYYY')) "FIRST",
       GREATEST(date_shipped,
       TO_DATE('15-SEP-1992','DD-MON-YYYY'),
       TO_DATE('20-SEP-1992', 'DD-MON-YYYY')) "LAST"
FROM s_ord
WHERE TO_CHAR(date_shipped, 'MON') = 'SEP';
DATE_SHIP FIRST     LAST
--------- --------- ---------
08-SEP-92 08-SEP-92 20-SEP-92
10-SEP-92 10-SEP-92 20-SEP-92
15-SEP-92 15-SEP-92 20-SEP-92
17-SEP-92 15-SEP-92 20-SEP-92
18-SEP-92 15-SEP-92 20-SEP-92
21-SEP-92 15-SEP-92 21-SEP-92
22-SEP-92 15-SEP-92 22-SEP-92
23-SEP-92 15-SEP-92 23-SEP-92
28-SEP-92 15-SEP-92 28-SEP-92
```

6.26.

```
SELECT 'The order from customer '|| customer_id || ' '||
     TO_CHAR(date_ordered, 'fmMONTH DD, YYYY') ||
     ' was shipped on ' ||
     TO_CHAR(date_shipped, 'fmMONTH DD, YYYY') || '.' "ORDERS"
FROM s_ord
WHERE TO_CHAR(date_ordered, 'MON') = 'AUG'
ORDER BY customer_id;
ORDERS
----------------------------------------------------------------------------
The order from customer 201 AUGUST 28, 1992 was shipped on SEPTEMBER 17, 1992.
The order from customer 202 AUGUST 31, 1992 was shipped on SEPTEMBER 10, 1992.
The order from customer 203 AUGUST 31, 1992 was shipped on SEPTEMBER 18, 1992.
The order from customer 204 AUGUST 31, 1992 was shipped on SEPTEMBER 10, 1992.
The order from customer 205 AUGUST 31, 1992 was shipped on SEPTEMBER 15, 1992.
The order from customer 210 AUGUST 31, 1992 was shipped on SEPTEMBER 10, 1992.
```

CHAPTER 7

Complex Queries and Set Operators

In all the queries considered so far, we have used a single SELECT statement to retrieve data from one or more tables. In this chapter we will consider nested queries that allow us to retrieve data based upon the results of another query. In addition, we will study the application of nested queries to manipulate tables based on the values of another table. Finally, we will study the set operators and some of their applications.

7.1   Subqueries

Nested queries, or *subqueries*, allow us to retrieve values from a table whose rows satisfy a WHERE condition that depends on values returned by another SELECT statement. The general syntax of a nested query is that of a SELECT statement included within another SELECT statement (see Fig. 7-1). The first SELECT statement is sometimes called the *main query* or *outer query*. Likewise, the nested query is sometimes called the *inner query* or *subquery*.

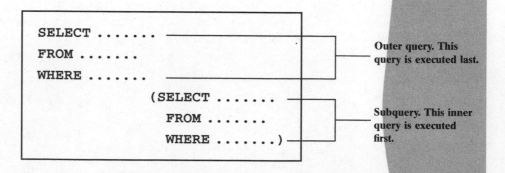

Fig. 7-1.   Basic syntax of a nested query or subquery.

As indicated in Fig. 7-1, the subquery must be enclosed in parentheses and must appear on the right-hand side of the condition of the WHERE clause of the outer query. In the figure shown above, we show only one subquery; however, it is possible, although highly improbable, to have up to 16 nested subqueries. Regardless of the number of subqueries, the order of execution is always from the innermost query to the outermost query. Subqueries are sometimes classified according to the number of rows that they return (single versus multiple rows) or the number of columns that are compared (single or multiple columns).

7.1.1   SINGLE-ROW SUBQUERIES

Subqueries that return a single value from a table are called *single row-subqueries*. The operators that can be used in the condition of the WHERE clause of the outermost query are called *single-row comparison operators* (See Table 7-1).

Table 7-1.   Single-row comparison operator.

Operator	Meaning
=	Equal to
<>	Not equal to or different than
>	Greater than or strictly greater than
>=	Greater or equal to
<	Less than or strictly less than
<=	Less than or equal to

EXAMPLE 7.1
Using the S_EMP table, display the last name, first name, and salary of all the employees whose salary is greater than the average salary.

To answer this query, first, we need to determine the average salary of all the employees. Second, we need to find those employees whose salary is greater than the average.

To determine the average salary of all employees, we can use the following query:

```
SELECT AVG(SALARY)
FROM s_emp;

AVG(SALARY)
----------
1542.48
```

Using the result of this query, we can find the employees who make more than the average salary by issuing the following command:

```
SELECT first_name, last_name, salary
FROM s_emp
WHERE salary > 1542.48;
FIRST_NAME           LAST_NAME            SALARY
-------------------- -------------------- ---------

Carmen               Martin               4500
Doris                Smith                2450
Michael              Norton               2400
Mark                 Quentin              2450
Joseph               Roper                2550
Molly                Brown                1600
Roberta              Hawkins              1650
Antoinette           Catskill             1700

8 rows selected.
```

These two SELECT statements can be combined into a single query that uses a subquery as follows:

```
SELECT first_name, last_name, salary  ←——————— Outer query

FROM s_emp

WHERE salary > (SELECT AVG(SALARY)  ←—————————— Subquery or
                                                 inner query

            FROM s_emp);
```

Notice that the subquery returns a single value—the average—that is used to evaluate the condition of the outer query.

7.1.2 MULTIPLE-ROW SUBQUERIES

Multiple-row subqueries return one or more rows that can be incorporated into the WHERE clause of the outer query using one of the multiple-row comparison operators shown in Table 7-2.

Table 7-2. Multiple-row comparison operators.

Operator	Meaning
IN	Equal to any value retrieved in a subquery.
NOT IN	Different than or not equal to any value retrieved in a subquery.
ANY	Compare value to every value returned by a subquery.
ALL	Compare value to every value returned by a subquery.

EXAMPLE 7.2
Display the name of department where there is at least one employee.

Since the inner query may retrieve more than one row, it is necessary to use the IN operator in the WHERE clause of the outer query. Notice the use of DISTINCT in the SELECT clause of the outer query to prevent the display of duplicate rows.

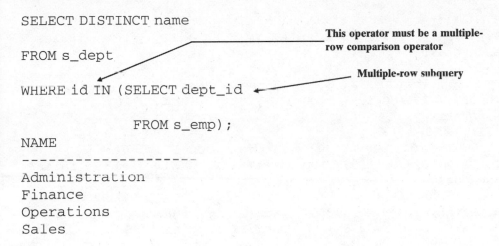

```
SELECT DISTINCT name

FROM s_dept

WHERE id IN (SELECT dept_id

            FROM s_emp);
NAME
--------------------
Administration
Finance
Operations
Sales
```

This operator must be a multiple-row comparison operator

Multiple-row subquery

7.1.3 MULTIPLE-COLUMN SUBQUERIES

This type of subquery allows the comparison of multiple columns between the inner and outer query. The WHERE condition of the outer table lists the columns that we want to compare. These columns are separated by commas. The subquery selects the corresponding columns from the inner table.

The syntax of this type of subquery is shown in Fig. 7-2.

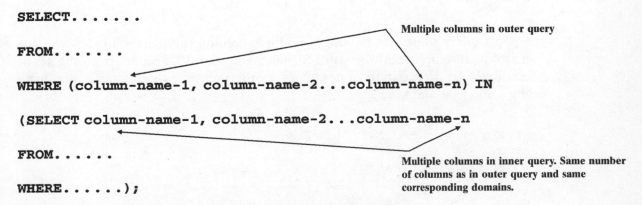

```
SELECT.......

FROM.......

WHERE (column-name-1, column-name-2...column-name-n) IN

(SELECT column-name-1, column-name-2...column-name-n

FROM......

WHERE......);
```

Multiple columns in outer query

Multiple columns in inner query. Same number of columns as in outer query and same corresponding domains.

Fig. 7-2. Syntax of a multiple-column subquery.

EXAMPLE 7.3

Display the first name, last name, department ID, salary, and start date of all employees who have the same salary and title of the employees who work for manager 10.

Before answering this query, add the following tuples to the S_EMP table.

```
INSERT INTO s_emp VALUES ('300', 'Smith', 'Albert', 'smithal',
    TO_DATE('09-MAY-1998','DD-MON-YYYY'), NULL, '10', 'Sales
Representative',
    '31', 1100, 10);
INSERT INTO s_emp VALUES ('301', 'Jones', 'Jenny', 'jonesjen',
    TO_DATE('31-AUG-1999','DD-MON-YYYY'), NULL, '10', 'Sales
Representative',
    '31', 1100, 10);
INSERT INTO s_emp VALUES ('302', 'Barker', 'Joel', 'barkerjo',
    TO_DATE('09-JUL-1999','DD-MON-YYYY'), NULL, '10', 'Sales
Representative',
    '31', 1400, NULL);
INSERT INTO s_emp VALUES ('303', 'Armstrong', 'Marta', 'armstmar',
    TO_DATE('26-MAR-1999','DD-MON-YYYY'), NULL, '10', 'Sales
Representative',
    '31', 1100, 10);
INSERT INTO s_emp VALUES ('304', 'Nichols', 'Jim', 'nichojim',
    TO_DATE('11-DEC-1999','DD-MON-YYYY'), NULL, '10', 'Sales
Representative',
    '31', 1400, 10);
INSERT INTO s_emp VALUES ('305', 'Ritchie', 'Diane', 'ritchdi',
    TO_DATE('13-FEB-1998','DD-MON-YYYY'), NULL, '10', 'Sales
Representative',
    '31', 1100, NULL);
INSERT INTO s_emp VALUES ('306', 'Good', 'Gwen', 'goodgw',
    TO_DATE('01-SEP-1998','DD-MON-YYYY'), NULL, '10', 'Sales
Representative',
    '31', 1400, NULL);
COMMIT;
```

This query illustrates the use of multiple-column subqueries. In this case, we first find all employees who work for manager_id = 10. Second, from the set of employees retrieved in the inner query, we then retrieve all employees that have the same title and salary.

```
SELECT first_name, last_name, dept_id, salary, start_date
FROM s_emp
WHERE (salary, title) IN
          (SELECT salary, title
           FROM s_emp
           WHERE manager_id = '10');
```

FIRST_NAME	LAST_NAME	DEP	SALARY	START_DAT
Blaine	Stephenson	45	860	17-MAR-91
Bonnie	Dancer	45	860	17-MAR-91
Albert	Smith	31	1100	09-MAY-98
Marta	Armstrong	31	1100	26-MAR-99
Diane	Ritchie	31	1100	13-FEB-98
Jenny	Jones	31	1100	31-AUG-99
Colin	Henderson	31	1400	14-MAY-90
Joel	Barker	31	1400	09-JUL-99
Gwen	Good	31	1400	01-SEP-98
Jim	Nichols	31	1400	11-DEC-99

7.2   Correlated Queries

Correlated queries are nested queries that offer a more powerful mechanism to retrieve data than the subqueries considered in the previous two sections. Unlike subqueries, in a correlated query the inner query always refers to the table mentioned in the FROM clause of the outer query. In addition, correlated queries differ from subqueries not only in the order of execution but also in the number of times that the queries are executed. Correlated queries make use of table aliases to refer to values specified in the outer query. In the content of correlated queries, some authors refer to table aliases as *correlation variables* or *correlation names*. In this book we will use these terms interchangeably. Fig 7-3 shows the basic syntax of correlated queries.

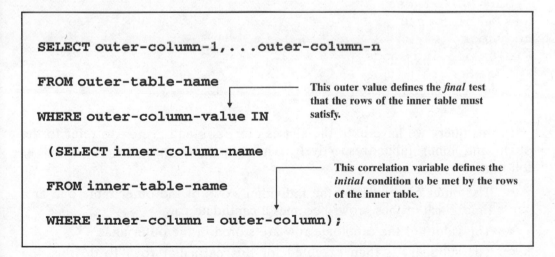

Fig 7-3.   Syntax of correlated queries.

In all correlated queries, execution always starts with the outer query. The outer query selects each of the individual rows of the *outer table* and considers them as candidate rows. For each one of these candidate rows, the correlated *inner query* is executed once. During the execution of the inner query the system looks for rows that satisfy the *inner* WHERE *condition* for the value specified *by the outer column*. All rows of the inner table that satisfy this condition form a temporary set. The system then tests the outer condition against the rows stored in the temporary set. All rows that satisfy the outer condition are then displayed. This process continues until all candidate rows have been processed.

EXAMPLE 7.4
Display all customers who placed an order in August 31, 1992.

Following are the correlated query that allows us to retrieve this data and its result:

```
SELECT name
FROM s_customer outer
WHERE TO_DATE('31-AUG-1992','DD-MM-YYYY')

    IN ( SELECT date_ordered

        FROM s_ord inner

        WHERE inner.customer_id = outer.id);
```

Correlation variable

```
NAME
--------------------
Deportivo Caracas
New Delhi Sports
Ladysport
Kim's Sporting Goods
Futbol Sonora
5 rows selected.
```

In this query we have used the aliases of outer and inner to refer to the outer and inner table, respectively. This particular query is evaluated as follows:

- The outer query selects the individual rows of the outer table one at a time. Each of these rows becomes a candidate row.
- The values of the candidate row are stored in the outer alias.
- The subquery is then executed for this particular row. To do this, the system goes through the entire inner table looking for rows that have the same outer.id, which, in this case, is the customer ID of the current row. All rows that have the same customer ID form a temporary set.
- Using the temporary set of the previous step, the system now uses the condition of the outer query to find all rows that have '31-AUG-1992'.

as their order date. Rows that satisfy that condition are displayed in the result table.

- The system repeats Steps 1 through 4 until all rows of the outer table have been tested.

7.3   Using Subqueries to Create Tables

There are situations where we would like to copy the structure of a table and none of its data or just copy part of a table along with the corresponding data. To do this, we can use a variation of the CREATE TABLE command. Fig. 7-4 shows the basic syntax of the variation of the CREATE TABLE statement that uses subqueries.

```
CREATE TABLE table-new-name AS
SELECT column-name-1, column-name-2,...column-name-n
FROM table-name
WHERE column-name = (SELECT column-name
                     FROM table-name
                     WHERE condition);
```

Fig. 7-4.   Syntax of the CREATE table command to copy a table or part of a table using subqueries.

7.3.1   COPYING THE STRUCTURE OF A TABLE

To copy the structure of a table and none of its data, we use the * and a Boolean condition that cannot be satisfied. The following example illustrates this.

EXAMPLE 7.5
Copy the structure of the S_EMP table and none of its data. Call the new table S_WORKER.

The corresponding CREATE TABLE command is as follows:

CREATE TABLE s_worker ◄——— **Name of the new table being created.**

AS SELECT * ◄——————— **The * allows us to select all columns of the S_EMP table.**

FROM s_emp

WHERE 1 <> 1; ◄——————— **This Boolean condition can never be satisfied.**

The * allows us to select all columns of the S_EMP table. Notice the use of the expression 1<>1 to form a Boolean condition that cannot be satisfied by any row of the table. Since no rows are retrieved, only the structure of the table is copied.

7.3.2   COPYING SELECTED COLUMNS OF A TABLE AND THEIR DATA

To copy a particular set of columns and their data, we just name the columns and the condition that need to be satisfied by the rows of the table that we are copying in the CREATE TABLE command shown above. The following example illustrates this.

EXAMPLE 7.6
Create a table that contains the first name, last name, and the department ID of all employees who have the title of VP. Call the table Vice_President.

```
CREATE TABLE Vice_President AS
SELECT first_name, last_name, dept_id
FROM s_emp
WHERE id IN (SELECT id
             FROM s_emp
             WHERE title LIKE '%VP%');
```

To verify that the structure and the data have been copied correctly we can use the following commands:

```
DESCRIBE Vice_President
```

Name	Null?	Type
FIRST_NAME		VARCHAR2(20)
LAST_NAME	NOT NULL	VARCHAR2(20)
DEPT_ID		VARCHAR2(3)

```
SELECT * FROM vice_president;
```

FIRST_NAME	LAST_NAME	DEP
Doris	Smith	41
Michael	Norton	31
Mark	Quentin	10
Joseph	Roper	50

4 rows selected.

7.4   Updating a Table Using Subqueries

It is possible to update the content of a table using subqueries. The syntax of this command is as follows:

```
UPDATE table-name
SET column = (SELECT column-name
             FROM table-name
             WHERE condition)
WHERE column-name = (SELECT column-name
                     FROM table-name
                     WHERE condition);
```

EXAMPLE 7.7

Assume that the manager of the warehouse in Slovakia has resigned and will be replaced temporarily by the V.P. Michael Norton. Update the S_EMP table to reflect this change.

Following is the UPDATE command to reflect this change:

```
UPDATE s_emp

SET manager_id = (SELECT id  ←

                 FROM s_emp                            3

                 WHERE last_name = 'Norton')

WHERE manager_id = (SELECT manager_id  ←——————  1

      2  ——→        FROM s_warehouse

                    WHERE country = 'Slovakia');
```

Processing this command in a bottom-up fashion, let's observe that the subquery indicated by No. 1 retrieves the manager_id for the warehouse located in Slovakia. The system uses this manager_id to retrieve the employees of the S_EMP table whose manager is the manager of the warehouse in Slovakia (see No. 2). Finally, the value returned by the subquery indicated by No. 3 is used to update the appropriate rows in the S_EMP table.

7.5   Inserting Values into a Table Using Subqueries

Subqueries also allow us to add rows of a table using a variation of the INSERT INTO table. When used in conjunction with subqueries, it is possible to insert rows into a table from another table. The syntax of this command is as follows:

```
INSERT INTO table-name (column-name-1,...,column-name-n)
SELECT column-name-1,...,column-name-n
FROM table-name
WHERE column-name = (SELECT column-name
                     FROM table-name
                     WHERE condition);
```

EXAMPLE 7.8
Insert into the table S_WORKER of Example 7.5 all the employees of the table S_EMP that work in `dept_id='10'`.

```
INSERT INTO s_worker
SELECT *
FROM s_emp
WHERE dept_id='10';
```

7.6 Deleting Rows from a Table Using Subqueries

Using subqueries in conjunction with the DELETE FROM command allows us to remove rows from a table using the information from another table. The basic syntax of this command is as follows:

```
DELETE FROM table-name
WHERE column-name = (SELECT column-name
                     FROM table
                     WHERE condition);
```

EXAMPLE 7.9
Assume that due to lack of business the warehouse located in Slovakia is being closed. Remove from the S_EMP table all employees working in this warehouse. Refresh the Sporting Goods tables before answering this question.

The corresponding DELETE FROM command is as follows:

```
DELETE FROM s_emp
WHERE manager_id = (SELECT manager_id
                    FROM s_warehouse
                    WHERE country = 'Slovakia');
```

7.7 Set Operators

The set operators of UNION, INTERSECT, and MINUS allow us to combine the results of separate SELECT statements. They are the SQL equivalent of the set operators INTERSECTION, UNION, and DIFFERENCE, respectively. Of all the three operators, the UNION is the most powerful and interesting.

7.7.1 THE UNION OPERATOR

The **UNION** operator allows us to present the result of multiple SELECT statements as a single SELECT statement. Fig. 7-5 shows the basic syntax of this command.

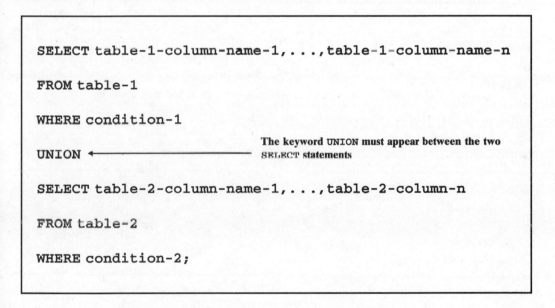

```
SELECT table-1-column-name-1,...,table-1-column-name-n

FROM table-1

WHERE condition-1
                            The keyword UNION must appear between the two
UNION ◄─────────────────    SELECT statements

SELECT table-2-column-name-1,...,table-2-column-n

FROM table-2

WHERE condition-2;
```

Fig. 7-5. Syntax of the UNION of two SELECT statements.

Before forming the union of two tables, the user needs to make sure that the results of the SELECT statements are union-compatible. That is, the result of each individual SELECT statement needs to satisfy the following conditions:

- The number of columns in each intermediate table must be the same.
- The data type of the corresponding columns must be the same. It is not necessary that the column names be identical. When forming the UNION, Oracle uses the first SELECT statement to determine the column heading of the resulting table.

- If the ORDER BY clause is used, it can appear only once and it must be the last clause of the last SELECT statement.
- The ORDER BY clause must reference a column by its relative column number, not by the column name.

The following example illustrates the use of the UNION operation.

EXAMPLE 7.10
Display the name of all customers of region_id 1 along with the department names that are located in that region_id.

The SELECT statements that participate in the UNION and their corresponding results are shown below. Notice that the result is sorted even though no ORDER BY clause was specified. The result of the UNION is already sorted because Oracle performs an internal sort to identify duplicate rows as required by the theoretical definition of UNION.

```
SELECT name
FROM s_customer
WHERE region_id ='1'
UNION
SELECT name
FROM s_dept
WHERE region_id ='1';
NAME
--------------------
Administration
Beisbol Si!
Finance
Ladysport
Operations
Sales
Sports Emporium
Sports Retail
.
.
17 rows selected.
```

7.7.2 THE INTERSECT OPERATOR

The **INTERSECT** operator allows us to identify rows that are common to two tables. This operator is also placed between two SELECT statements. The syntax of this operator is as follows:

```
SELECT table-1-column-name-1,...,table-1-column-name-n

FROM table-1

WHERE condition-1

INTERSECT  ◄────────────────    The keyword INTERSECT must appear between
                                the two SELECT statements.

SELECT table-2-column-name-1,...,table-2-column-n

FROM table-2

WHERE condition-2;
```

The intermediate results of the SELECT statements must satisfy the conditions for union compatibility. The following example illustrates the use of this operator.

EXAMPLE 7.11
Display the ID of all sales representatives who have been assigned to a customer.

The corresponding query and its result are as follows:

```
COLUMN sales_rep_id HEADING 'Sales Reps' FORMAT A11
SELECT sales_rep_id
FROM s_customer
INTERSECT
SELECT id
FROM s_emp;

Sales Reps
-----------
11
12
13
14

4 rows selected.
```

7.7.3 THE MINUS OPERATOR

The MINUS operator allows us to determine the rows that are present in one table but not in another. Unlike the UNION and INTERSECT operators, the MINUS operator is not commutative. That is, the result of table A MINUS table B is in general different than the result of table B MINUS table A. The following example illustrates the use of this operator.

EXAMPLE 7.12
Due to their in-house training, some sales representatives have not been assigned a customer yet. Display the name of these sales representatives.

The corresponding query and its result are as follows:

```
SELECT id
FROM s_emp
MINUS
SELECT sales_rep_id
FROM s_customer;

ID
---
1
10
15
16
.
.
.
20 rows selected.
```

 Solved Problems

7.1. Display the department name of the employee whose ID is number 2.

The query to retrieve this information and its result are shown below.

```
SELECT name
FROM s_dept
WHERE id = (SELECT dept_id
            FROM s_emp
            WHERE id = '2');
NAME
--------------------
Operations
```

In this query, notice that the subquery retrieves the department ID for the given employee. The main query then uses this department ID to display the corresponding department name.

7.2. Display the last name, first name, and salary of all employees who work in the same department as the employee whose last name is Brown.

The query and its result are shown below.

```
SELECT first_name, last_name, salary
FROM s_emp
WHERE dept_id IN (SELECT dept_id
                  FROM s_emp
                  WHERE last_name = 'Brown');
FIRST_NAME              LAST_NAME            SALARY
----------------------  -------------------- ---------
Doris                   Smith                 2450
Molly                   Brown                 1600
George                  Brown                  940
Elaine                  Hardwick              1400
```

In this case, the subquery returns more than one row because more than one employee works in the same department as Brown. In addition, observe that there are two employees whose last name is Brown that work in the same department. Therefore, in the main query it is necessary to use the IN operator instead of the equal sign.

7.3. Display the name, city, and country of all customers whose representative is Andre Dameron.

The query and its result are as follows:

```
SELECT name, city, country
  FROM s_customer
  WHERE sales_rep_id = (SELECT id
                        FROM s_emp
                        WHERE last_name ='Dameron');

NAME                   CITY                    COUNTRY
--------------------   --------------------    ---------------
Toms Sporting Goods    Harrisonburg            US
Athletic Attire        Harrisonburg            US
.
.
5 rows selected.
```

7.4. Display the first name, last name and title of any employee employed by an existing department.

The query and its result are as follows:

```
SELECT first_name, last_name
FROM s_emp
WHERE dept_id = ANY (SELECT id FROM s_dept);
```

```
FIRST_NAME            LAST_NAME
--------------------  --------------------
Carmen                Martin
Doris                 Smith
Michael               Norton
Mark                  Quentin
Joseph                Roper
.

.
24 rows selected.
```

In this example, we have used the keyword ANY, that can be used with any of the comparison operators whether or not the subquery returns one or more rows. When ANY is used with the comparison operators, the Boolean condition evaluates to TRUE if the expression is true for *any* of the values returned by the subquery. In this case, the subquery reduces to the following:

```
SELECT first_name, last_name
FROM s_emp
WHERE dept_id = ANY ('Finance', 'Sales', 'Operations',
                     'Administration');
```

7.5. Find the employees with the lowest salary.

```
SELECT first_name, last_name
FROM s_emp
WHERE salary <= ALL (SELECT salary
                     FROM s_emp);
FIRST_NAME            LAST_NAME
--------------------  --------------------
Donald                Patterson
Roger                 Pearl
```

In this exercise, we have the keyword ALL, which can also be used with any of the comparison operators whether or not the subquery returns one or more rows. When ALL is used, the condition is evaluated to TRUE if the expression is TRUE *for all* the values returned by the subquery. In this case, there are two employees whose salary is less than or equal to the salary of all other employees.

7.6. Display the first name, last name, and department ID of any employee whose salary and commission percentage is the same as employee Jason Sanders. Before answering this question, insert the following tuples into the S_EMP table:

```
INSERT  INTO  s_emp  (id,  last_name,  first_name,  userid,  start_date,
manager_id, title, dept_id, salary, commission_pct)
VALUES  ('514',  'Chloe',  'Wendt',  'wendtch',TO_DATE('18-FEB-1991','DD-
MON-YYYY'),'3', 'Sales Representative','33', 1515, 10);
INSERT  INTO  s_emp  (id,  last_name,  first_name,  userid,  start_date,
manager_id,  title,  dept_id,  salary,  commission_pct) VALUES  ('611',
'Ritchie',  'Erin',  'ritchri',TO_DATE('18-FEB-1991','DD-MON-YYYY'),'3',
'Sales Representative','33', 1515, 10);
```

The query and its result are as follows:

```
SELECT last_name,first_name, dept_id
FROM s_emp
WHERE (salary, commission_pct)
IN (SELECT salary, commission_pct
    FROM s_emp
    WHERE dept_id IN (SELECT dept_id FROM s_emp
                      WHERE last_name = 'Sanders'));


LAST_NAME            FIRST_NAME            DEP
-------------------- --------------------- ---
Sanders              Jason                 33
Ritchie              Erin                  33
Chloe                Wendt                 33
```

Notice that in this query the innermost subquery retrieves the department ID of Jason Sanders. The next subquery retrieves the salary and commission percentage for this employee. Finally, the outer subquery retrieves all employees that match Jason Sanders' salary and commission.

7.7. Display the name, city, country, and sales representative of all customers who placed an order on AUG-31-1992.

The query and its result are shown below. To answer this query, we have taken advantage of the fact that each order has the name of the customer and its sales representative. Notice that the result has been formatted to fit the page.

```
SELECT name, city, country, sales_rep_id
FROM s_customer
WHERE (id, sales_rep_id) IN
(SELECT customer_id, sales_rep_id AS "Rep"
 FROM s_ord
 WHERE date_ordered='31-AUG-1992');
NAME                CITY            COUNTRY         Rep
Ladysport           Seattle         US              11
Futbol Sonora       Nogales         Mexico          12
```

7.8. For each sales representative, display the sum of his or her total orders if this amount exceeds the "average" order.

The query and its result are shown below.

```
SELECT sales_rep_id AS "Rep", SUM(total) AS "Total Orders"
FROM s_ord
GROUP BY sales_rep_id
HAVING SUM(total) > (SELECT AVG(total)
                     FROM s_ord);
Rep Total Orders
--- ------------
11      1629443.4
13         182000
14       158529.6
```

In this case, the subquery calculates the average total of all orders. This result is then used by the main query to display the sales representatives whose total orders exceed the "average" order.

7.9. Display the name, city, country, and rating of all customers whose orders exceed the "average" order.

The query and its result are shown below. Notice that the value returned by the subquery is used in conjunction with a join condition to retrieve the required information about the customers. The output has been modified to fit the screen.

```
SELECT name, city, country, credit_rating AS "Rating"
FROM S_customer, s_ord
WHERE total > (SELECT AVG(total)
            FROM s_ord)
            AND s_ord.customer_id = s_customer.id;
```

NAME	CITY	COUNTRY	Rating
Ladysport	Seattle	US	EXCELLENT
Helmut's Sports	Prague	Czechoslovakia	EXCELLENT
Hamada Sport	Alexandria	Egypt	EXCELLENT
Sports Emporium	San Francisco	US	EXCELLENT

7.10. Use a correlated subquery to display the name of all departments that have at least one employee.

The query and its result are shown below. Notice that in this query we have used the EXISTS operator. The EXISTS operator can be used whenever we are interested in knowing whether or not the subquery returns a row and not in the values of any particular row. This operator returns a TRUE value if the subquery returns any row. Observe the use of the DISTINCT clause to avoid duplicate department names in the result.

```
SELECT DISTINCT name
FROM s_dept D
WHERE EXISTS (SELECT E.dept_id
            FROM s_emp E
            WHERE E.dept_id = D.id);
NAME
--------------------
Administration
Finance
Operations
Sales
```

7.11. Display the last name and first name of all employees who do not have customers.

The query and its result are as follows:

```
SELECT last_name, first_name
FROM s_emp Outer
WHERE id NOT IN (SELECT sales_rep_id
                 FROM s_customer Inner
                 WHERE inner.sales_rep_id = outer.id);
LAST_NAME              TITLE
-------------------- ---------------------
Martin                President
Smith                 VP, Operations
Norton                VP, Sales
Quentin               VP, Finance
.
.
.
22 rows selected.
```

7.12. Is there any country for which there is no sales representative? If so, display the name of the country. Use a correlated query and the NOT EXISTS operator.

The query and its result are as follows:

```
SELECT country
FROM s_customer C
WHERE NOT EXISTS (SELECT id
                  FROM s_emp E
                  WHERE E.id = C.sales_rep_id);


COUNTRY
--------------------
Nigeria
```

7.13. Write a query to display the customers and sales representatives that are located or are assigned to Venezuela. Use the UNION operator.

The query and its result are shown below.

```
SELECT C.name
FROM s_customer C
WHERE country = 'Venezuela'
UNION
SELECT last_name
FROM s_emp
WHERE id IN (SELECT sales_rep_id
FROM s_customer
WHERE country = 'Venezuela');
NAME
--------------------
Deportivo Caracas
Gilson
```

7.14. Display the ID of the sales representatives for Venezuela and Russia. Use the UNION operator.

```
SELECT id
FROM s_emp E
WHERE id IN (SELECT sales_rep_id
             FROM s_customer C
             WHERE country = 'Venezuela')
UNION
SELECT id
FROM s_emp E
WHERE id IN (SELECT sales_rep_id
             FROM s_customer C
             WHERE country = 'Russia');
ID
---
11
12
```

7.15. Create a table that contains the name, city, state, country, and region of all customers with POOR credit. Call the table Low_Rating.

The corresponding CREATE TABLE command is shown below.

```
CREATE TABLE low_rating
AS SELECT name, city, country, region_id
FROM s_customer
WHERE credit_rating ='POOR';
```

7.16. Create a table called PC users with the following columns: first name, last name, and user ID of all employees of the SG company. Make sure that no data is copied into the table being created and that the table is created correctly.

```
CREATE TABLE pc_users AS
SELECT first_name, last_name, userid
FROM s_emp
WHERE id <>id;

DESC pc_users;
```

Name	Null?	Type
FIRST_NAME		VARCHAR2(20)
LAST_NAME	NOT NULL	VARCHAR2(20)
USERID	NOT NULL	VARCHAR2(8)

7.17. Create a table with same structure of the s_dept table, but rename the columns as indicated below. Call the new table WORK_UNIT.

Name in S_DEPT Table	Name in the Work_Unit Table
Id	Unit_id
Name	Unit_name
Region_id	Global_area

The statement to create the work_unit table is as follows:

```
CREATE TABLE work_unit (unit_id, unit_name, global_area)
AS SELECT id, name, region_id
FROM s_dept;
```

We can verify that the table has the required structure by issuing the following command:

```
DESC work_unit;
Name                                Null?     Type
----------------------------------- --------- ----
UNIT_ID                             NOT NULL  VARCHAR2(3)
UNIT_NAME                           NOT NULL  VARCHAR2(20)
GLOBAL_AREA                                   VARCHAR2(3)
```

7.18. The table of the previous solved problem was created, and the data from the s_dept table was copied into it. Write a subquery to delete all rows from the work_unit table.

The corresponding subquery is as follows. Notice that the subquery returns every ID of the s_dept table. Each one of these IDs are used as the deletion criteria in the work_unit table.

```
DELETE FROM work_unit
WHERE unit_id IN (SELECT id
                  FROM s_dept);
```

7.19. Due to an excellent performance during the previous year, all employees whose manager is located in Seattle, Washington, got a salary increase of $1000. Write the corresponding query to update the employees' information.

The corresponding query is shown below.

```
UPDATE s_emp
SET salary = salary + 1000
WHERE manager_id =(SELECT manager_id
                   FROM s_warehouse
                   WHERE city = 'Seattle' AND state ='WA');
```

Supplementary Problems

7.20. Display the department name of the employee whose last name is Dameron.

7.21. Display the last name, first name, and start date of the employees who have the lowest salary. Do not use the same method shown in Solved Problem 7.5.

7.22. Display the first and last name for all employees who work for Michael Norton.

7.23. Display the name of all departments with no employees.

7.24. Display the name, country, and region of all customers whose sales representative is also a manager of a warehouse. How many customers satisfy this condition?

7.25. Display the name, city, country, and sales representative of all customers who placed an order during the month of July 1992.

7.26. Display the name of each sales representative for whom the sum of all his or her orders exceeds the "average" order.

7.27. Write a correlated query to display the name of any department that has no employees. Use the NOT EXISTS operator. Refer to Solved Problem 7.10.

7.28. Use a correlated query to display the last name and first name of all sales representatives that have customers.

7.29. Display all sales representatives who have customers with a credit rating of GOOD. Use a correlated query and the EXISTS operator.

7.30. Display the names of all customers and the sales representatives of the company.

7.31. Display the name of the sales representatives for Venezuela and Russia. Use the UNION operator.

7.32. Delete all sales representatives who have customers in Harrisonburg, Virginia. Run the script SG_NO_CONSTRAINTS.SQL before answering this question.

7.33. Delete all customers that do not have any current order.

Answers to Supplementary Problems

7.20.

```
SELECT name
FROM s_dept
WHERE id = (SELECT dept_id
            FROM s_emp
            WHERE LAST_NAME = 'Dameron');
```

7.21.

```
SELECT last_name, first_name, start_date
FROM s_emp
WHERE salary = (SELECT MIN(salary)
                FROM s_emp);
```

7.22.

```
SELECT first_name, last_name
FROM s_emp
WHERE manager_id = (SELECT id
                     FROM s_emp
                     WHERE last_name = 'Norton');
```

7.23.

```
SELECT name
FROM s_dept
WHERE id NOT IN (SELECT dept_id
                  FROM s_emp);
```

7.24.

```
SELECT name,city,country
FROM s_customer
WHERE (sales_rep_id, region_id) IN
(SELECT manager_id, region_id
 FROM s_warehouse);
```
There are no sales representatives that are also managers.

7.25.

```
SELECT name, city, country, sales_rep_id
FROM s_customer
WHERE (id, sales_rep_id) IN
(SELECT customer_id, sales_rep_id
 FROM s_ord
 WHERE date_ordered BETWEEN '01-JUL-1992' AND
                            '31-AUG-1992');
```

7.26.

```
SELECT last_name
FROM s_emp
WHERE id IN (SELECT sales_rep_id
             FROM s_ord
             GROUP BY sales_rep_id
             HAVING SUM(total) > (SELECT AVG(total)
                                   FROM s_ord));
```

7.27.

```
SELECT name
FROM s_dept D
WHERE NOT EXISTS (SELECT E.dept_id
                   FROM s_emp E
                   WHERE E.dept_id = D.id);
```

7.28.

```
SELECT last_name, first_name
FROM s_emp Outer
WHERE id IN (SELECT sales_rep_id
                FROM s_customer Inner
                WHERE inner.sales_rep_id = outer.id)
AND Title = 'Sales Representative';
```

7.29.

```
SELECT last_name
FROM s_emp E
WHERE EXISTS (SELECT name
                FROM s_customer C
                WHERE C.sales_rep_id = E.id
                AND C.credit_rating='GOOD');
```

7.30.

```
SELECT C.name
FROM s_customer C
UNION
SELECT last_name
FROM s_emp
WHERE title ='Sales Representative';
```

7.31.

```
SELECT last_name
FROM s_emp
WHERE id IN (SELECT id
                FROM s_emp E
                WHERE id IN (SELECT sales_rep_id
                                FROM s_customer C
                                WHERE country = 'Venezuela')
UNION
SELECT id
FROM s_emp E
WHERE id IN (SELECT sales_rep_id
                FROM s_customer C
                WHERE country = 'Russia'));
```

7.32.

```
DELETE
FROM s_emp
WHERE id IN (SELECT sales_rep_id
                FROM s_customer
                WHERE city = 'Harrisonburg' AND state ='VA');
```

Note: This query will generate an error because we are violating the referential integrity constraint. This will only work in the SG_NO_Constraints.sql database.

7.33.

```
DELETE FROM s_customer
WHERE NOT EXISTS (SELECT *
                  FROM s_ord
                  WHERE customer_id = s_customer.id);
```

CHAPTER 8

Basic Security Issues Using SQL

In this chapter we consider some of the elementary aspects of data security within the framework and capabilities of the SQL language to authenticate users and to protect data from unauthorized use.

8.1   Data Security

In any corporation data is the most valuable resource. Therefore, it needs to be controlled, managed, protected, and secured. In the context of RDBMS by *security* we will be referring to the protection of the database against un-authorized access or the intentional or unintentional disclosure, alteration, or destruction of the database. Although security of a DBMS requires that we pay attention to other issues such as its physical protection and network protection, in this book, we will concentrate only on some of the basic computer-based countermeasures. In particular, we will address the topics of authentication and authorization.

8.1.1   AUTHENTICATION

By *authentication*, we will refer to any mechanism that determines whether a user is who he or she claims to be. Authentication can be carried out at the operating system level or at the RDBMS. In either case, the system administrator (SYSAD) or database administrator (DBA) creates for every user an individual accounts or username. In addition, to these accounts users are also assigned passwords. A *password* is a sequence of characters, numbers, or a combination of both that is supposedly known only to the system and its legitimate user. RDBMS store usernames and passwords in an encrypted form in the data dictionary. To access the database, a user must run an application and connect to the database using his or her account or username and the appropriate password. For example, for the exercises of this book, we have connected to the Oracle database via the SQL Plus application using `scott` as the username and `tiger` as the password, respectively.

Since the password is the first line of defense against unauthorized use by outsiders, it needs to be kept confidential by its legitimate user. It is highly recommended that users change their password frequently. Passwords should be, at the very least, six characters long and made up of a combination of letters, numbers, and some other allowable keyboard symbols. Users should avoid common names such as nicknames or proper names. To change a password in Oracle, a user can issue the following command:

ALTER USER user-name IDENTIFIED by new-password;

EXAMPLE 8.1
Log into PO8 as scott/tiger and change the password to RJ89.

The corresponding instruction is as follows:

```
ALTER USER Scott IDENTIFIED BY RJ89;
```

It should be obvious that after changing his or her password, the user will no longer be able to use the previous password. Users can change their passwords as many times as they want.

8.1.2 AUTHORIZATION

By *authorization* we will understand the granting of a right or privilege to a user that allows him or her to have access to the system or objects within the system. The basic types of privileges associated with any user are the system and objects privileges. *System privileges* allow the user to gain access to the database. *Object privileges* allow the user to manipulate objects within the database. When a database user is created, the user is associated with a *schema* or a collection of objects in the database to which he or she has access. The system administrator determines and controls the access rights of user through the user's *security domain*. The settings of this domain limit what the user can or cannot do in the database. In this sense, the security domain includes information about:

- The type of authentication for this user (through the operating system or the network services)
- The amount of system resources available to this user, including tablespaces (similar to directories in a Windows or DOS environment) and their default values

- The database objects that the user has access to and the operations that the user can perform on these objects

Before a user can grant any system privileges to any other user, he or she must have administrative privileges. Table 8-1 lists some of the basic system privileges.

Table 8-1.   Partial list of system privileges.

THIS PRIVILEGE	ALLOWS THE USER TO
CREATE SESSION	Connect to database.
CREATE TABLE	Create table in own schema and use commands such as ALTER, DROP, TRUNCATE on the tables.
SELECT [ANY TABLE]	Query tables in own schema. If ANY is granted, user can access tables in other schema.
CREATE SEQUENCE	Create sequence in own schema.
CREATE VIEW	Create view in own schema.

8.1.2.1   Creating Users

To create a user, we can use the following simplified version of the CREATE USER command.

```
CREATE USER user-name IDENTIFIED BY user-password
DEFAULT TABLESPACE tablespace-name
TEMPORARY TABLESPACE temptablespace-name
QUOTA integer M on tablespace-name
QUOTA integer N on temptablespace-name;
```

This command assigns to the user a default and a temporary tablespace. As mentioned, A *tablespace* is logical storage unit similar to a directory in Windows or DOS. This command also establishes the amount of memory allocated to the user (his or her quota) in each of these tablespaces.

As indicated before, to create a user, it is necessary to have administrative privileges. To be able to do this, it is necessary to log in to PO8 using SYSTEM as the username and MANAGER as the password. This is a built-in account in Oracle with administrative privileges.[1]

---

[1] In the following sections, unless otherwise indicated, we will assume that the reader has logged in to the Oracle database using this built-in account.

EXAMPLE 8.2
Create the user `hayley` with password `whm123bng`

The command to create this user is as follows:

```
CREATE USER hayley IDENTIFIED BY whm123bng
DEFAULT TABLESPACE user_data
TEMPORARY TABLESPACE temporary_data
QUOTA 5M on user_data QUOTA 1M on temporary_data;
```

The tablespaces `user_data` and `temporary_data` come with the default database created for PO8. We will use them in this section without further consideration since their explanation is beyond the scope of this book.

8.1.2.2   Dropping Users

At times, it may be necessary to remove a user from the database—for instance, if an employee resigns or is fired. The instruction that allows us to do this is the following:

DROP USER user-name [CASCADE];

If the `CASCADE` option is used when dropping a user, not only the user but also all of the user's objects in his or her schema will be dropped.

EXAMPLE 8.3
Drop the user Hayley but leave all her objects in her schema.

```
DROP USER hayley;
```

8.1.2.3   Monitoring Users

To display information about the user, there are several views (to be explained later in the chapter) that allow the database administrator to gather information about the database users. Views can be queried as any other ordinary table. Table 8-2 lists some of the views that provide information about users.

Table 8-2.   Partial list of views that provide information about a user.

THIS VIEW	CAN BE USED TO OBTAIN INFORMATION ABOUT
ALL_USERS	All the users that have been created.
USER_USERS	The user currently logged-in.
USER_TABLES	All the tables owned by the current user.
USER_TS_QUOTAS	Tablespace quotas for the current user.
USER_OBJECTS	Objects owned by the user.

8.1.2.4 Granting System Privileges to Users

Once a user has been created, the system administrator may grant the user a set of privileges. Table 8-3 lists some of the most common privileges assigned to a user.

Table 8-3. Partial list of common privileges granted to users.

THIS PRIVILEGE	ALLOWS THE USER TO
CREATE SESSION	Connect to the database.
CREATE TABLE	Create tables in his or her schema.
CREATE VIEW	Create view in his or her schema.
CREATE SEQUENCE	Create sequence in his or her schema.

The command to grant privileges to a user is the following:

```
GRANT priv-1 [,priv-2,...priv-n] TO USER user-name;
```

The first privilege that should be granted to a user is the one that allows the user to connect to the database. As indicated in Table 8-3, the name of this privilege is CREATE SESSION.

EXAMPLE 8.4
Re-create the user hayley and grant her the CREATE SESSION privilege.

The corresponding command is as follows:

```
GRANT create session TO hayley;
```

If user hayley tries to log in to the database, the login will succeed. However, if she tries to create a table, she will not be able to do it because she lacks the privileges to do so.

EXAMPLE 8.5
Grant the necessary privileges to the user hayley to create tables and views.

The command that allows us to do this is as follows:

```
GRANT create table, create view TO hayley;
```

After this statement, the user hayley can connect to the database and create tables in it.

To avoid the tedious task of granting individual privileges to different users, database administrators create groups of related privileges and grant them to the users according to the users' needs. Each group of privileges is called a *role*. For instance, data entry operators may require a certain set of privileges, while programmers require a different set. The database administrator can then create separate roles for the entry operators and for the programmers. The DBA then assigns the privileges to each of these roles and grants them to the two groups of users.

The command that allows us to create a role is as follows:

CREATE ROLE role-name;

To grant privileges to a role that has already been created, the DBA can use the GRANT command as follows:

GRANT privilege-1 [, privilege...] TO role-name;

The following example illustrates this.

EXAMPLE 8.6

Create a role that allows a user to create a session and a table. At the same time create another role that allows a user to create a session and create a view but not a table. Call these roles role_tables and role_views, respectively.

```
CREATE ROLE role_tables;
GRANT create session, create table to role_tables;
CREATE ROLE role_views;
GRANT create session, create view to role_views;
```

After these roles have been created, the DBA can assign them to any user by using the GRANT command. Assuming there are users Nancy Wendt (wendtnan) and Denise Fernandez (fernande) who needed to access the database and create tables but not views, the DBA could grant them these privileges using the following command:

```
GRANT role_tables to wendtan, fernande;
```

Once a privilege has been granted to a user or a role, it can also be taken away from the user or the role. The instructions that allows the DBA to take away a specific set of privileges from a user or a role are the following:

```
REVOKE priv-1 [,priv-2...priv-n ]
FROM [ user-1 [, user-2...,user-n]]
```
← Command to revoke individual privileges from a use or users

```
                        or
```

```
REVOKE priv-1 [,priv-2...priv-n ]
FROM [ role-1 [, role-2...,role-n]];
```
← Command to revoke individual privileges from a role or roles

Users who have been granted privileges can consult some of the individual views available for this purpose. Table 8-4 lists some of these views

Table 8-4. Partial list of views that provide information about privileges granted or received.

THIS VIEW	ALLOWS THE USER TO
USER_SYS_PRIVS	Check system privileges granted to the current user.
USER_TAB_PRIVS_RECD	Check grants on objects for which the user is the grantee.
USER_ROLE_PRIVS	Roles granted to the user.

8.1.2.5 GRANTING OBJECTS PRIVILEGES TO USERS

So far, we have considered system privileges. However, the DBA can also grant privileges on specific objects. This type of privilege is called an *object privilege*. Object privileges allow particular actions on the object. Table 8-5 lists several objects and their privileges.

Table 8-5 Partial list of object privileges for tables and views.

OBJECT PRIVILEGE	TABLE	VIEW
ALTER	✓	
DELETE	✓	✓
INSERT	✓	✓
REFERENCES	✓	
RENAME	✓	✓
SELECT	✓	✓
UPDATE	✓	✓

The command that allows us to grant privileges on a particular object to a user or role is the following:

```
GRANT obj-priv-1 [,obj-priv-2...,obj-priv-n]
ON object-1 [,object-2,...,object-n]
TO user-1[,user-2,...,user-n]
[WITH GRANT OPTION];
```

or

```
GRANT obj-priv-1 [,obj-priv-2...,obj-priv-n]
ON object-1 [,object-2,...,object-n]
TO role-1 [,role-2,...,role-n]
[WITH GRANT OPTION];
```

If the `WITH GRANT OPTION` option is used, the user or role to which the privileges are granted can then, in turn, grant these privileges to another user. Any user who owns an object can grant privileges to another user.

> **EXAMPLE 8.7**
> Log in as `scott` and write the commands that allows `scott` to grant `SELECT` privileges to user `hayley` on the table S_EMP and S_DEPT.

```
GRANT select
ON s_emp
TO hayley;
GRANT select
ON s_dept
TO hayley;
```

Users who have been granted privileges on objects owned by another user can always refer to these objects by preceding the object name with that of its owner and separating them with a period.

```
Owner-name.object-name
```

For example, had the user hayley logged on, she could access the table S_EMP by preceding the table name with that of its owner scott. She could refer to this table as follows:

```
SELECT *

FROM scott.s_emp;
```
Notice the period separating the name of the owner of the object from the name of the object.

8.2   Hiding Data Through Views

A mechanism that allows users to exclude data that other users should not see is that of a *view*. By this term, we are referring to a stored query that, when executed, derives its data from other tables (the base or underlying tables). Literally stored in the data dictionary, the view does not contain data nor is it allocated any storage space. When a user references a view, the RDBMS retrieves its definition from the dictionary and executes or "runs" the query.

Views provide a level of security because they allow us to hide data "behind" the query. That is, users who execute the query will only see the result of the query, not the tables or views from which the data is extracted. In this sense, views are a tailored presentation of the data contained in one or more tables or views. Notice that a view can be based in some other views, providing an extra level of protection.

8.2.1   CREATING VIEWS

Since views may be derived from tables, there are many similarities between these two objects. From a practical point of view, the user cannot easily differentiate views from tables. Users with the appropriate privileges can query views like any other table. In addition, users can, with some restrictions, update, insert into, and delete data from a view. Like any other database object, to create a view in his or her own schema, the user must have the system privilege CREATE VIEW.

The syntax of this command is shown below.

```
CREATE VIEW view-name [(alias-1, alias-2,...,alias-n)]
AS query
WITH [READ ONLY | WITH CHECK OPTION [CONSTRAINT constraint-name];
```

The aliases are names for the expressions selected by the view's query. The number of aliases must match the number of expressions selected by the view. The WITH READ OPTION option prevents insertions, deletions, or updates of the underlying tables through the view. The WITH CHECK OPTION option specifies that inserts and updates performed through the view must result in rows that the view query can select.[2] The following examples illustrate this.

> **EXAMPLE 8.8**
> Create a view that contains the following attributes of the s_customer table (the base table): name, city, state, country. Call the view European_client.

```
CREATE view European_client
AS SELECT name, city, country, region_id
FROM s_customer
WHERE region_id = '5'
WITH CHECK OPTION;
```

To display the contents of this view, the user can issue the following command:

```
SELECT *
FROM european_client;
```

---

[2] Actually, this option cannot make this guarantee if there is a subquery in the query of this view or any of the underlying views on which this view is based.

The result of this query is as follows:

```
NAME                    CITY                COUNTRY              REG
-------------------     ---------------     -------------------  ---
Sportique               Cannes              France               5
Muench Sports           Munich              Germany              5
Helmut's Sports         Prague              Czechoslovakia       5
Sports Russia           Saint Petersburg    Russia               5
```

EXAMPLE 8.9
Create a view called `Sales Person` that displays the last name and name of the department for all employees of the SG database who are sales representatives. Name the headings `Employee` and `Department`.

The query that allows us to display this information is a join of the S_EMP and S_DEPT tables on the common attribute dept_id (of the S_EMP) and id (S_DEPT). The corresponding command is as follows:

```
CREATE VIEW Sales_Person (Employee, Department)
AS SELECT E.last_name, D.name
FROM s_emp E, s_dept D
WHERE E.dept_id = D.id
AND E.title = 'Sales Representative';
```

The output of the execution of this view is as follows:

```
SELECT *
FROM SALES_PERSON;


EMPLOYEE                DEPARTMENT
-------------------     ------------
Henderson               Sales
Gilson                  Sales
Sanders                 Sales
Dameron                 Sales
```

This example clearly illustrates the power of views to hide data. Notice that as far as the user is concerned, there are no practical differences between this view and any other table. In fact, if we describe this view (see below), we will not have any idea that its base table is the join of two tables. Observe also how the aliases help to hide the data even more, since there is no mention of the real name of the original columns.

```
DESC sales_person;
  Name                            Null?      Type
  ------------------------------  ---------  ----
    EMPLOYEE                      NOT NULL   VARCHAR2(20)
    DEPARTMENT                    NOT NULL   VARCHAR2(20)
```

8.2.2 UPDATING VIEWS

As indicated before, a user can update a view if he or she has the appropriate privileges. The command to update a view is similar to that of updating a table (see Chapter 1, Section 1.16.1). However, in some instances, to preserve the integrity of the data, it is necessary to ensure that any update performed through the view will not affect the data that the view is able to select. This type of update can be prevented by creating the view with the WITH CHECK option as we did in Example 8.8. The following example illustrates this.

EXAMPLE 8.10

Update the query of Example 8.8 by changing the region_id from five to two for all customers located in Russia.

The corresponding command is as follows:

```
UPDATE European_client
SET region_id ='2'
WHERE country = 'Russia';
```

Notice that if we try to execute this command, we get an error. This error reads something like this:

```
UPDATE European_client
SET region_id ='2'
WHERE country = 'Russia';
UPDATE European_client
       *
ERROR at line 1:
ORA-DDD: view WITH CHECK OPTION where-clause violation.
```

In this case, DDD stands for a manufacturer internal error. This error occurs because we are trying to change a row that is retrieved by the query. That is, if we update the corresponding row, the query can no longer retrieve it, since it will change the region_id from five to two. If we were not using the option WITH CHECK OPTION, we would have been able to update the view and its underlying table.

Solved Problems

8.1. Write the command to change the password of the user Jose Luis Fernandez (fernajol) from 1plummer82 to 3wnatasha2.

To change the password of this user, we need to issue the following command:

```
ALTER USER fernajol IDENTIFIED BY 3wnatasha2;
```

8.2. Create the user `acm123mca` with password `bnd26cufm`. Use the `user_data` and `temporary_data` tablespaces provided by P08, and provide to this user `10M` of storage space in `user_data` and `5M` of storage space in `temporary_data`.

The command to create this user using the tablespaces provided by P08 is as follows:

```
CREATE USER acm123mca IDENTIFIED BY bnd26cufm
DEFAULT TABLESPACE user_data
TEMPORARY TABLESPACE temporary_data
QUOTA 10M on user_data QUOTA 5M on temporary_data;
```

8.3. Create the role `role_tables and_views`.

The command to create this role is as follows:

```
CREATE ROLE role_tables_and_views;
```

8.4. Grant to the role of the previous question the privileges to connect to the database and the privileges to create tables and views.

The privilege to connect to the database is the CREATE SESSION. The privileges to create tables and views are CREATE TABLE and CREATE VIEW, respectively.

The command to grant these privileges to the given role is as follows:

```
GRANT create session, create table, create view
TO role_tables_and_views;
```

8.5. Grant the role of the previous question to the users `fernajol` and `acm123mca`. After granting the role to these two users, what will they be able to do?

```
GRANT role_tables_and_views TO fernajol, acm123mca;
```

Both users can connect to the database and be able to create tables and views.

8.6. The users `fernajol` and `acm123mca` do not have SELECT privileges on the tables S_INVENTORY and S_ITEM that were created by the user `scott`. Write the command that would allow `scott` to grant these users SELECT privileges on these two tables.

The user `scott` would have to issue the following commands to allow these two users to do selections on the given tables:

```
GRANT select ON s_inventory TO fernajol, acm123mca;
                        and
GRANT select ON s_item TO fernajol, acm123mca;
```

8.7. User `fernajol` has been transferred and no longer needs the privileges that were granted to him through the role `role_tables_and_views`. Make sure that he can no longer create tables and views or have access to the tables of the previous question. However, user `fernajol` should still be able to connect to the database. Write the command to accomplish these tasks.

The following commands revoke the privileges mentioned above from the user fernajol:

```
REVOKE select ON scott.s_inventory FROM fernajol;
REVOKE select ON scott.s_item FROM fernajol;
REVOKE create table, create view FROM fernajol;
```

8.8. Assume that the user `fernajol` finished all his tasks and has moved to another company. Since the objects that he created are no longer of any use, write the command that allows the DBA to remove this user and all his objects.

The corresponding command is as follows:

```
DROP USER fernajol CASCADE;
```

Notice that to drop the user and his objects, the `CASCADE` option is necessary.

8.9. Assume that the DBA suspects that a person currently logged in may be an impostor impersonating the legal user `dulldns`. Is there any way to terminate the session of this person?

Yes, there is. However, before ending the session, the DBA needs to obtain some information such as the *session id* and the *serial number* of the user session. The DBA can obtain this information from the V$SESSION view. Following is a query to retrieve that information and its output:

```
SELECT sid,serial#,username FROM v$session;
     SID    SERIAL# USERNAME
--------- --------- ----------------------------
        1         1 dulldns
        2         3 scott
        .
        .
        9        11 SYSTEM
```

With this information, the DBA can kill the session by issuing the following command:

```
ALTER SYSTEM KILL SESSION '1,1';
```

8.10. As a user, how can I find out the default and temporary tablespaces to which I have been assigned?

The data dictionary view that allows any user to find out this information is USER_USERS. This view, in addition to the previous information, informs the user about his or her user ID, and the time the account was created.

Supplementary Problems

8.11. Change the password of user Danielle Armstrong (`armstdan`) from `burg8two` to `1span2nts`.

8.12. How do we delete a view?

8.13. Create the user `gomezlila` with password `titus2`. Use the tablespaces `user_data` and `temporay_data` provided by PO8. Assign to this user `12M` of storage in `user_data` and `6M` of storage in `temporary_data`.

8.14. Create the role `role_tables`.

8.15. Grant to the role of the previous question the privileges to connect to the database and the privileges to create tables only.

8.16. Grant the role of the previous question to the users `math7gnm` and `halmat14`.

8.17. Allow the users `math7gnm` and `halmat14` to have SELECT privileges on the S_WAREHOUSE and S_REGION tables created by user `scott`.

8.18. Revoke all the privileges granted to `math7gnm`.

8.19. Remove user `math7gnm` and all his objects from the database.

8.20. Can a user that is currently connected to the database be dropped?

Answers to Supplementary Problems

8.11.

```
ALTER user armstdan IDENTIFIED BY 1span2nts.
```

8.12. Like like most of the database objects, views can be deleted using the DROP command. The syntax of this command is very similar to that of dropping a table. For instance, to drop the view european_client, we can issue the following command:

```
DROP VIEW european_client;
```

Notice that it does not make sense to use the CASCADE option, because it is not possible to define integrity constraints on the view.

8.13.

```
CREATE USER gomezlila IDENTIFIED BY titus2
DEFAULT TABLESPACE user_data
TEMPORARY TABLESPACE temporary_data
QUOTA 12M on user_data QUOTA 6M on temporary_data;
```

8.14.

```
CREATE ROLE role_tables;
```

8.15.

```
GRANT create session, create table
TO role_tables;
```

8.16.

```
GRANT role_tables TO math7gnm, halmat14;
```

8.17.

```
GRANT select ON s_inventory TO math7gnm, halmat14;
                              and
GRANT select ON s_item TO math7gnm, halmat14;
```

8.18.

```
REVOKE create session FROM math7gnm;
REVOKE create table FROM math7gnm;
REVOKE select scott.s_warehouse FROM math7gnm;
REVOKE select scott.s_item FROM math7gnm;
```

8.19.

```
DROP USER math7gnm CASCADE;
```

8.20. No, a user that is currently logged in cannot be dropped. However, the DBA can kill his or her session and then drop the user.

APPENDIX A

Using Personal Oracle

What is Personal Oracle?

Personal Oracle is the PC version of the Oracle 8 database. Personal Oracle is a complete Relational Database Management System. Personal Oracle is bundled with a set of Oracle database administration tools such as the Personal Oracle 8 Navigator for Windows 95, Oracle backup and recovery tools, Oracle utilities, Oracle Objects for OLE, Oracle 8 ODBC driver, and the Oracle online documentation.

Where to get Personal Oracle?

You can download a 90-day free trial copy from the Oracle World Wide Web server at http://www.oracle.com, or you can order a trial copy from the same site for a small fee.

Main components

Although Personal Oracle has several administrative tools, we can create, access, and manipulate an Oracle database using SQL and the Oracle Corporation's proprietary interface, SQL*Plus.

Starting Personal Oracle

1. Click on *Start* on the Windows taskbar.
2. Click on *Oracle 8 Personal Edition*. On the submenu, click on *Start Database*. If you are required to enter a password, use the word ORACLE as the password.
3. Click on *Programs*
4. Click on *Oracle for Windows NT*.

5. Click on *SQL*Plus 8.0*. You should see the following log-on screen.

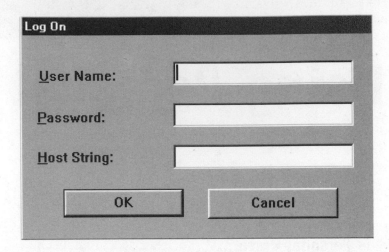

6. Enter SCOTT as the username and TIGER as the password. Do not type anything on the Host String field. You should be able to log in with the scott/tiger built-in account. However, should you experience any difficulty with that account, try using SYSTEM as the user name and MANAGER as the password.

Note: You can combine both steps by entering scott/tiger or system/manager in the user name box.

7. If successful, you should see the following screen. Notice that only portion of the screen is shown.

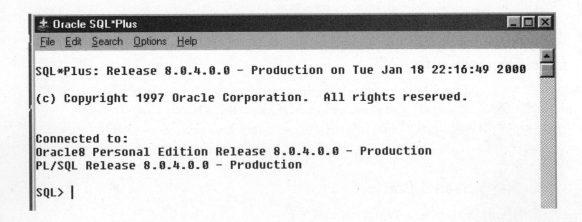

8. You are now ready to start working with SQL*Plus. In this appendix, we will refer to the prompt SQL> as the "sequel" prompt.

9. To exit SQL*Plus at any time, type EXIT.

The editor within SQL*Plus is a line editor. That is, you can only edit the "current" line. In SQL*Plus, the current line is indicated by an *. The instructions typed by a user are stored in a temporary storage area or buffer. The buffer holds only one complete instruction. To display the contents of the buffer at any one time, the user needs to type list or l at the sequel prompt. To execute the instruction in the buffer, type a forward slash at the sequel prompt and press the Enter key. The following sections illustrate some of the basic actions that you can perform with this editor.

Adding a New Line to the Buffer

To add a new line to the current buffer, it is necessary to insert first a new line at the proper place in the buffer. Lines are inserted by typing i or I at the sequel prompt and pressing the Enter key. This puts the user in "input" mode. The user can then continue typing until he or she decides to exit the input mode by pressing the Enter key twice in a row. The reader should be aware that new lines are always inserted *after* the current line. To make any line of the buffer the current line, the user needs to type the corresponding line number after the sequel prompt. The current line in the buffer is always preceded by an *.

In the section of code shown below, let's assume that we need to add the clause **WHERE sal > 1000** *after* the FROM emp clause:

```
SQL > list
1   SELECT empno, ename
2* FROM emp
```

Since the current line is the last line, there is no need to type a line number. To insert a new line, we type I or i. The system responds as follows:

```
SQL > list
1   SELECT empno, ename
2* FROM emp
SQL > i
3
```

After typing the missing clause and pressing Enter, the system responds by adding another line, as shown below. Press the Enter key again to exit the insert mode.

```
SQL > list
1   SELECT empno, ename
2* FROM emp
SQL > i
3    WHERE sal > 1000
4
SQL >
```

We can verify that the new line has been entered correctly by typing **L** to display the current content of the buffer.

Changing Characters in the Current Line

To change a character or sequence of characters in the current line, use the command at the sequel prompt. This command can take either of the following forms:

$$Change\ /old\text{-}value/new\text{-}value/$$

or

$$C\ /old\text{-}value/new\text{-}value/$$

where `old-value` is the character or sequence of characters in the current line that we want to change and `new-value` is the character or sequence of characters with which we want to replace the `old-value`. The following example illustrates the use of this command.

Assume that the `empno` attribute was misspelled in the command that follows:

```
SQL > list
1  SELECT emno, ename   ◄————   This line has an error
2* FROM emp   ◄————   Current line
SQL >
```

Since the error occurred in line number 1 of the buffer, it is necessary to make this line the current line of the buffer. Therefore, at the sequel prompt we type 1 and press the Enter key. The sequence of commands to correct this error is as follows:

```
SQL > list
1  SELECT emno, ename   ◄————   Need to make this line the current line
2* FROM emp
SQL > 1
1* SELECT emno, ename   ◄————   This * indicates that this line is the current line.
SQL > c /m/mp/   ◄————   This command changes the first occurrence of the letter m by the
                         letters mp.
1 * SELECT empno, ename
SQL > /   ◄————   Use a / to execute the command currently stored in the buffer.
```

The CHANGE command replaces the first occurrence of the letter m by the letters mp. The user can display the entire buffer by typing 1 or L; he or she can then execute the command by typing / at the sequel prompt.

Appending Character to the End of Line

To append a character or sequences of characters to the end of the current line, use the Append command at the sequel prompt. The syntax is as follows:

APPEND character-sequence

or

A character-sequence

Assume that we need to add the attribute JOB to the SELECT clause of the previous example. If line 1 is already the current line, the APPEND command to accomplish this may look as follows:

```
1 * SELECT empno, ename

SQL > A , job    ◄──────  APPEND command

1* SELECT empno, ename, job  ◄──────  Attribute job has been added to the end
                                        of the current line.
```

Users who are not accustomed to working with line editors can use tools such as Notepad to write the SQL commands and then copy and paste them into SQL*Plus. Alternatively, the user can instruct SQL*Plus to use his or her editor of choice as default by issuing the following command:

DEFINE_EDITOR = full-path-to-editor

If the user wants to use the Notepad editor, then he or she can issue the following command:

DEFINE_EDITOR = NOTEPAD

To use the editor at any one time, the user should type EDIT at the sequel prompt. The user can copy and paste commands either from the SQL*Plus environment to NOTEPAD or vice versa.

Controlling the Session Environment

The behavior of the SQL*Plus environment can be controlled by setting the appropriate system variables. Any system variable can be set using the following syntax:

SET system-variable = new-value

Table A-1 shows a partial list of the most common system variables. The user can view the entire list of system variables by typing SHOW ALL at the sequel prompt. To view the settings of a particular variable, the user can use the following command:

```
SHOW system-variable.
```

Table A-1.   Partial list of system variables.

System Variable	Description	Example
FEEDBACK n	Notifies the user when a query or report returns a minimum of n rows. This variable can be set to ON or OFF. Default value is 6.	SET FEEDBACK 10 Notifies the user when a minimum of 10 rows.
PAUSE *text*	Displays *text* after a full screen of output as a result of a query or report.	SET PAUSE continue
PAUSE ON | OFF	Make screen display stop in between pages of display. If PAUSE has text display it.	SET PAUSE ON
PAGESIZE	Determines the number of lines per page. Default value is 80.	SET PAGE 24
LINESIZE	Determines the characters per line.	SET LINESIZE 60
UNDERLINE	Default character to separate column headings from column values.	SET UNDERLINE '*' Use an * to separate column headings from column values.

Executing Scripts Files

A text file that contains SQL or a combination of SQL and SQL*Plus is called a *script file*. To execute the statements contained in script file SG.SQL located in drive A, we can use either of the following commands:

```
START "a:SG.sql"
```

or

```
@"a:SG.sql"
```

Saving the Content of the Buffer to a File

To save the content of the buffer to a file, use the following command:

```
SAVE filename [REPLACE]
```

The option REPLACE should be used to replace the content of an existing file. If the file does not exist, this option creates a new filename. If the user does not specify any extension in the filename, Oracle creates the file with an .SQL extension.

Retrieving a File into the Buffer

To retrieve a file into the buffer, use the following command:

```
GET full-path-to-file filename
```

SQL Reserved Words

ACCESS	DEFAULT	INTEGER	OPTION	START
ADD	DELETE	INTERSECT	OR	SUCCESSFUL
ALL	DESC	INTO	ORDER	SYNONYM
ALTER	DISTINCT	IS	PCTFREE	SYSDATE
AND	DROP	LEVEL	PRIOR	TABLE
ANY	ELSE	LIKE	PRIVILEGES	THEN
AS	EXCLUSIVE	LOCK	PUBLIC	TO
ASC	EXISTS	LONG	RAW	TRIGGER
AUDIT	FILE	MAXEXTENTS	RENAME	UID
BETWEEN	FLOAT	MINUS	RESOURCE	UNION
BY	FOR	MODE	REVOKE	UNIQUE
CHAR	FROM	MODIFY	ROW	UPDATE
CHECK	GRANT	NOAUDIT	ROWID	USER
CLUSTER	GROUP	NOCOMPRESS	ROWLABEL	VALIDATE
COLUMN	HAVING	NOT	ROWNUM	VALUES
COMMENT	IDENTIFIED	NOWAIT	ROWS	VARCHAR
COMPRESS	IMMEDIATE	NULL	SELECT	VARCHAR2
CONNECT	IN	NUMBER	SESSION	VIEW
CREATE	INCREMENT	OF	SET	WHENEVER
CURRENT	INDEX	OFFLINE	SHARE	WHERE
DATE	INITIAL	ON	SIZE	WITH
DECIMAL	INSERT	ONLINE	SMALLINT	

Syntax Diagrams of a Subset of SQL

`expr ::=`

Possible expressions denoted by "expr" in the following syntax diagrams.

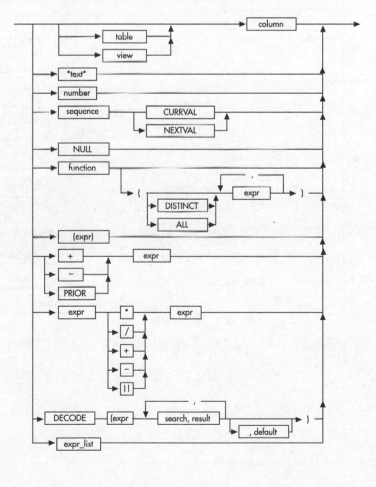

`expr_list ::=`

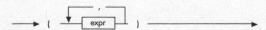

```
condition ::=
```

Possible conditions denoted by `condition` in following syntax diagrams.

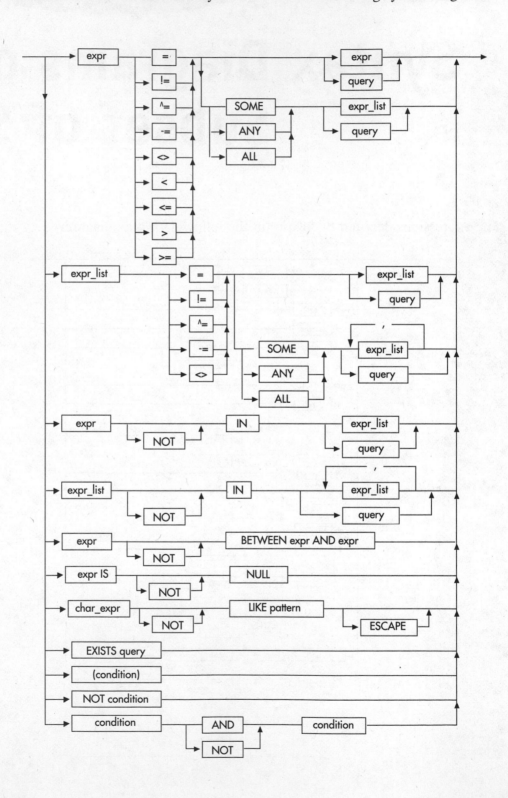

ALTER ROLE

Changes the authorization needed to enable a role.

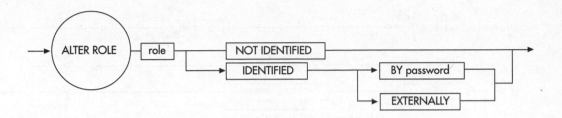

ALTER SEQUENCE

Redefines an existing sequence.

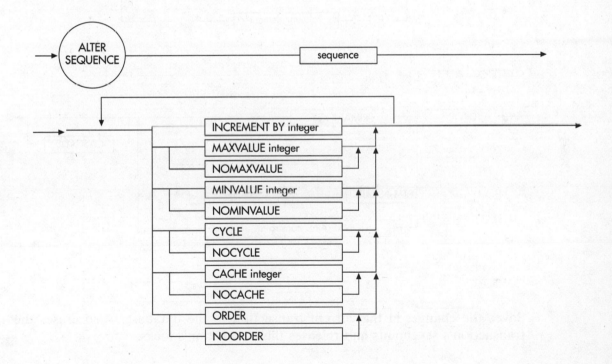

ALTER TABLE

Redefines the columns, constraints, or storage allocations of an existing table.

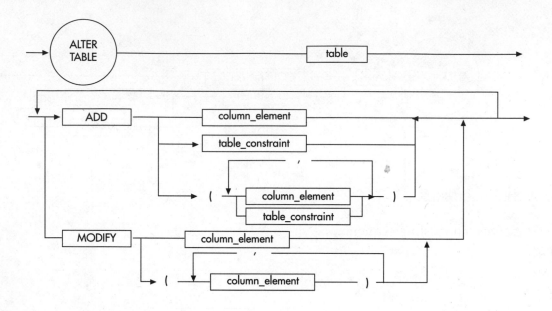

drop_clause ::=

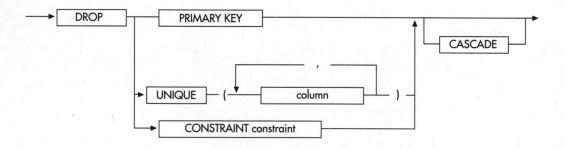

COMMIT

Saves the changes in the current transaction to the database. Also erases the transaction's savepoints and releases the transaction's locks.

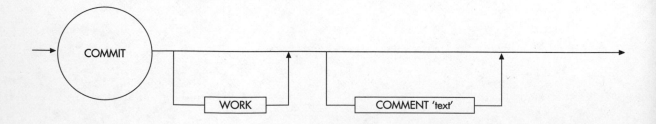

CREATE INDEX

Creates a new index on the specified columns in a table or cluster.

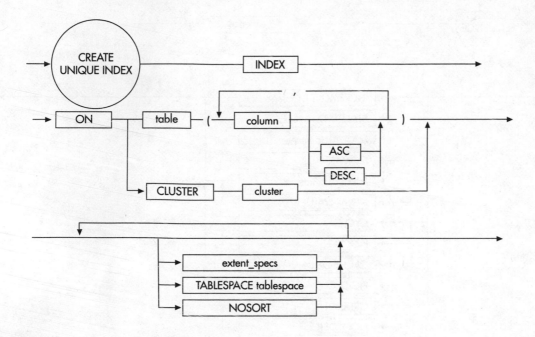

CREATE ROLE

Creates a security role.

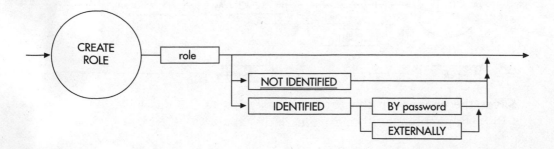

CREATE SEQUENCE

Creates a new sequence suitable for generation of primary keys.

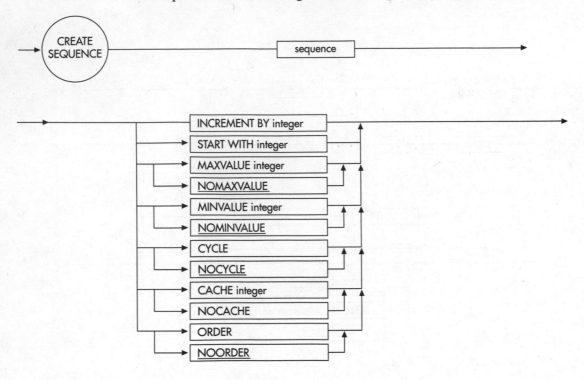

CREATE SYNONYM

Creates a new synonym for a table, view, sequence, or for another synonym.

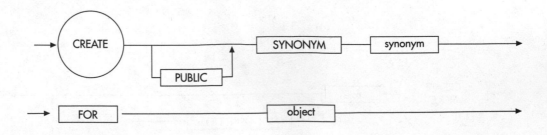

CREATE TABLE

Creates a new table, defining its columns, constraints, and storage.

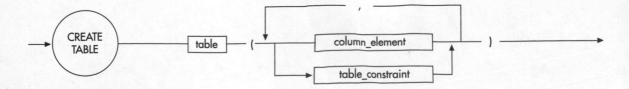

column_element ::=

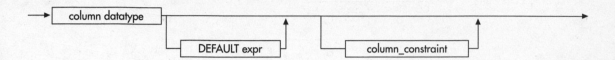

column_constraint ::=

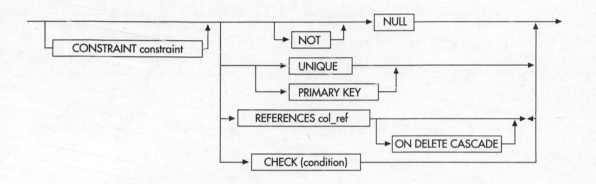

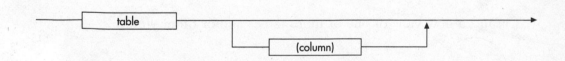

col_ref ::=

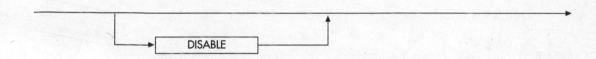

integrity_constraint ::=

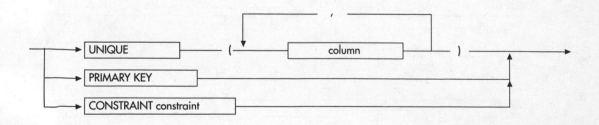

`table_constraint ::=`

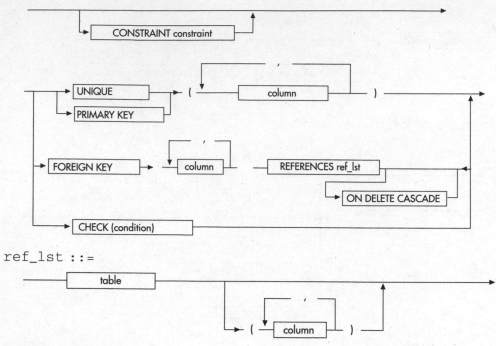

`ref_lst ::=`

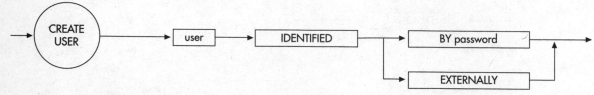

CREATE USER

Defines a database user.

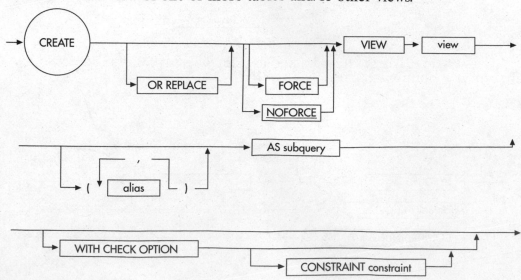

CREATE VIEW

Creates a new view of one or more tables and/or other views.

DELETE

Removes rows from a table or view that meets the WHERE condition.
Removes all rows if no WHERE clause is specified.

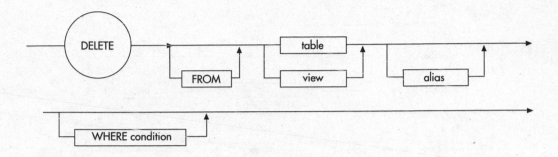

DROP

Removes objects and constraints from the database. The appropriate privileges
are required for the action.

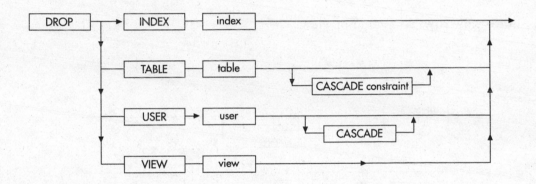

GRANT (System Privileges and Roles)

Gives system privileges to users and to roles. Gives roles to users and other
roles.

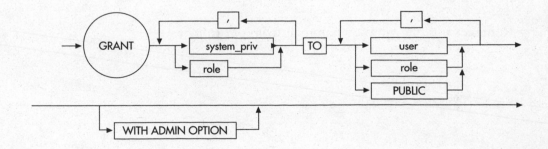

GRANT (Object Privileges)

Gives privileges for a particular object (a table, view, synonym, package, procedure, etc.) to users and to roles.

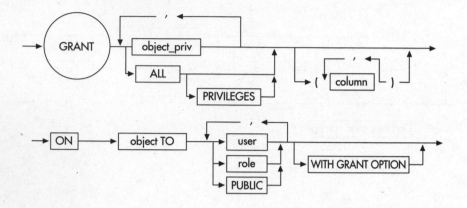

INSERT

Adds new rows to a table or view.

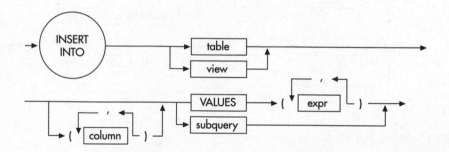

RENAME

Renames a table, view, or synonym from *old* to *new*.

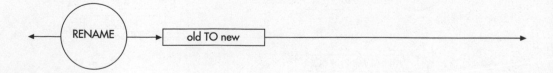

REVOKE (System Privileges and Roles)

Revokes system privileges and roles from users and from roles. Reverses the
action of the GRANT (System Privileges and Roles) command.

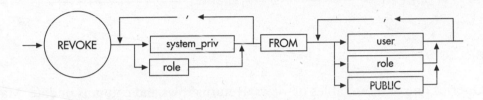

REVOKE (Object Privileges)

Revokes object privileges from users and from roles. Reverses the action of the
GRANT (Object Privileges) command.

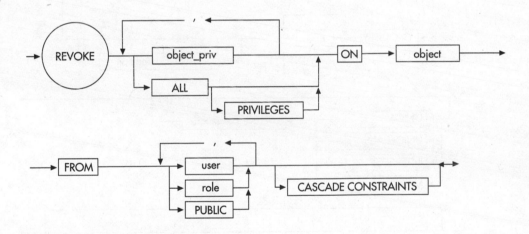

ROLLBACK (Transaction Control)

Undoes all changes made since the savepoint. Undoes all changes in the current
transaction if no savepoint is specified.

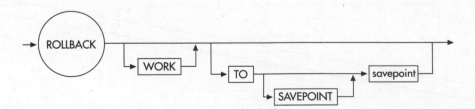

SAVEPOINT (Transaction Control)

Identifies a savepoint in the current transaction to which changes can be rolled back.

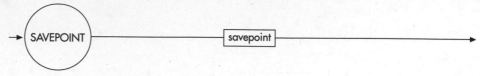

SELECT

Queries one or more tables or views. Returns rows and columns of data. May be used as statement or as a subquery in another statement.

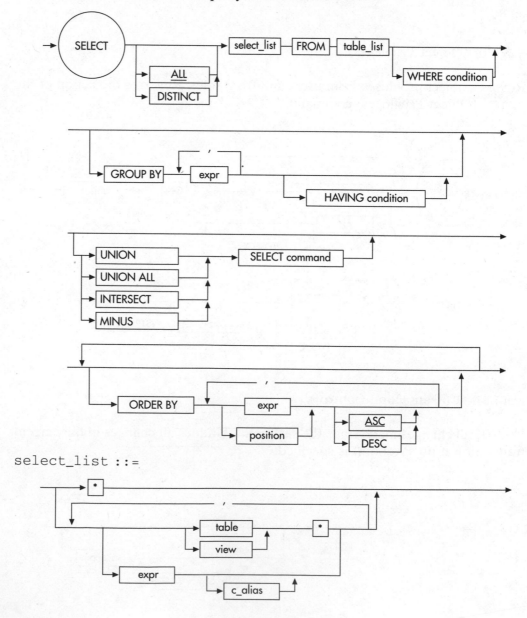

select_list ::=

`table_list ::=`

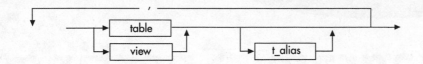

`update_list ::=`

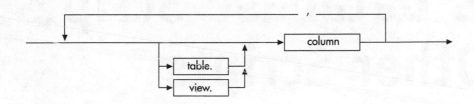

TRUNCATE

Removes all rows from a table or cluster.

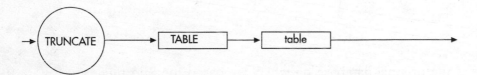

UPDATE

Changes the values of columns in rows that meet the WHERE condition in a table or view. Changes all rows if no WHERE condition is specified.

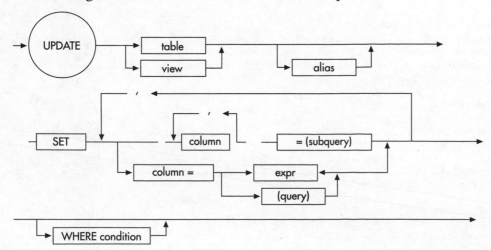

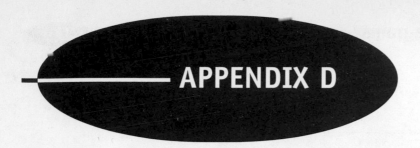

E-R Diagram, Sporting Goods Database Scripts, and Other Scripts

This is the original database on which we based the Sporting Goods database. We have adapted these tables to fit the scope of this book. The tables may be downloaded free of charge from http://www.cs.jmu.edu/sqldata. This E-R diagram is reproduced with permission of Oracle Corporation.

```
Rem Sporting Goods Database
Rem
Rem
Rem SCRIPT - FUNCTION
Rem Create and populate tables and sequences to support the Sporting Goods business
scenario.
Rem This database is a modified version of the database used in some of the classes of
Rem the ORACLE Corporation.
Rem
Rem NOTES
Rem
Rem MODIFIED
Rem Originally created: GDURHAM Mar 15, 1993 -- ORACLE Corporation
Rem
Rem Modified and reprinted with permission from The ORACLE Corporation
Rem by Drs. Ramon A. Mata-Toledo and Pauline K. Cushman on Dec 15, 1999.

set feedback off
Rem if your are using Oracle 7 change the next statement to set compativility v7
set compatibility v8
```

The Summit Sporting Goods ER Diagram

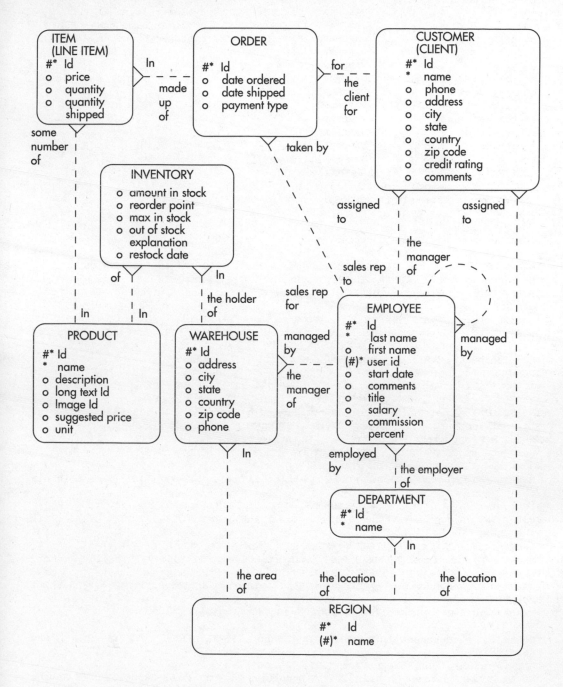

Rem Start of the creation and population of tables. Please wait.

prompt
prompt creating table s_customer

Rem*************** S_CUSTOMER TABLE *********************************
Rem**

```
DROP TABLE s_customer CASCADE CONSTRAINTS;
CREATE TABLE s_customer
(id                        VARCHAR2(3)   CONSTRAINT s_customer_id_nn NOT NULL,
 name                      VARCHAR2(20)  CONSTRAINT s_customer_name_nn NOT NULL,
 phone                     VARCHAR2(20)  CONSTRAINT s_customer_phone_nn NOT NULL,
 address                   VARCHAR2(20),
 city                      VARCHAR2(20),
 state                     VARCHAR2(15),
 country                   VARCHAR2(20),
 zip_code                  VARCHAR2(15),
 credit_rating             VARCHAR2(9),
 sales_rep_id              VARCHAR2(3),
 region_id                 VARCHAR2(3),
 comments                  VARCHAR2(255),
 CONSTRAINT s_customer_id_pk PRIMARY KEY (id),
 CONSTRAINT s_customer_credit_rating_ck
 CHECK (credit_rating IN ('EXCELLENT', 'GOOD', 'POOR'))
);

prompt populating table s_customer

INSERT INTO s_customer VALUES ('301', 'Sports,Inc', '540-123-4567','72 High St',
'Harrisonburg', 'VA','US', '22809','EXCELLENT', '12', '1', NULL);
INSERT INTO s_customer VALUES ('302', 'Toms Sporting Goods', '540-987-6543','6741
Main St',
'Harrisonburg', 'VA','US', '22809','POOR', '14', '1', NULL);
INSERT INTO s_customer VALUES ('303', 'Athletic Attire', '540-123-6789','54 Market
St',
'Harrisonburg', 'VA','US', '22808','GOOD', '14', '1', NULL);
INSERT INTO s_customer
VALUES ('304', 'Athletics For All', '540-987-1234','286 Main St', 'Harrisonburg',
'VA', 'US', '22808','EXCELLENT', '12', '1', NULL);
INSERT INTO s_customer VALUES ('305', 'Shoes for Sports', '540-123-9876','538 High
St','Harrisonburg', 'VA','US', '22809','EXCELLENT', '14', '1', NULL);
INSERT INTO s_customer VALUES ('306', 'BJ Athletics', '540-987-9999','632 Water St',
'Harrisonburg', 'VA','US', '22810','POOR', '12', '1', NULL);

INSERT INTO s_customer VALUES ('403', 'Athletics One', '717-234-6786','912 Columbia
Rd',
'Lancaster', 'PA','US', '17601','GOOD', '14', '1', NULL);
INSERT INTO s_customer VALUES ('404', 'Great Athletes', '717-987-2341','121 Litiz
Pike',
'Lancaster', 'PA','US', '17602','EXCELLENT', '12', '1', NULL);
INSERT INTO s_customer VALUES ('405', 'Athletics Two', '717-987-9875','435 High Rd',
'Lancaster', 'PA','US', '17602','EXCELLENT', '14', '1', NULL);
INSERT INTO s_customer VALUES ('406', 'Athletes Attic', '717-234-9888','101
Greenfield Rd',
'Lancaster', 'PA','US', '17601','POOR', '12', '1', NULL);

INSERT INTO s_customer VALUES ('201', 'One Sport', '55-112066222','82 Via Bahia', 'Sao
Paolo',
NULL, 'Brazil', NULL,'EXCELLENT', '12', '2', NULL);
INSERT INTO s_customer VALUES ('202', 'Deportivo Caracas', '58-28066222','31 Sabana
Grande',
'Caracas', NULL, 'Venezuela', NULL,'EXCELLENT', '12', '2', NULL);
INSERT INTO s_customer VALUES ('203', 'New Delhi Sports', '91-11903338','11368
Chanakya',
'New Delhi', NULL, 'India', NULL,'GOOD', '11', '4', NULL);
INSERT INTO s_customer VALUES ('204', 'Ladysport', '1-206-104-0111','281 Queen
Street',
'Seattle', 'Washington', 'US', NULL,'EXCELLENT', '11', '1', NULL);
```

```
INSERT INTO s_customer VALUES ('205', 'Kim''s Sporting Goods', '852-3693888','15 Henessey Road',
'Hong Kong', NULL, NULL, NULL,'EXCELLENT', '11', '4', NULL);
INSERT INTO s_customer VALUES ('206', 'Sportique', '33-93425722253','172 Rue de Place',
'Cannes', NULL, 'France', NULL,'EXCELLENT', '13', '5', NULL);
INSERT INTO s_customer VALUES ('207', 'Tall Rock Sports', '234-16036222','10 Saint Antoine',
'Lagos', NULL, 'Nigeria', NULL,'GOOD', NULL, '3', NULL);
INSERT INTO s_customer VALUES ('208', 'Muench Sports', '49-895274449','435 Gruenestrasse',
'Munich', NULL, 'Germany', NULL,'GOOD', '13', '5', NULL);

INSERT INTO s_customer VALUES ('209', 'Beisbol Si!', '809-352666','415 Playa Del Mar',
'San Pedro de Macoris', NULL, 'Dominican Republic', NULL, 'EXCELLENT', '11', '6', NULL);
INSERT INTO s_customer VALUES ('210', 'Futbol Sonora', '52-404555','5 Via Saguaro', 'Nogales',
NULL, 'Mexico', NULL,'EXCELLENT', '12', '2', NULL);
INSERT INTO s_customer VALUES ('211', 'Helmut''s Sports', '42-2111222','45 Modrany', 'Prague',
NULL, 'Czechoslovakia', NULL,'EXCELLENT', '11', '5', NULL);
INSERT INTO s_customer VALUES ('212', 'Hamada Sport', '20-31209222','47A Corniche',
'Alexandria', NULL, 'Egypt', NULL,'EXCELLENT', '13', '3', NULL);
INSERT INTO s_customer VALUES ('213', 'Sports Emporium', '1-415-555-6281','4783 168th Street',
'San Francisco', 'CA', 'US', NULL,'EXCELLENT', '11', '1', NULL);
INSERT INTO s_customer VALUES ('214', 'Sports Retail', '1-716-555-7777','115 Main Street',
'Buffalo', 'NY', 'US', NULL, 'POOR', '11', '1', NULL);
INSERT INTO s_customer VALUES ('215', 'Sporta Russia', '7-0953892444','7070 Yekatamina',
'Saint Petersburg', NULL, 'Russia', NULL,'POOR', '11', '5', NULL);
COMMIT;

prompt Finished populating the s_customer table - processing continues
prompt

prompt creating table s_dept
Rem************* S_CUSTOMER TABLE *******************************
Rem******************************************************************

DROP TABLE s_dept CASCADE CONSTRAINTS;
CREATE TABLE s_dept
(id          VARCHAR2(3)  CONSTRAINT s_dept_id_nn NOT NULL,
 name        VARCHAR2(20) CONSTRAINT s_dept_name_nn NOT NULL,
 region_id   VARCHAR2(3),
 CONSTRAINT s_dept_id_pk PRIMARY KEY (id),
 CONSTRAINT s_dept_name_region_id_uk UNIQUE (name, region_id)
);

prompt populating table s_dept

INSERT INTO s_dept VALUES ('10', 'Finance', '1');
INSERT INTO s_dept VALUES ('31', 'Sales', '1');
INSERT INTO s_dept VALUES ('32', 'Sales', '2');
INSERT INTO s_dept VALUES ('33', 'Sales', '3');
INSERT INTO s_dept VALUES ('34', 'Sales', '4');
INSERT INTO s_dept VALUES ('35', 'Sales', '5');
INSERT INTO s_dept VALUES ('41', 'Operations', '1');
```

```
INSERT INTO s_dept VALUES ('42', 'Operations', '2');
INSERT INTO s_dept VALUES ('43', 'Operations', '3');
INSERT INTO s_dept VALUES ('44', 'Operations', '4');
INSERT INTO s_dept VALUES ('45', 'Operations', '5');
INSERT INTO s_dept VALUES ('50', 'Administration', '1');
COMMIT;

prompt Finished populating the s_dept table - processing continues
prompt

prompt creating table s_emp
Rem************** S_TEMP TABLE *******************************
Rem****************************************************************

DROP TABLE s_emp CASCADE CONSTRAINTS;
CREATE TABLE s_emp
(id              VARCHAR2(3)  CONSTRAINT s_emp_id_nn NOT NULL,
 last_name       VARCHAR2(20) CONSTRAINT s_emp_last_name_nn NOT NULL,
 first_name      VARCHAR2(20),
 userid          VARCHAR2(8) CONSTRAINT s_emp_userid_nn NOT NULL,
 start_date      DATE CONSTRAINT s_emp_start_date_nn NOT NULL,
 comments        VARCHAR2(255),
 manager_id      VARCHAR2(3),
 title           VARCHAR2(25),
 dept_id         VARCHAR2(3),
 salary          NUMBER(11, 2),
 commission_pct  NUMBER(4, 2),
 CONSTRAINT s_emp_id_pk PRIMARY KEY (id),
 CONSTRAINT s_emp_userid_uk UNIQUE (userid),
 CONSTRAINT s_emp_commission_pct_ck CHECK (commission_pct IN (10, 12.5, 15, 17.5,
 20))
);

prompt populating table s_emp

INSERT INTO s_emp VALUES ('1', 'Martin','Carmen','martincu',TO_DATE('03-MAR-
1990','DD-MON-YYYY'), NULL,NULL, 'President', '50', 4500, NULL);
INSERT INTO s_emp VALUES ('2','Smith','Doris','smithdj',TO_DATE('08-MAR-1990','DD-
MON-YYYY'),NULL,'1', 'VP, Operations','41', 2450,NULL);
INSERT INTO s_emp VALUES ('3', 'Norton','Michael','nortonma',TO_DATE('17-JUN-
1991','DD-MON-YYYY'),NULL,'1', 'VP, Sales', '31', 2400,NULL);
INSERT INTO s_emp VALUES ('4', 'Quentin', 'Mark','quentiml',TO_DATE('07-APR-
1990','DD-MON-YYYY'),NULL,'1', 'VP, Finance', '10', 2450, NULL);
INSERT INTO s_emp VALUES ('5', 'Roper', 'Joseph','roperjm',TO_DATE('04-MAR-
1990','DD-MON-YYYY'),NULL,'1', 'VP, Administration', '50', 2550, NULL);
INSERT INTO s_emp VALUES ('6', 'Brown', 'Molly','brownmr',TO_DATE('18-JAN-
1991','DD-MON-YYYY'),NULL,'2', 'Warehouse Manager', '41', 1600, NULL);
INSERT INTO s_emp VALUES ('7', 'Hawkins', 'Roberta','hawkinrt',TO_DATE('14-MAY-
1990','DD-MON-YYYY'),NULL,'2', 'Warehouse Manager','42', 1650, NULL);
INSERT INTO s_emp VALUES ('8', 'Burns', 'Ben','burnsba',TO_DATE('07-APR-1990','DD-
MON-YYYY'),NULL,'2', 'Warehouse Manager','43', 1500, NULL);

INSERT INTO s_emp VALUES ('9', 'Catskill', 'Antoinette','catskiaw',TO_DATE('09-FEB-
1992','DD-MON-YYYY'),NULL,'2', 'Warehouse Manager','44', 1700,NULL);
INSERT INTO s_emp VALUES ('10', 'Jackson', 'Marta','jacksomt',TO_DATE('27-FEB-
1991','DD-MON-YYYY'),NULL,'2', 'Warehouse Manager','45', 1507,NULL);
INSERT INTO s_emp VALUES ('11', 'Henderson', 'Colin','hendercs',TO_DATE('14-MAY-
1990','DD-MON-YYYY'),NULL,'3', 'Sales Representative', '31', 1400, 10);
INSERT INTO s_emp VALUES ('12', 'Gilson', 'Sam', 'gilsonsj',TO_DATE('18-JAN-
1992','DD-MON-YYYY'),NULL,'3', 'Sales Representative','32', 1490, 12.5);
INSERT INTO s_emp VALUES ('13', 'Sanders', 'Jason', 'sanderjk',TO_DATE('18-FEB-
```

```
1991','DD-MON-YYYY'),NULL,'3', 'Sales Representative','33', 1515, 10);
INSERT INTO s_emp VALUES ('14', 'Dameron', 'Andre', 'dameroap',TO_DATE('09-OCT-
1991','DD-MON-YYYY'),NULL,'3', 'Sales Representative','35', 1450, 17.5);
INSERT INTO s_emp VALUES ('15', 'Hardwick', 'Elaine', 'hardwiem',TO_DATE('07-FEB-
1992','DD-MON-YYYY'),NULL,'6', 'Stock Clerk','41', 1400, NULL);
INSERT INTO s_emp VALUES ('16', 'Brown', 'George', 'browngw',TO_DATE('08-MAR-
1990','DD-MON-YYYY'),NULL,'6', 'Stock Clerk','41', 940, NULL);

INSERT INTO s_emp VALUES ('17', 'Washington', 'Thomas', 'washintl',TO_DATE('09-FEB-
1991','DD-MON-YYYY'),NULL,'7', 'Stock Clerk', '42', 1200, NULL);
INSERT INTO s_emp VALUES ('18', 'Patterson', 'Donald', 'patterdv',TO_DATE('06-AUG-
1991','DD-MON-YYYY'),NULL,'7', 'Stock Clerk','42', 795, NULL);
INSERT INTO s_emp VALUES ('19', 'Bell', 'Alexander', 'bellag',TO_DATE('26-MAY-
1991','DD-MON-YYYY'),NULL,'8', 'Stock Clerk','43', 850, NULL);
INSERT INTO s_emp VALUES ('20', 'Gantos', 'Eddie', 'gantosej',TO_DATE('30-NOV-
1990','DD-MON-YYYY'),NULL,'9', 'Stock Clerk','44', 800, NULL);
INSERT INTO s_emp VALUES ('21', 'Stephenson', 'Blaine', 'stephebs',TO_DATE('17-MAR-
1991','DD-MON-YYYY'),NULL,'10', 'Stock Clerk','45', 860, NULL);

INSERT INTO s_emp VALUES ('22', 'Chester', 'Eddie', 'chesteek',TO_DATE('30-NOV-
1990','DD-MON-YYYY'), NULL, '9', 'Stock Clerk','44', 800, NULL);
INSERT INTO s_emp VALUES ('23', 'Pearl', 'Roger', 'pearlrg',TO_DATE('17-OCT-
1990','DD-MON-YYYY'), NULL, '9', 'Stock Clerk','34', 795, NULL);
INSERT INTO s_emp VALUES ('24', 'Dancer', 'Bonnie', 'dancerbw',TO_DATE('17-MAR-
1991','DD-MON-YYYY'), NULL, '7', 'Stock Clerk','45', 860, NULL);
INSERT INTO s_emp VALUES ('25', 'Schmitt', 'Sandra', 'schmitss',TO_DATE('09-MAY-
1991','DD-MON-YYYY'), NULL, '8', 'Stock Clerk','45', 1100, NULL);
COMMIT;

prompt Finished populating the s_emp table - processing continues
prompt

prompt creating table s_inventory
Rem************* S_INVENTORY TABLE *******************************
Rem****************************************************************

DROP TABLE s_inventory CASCADE CONSTRAINTS;
CREATE TABLE s_inventory
(product_id              VARCHAR2(7)  CONSTRAINT  s_inventory_product_id_nn  NOT
                                      NULL,
 warehouse_id            VARCHAR2(7)  CONSTRAINT s_inventory_warehouse_id_nn NOT
                                      NULL,
 amount_in_stock         NUMBER(9),
 reorder_point           NUMBER(9),
 max_in_stock            NUMBER(9),
 out_of_stock_explanation VARCHAR2(255),
 restock_date            DATE,
 CONSTRAINT s_inventory_prodid_warid_pk PRIMARY KEY (product_id, warehouse_id)
 );

prompt populating table s_inventory

INSERT INTO s_inventory VALUES ('10011', '101', 650, 625, 1100, NULL, NULL);
INSERT INTO s_inventory VALUES ('10012', '101', 600, 560, 1000, NULL, NULL);
INSERT INTO s_inventory VALUES ('10013', '101', 400, 400, 700, NULL, NULL);
INSERT INTO s_inventory VALUES ('10021', '101', 500, 425, 740, NULL, NULL);
INSERT INTO s_inventory VALUES ('10022', '101', 300, 200, 350, NULL, NULL);
INSERT INTO s_inventory VALUES ('10023', '101', 400, 300, 525, NULL, NULL);
INSERT INTO s_inventory VALUES ('20106', '101', 993, 625, 1000, NULL, NULL);
INSERT INTO s_inventory VALUES ('20108', '101', 700, 700, 1225, NULL, NULL);
INSERT INTO s_inventory VALUES ('20201', '101', 802, 800, 1400, NULL, NULL);
```

```
INSERT INTO s_inventory VALUES ('20510', '101', 1389, 850, 1400, NULL, NULL);
INSERT INTO s_inventory VALUES ('20512', '101', 850, 850, 1450, NULL, NULL);
INSERT INTO s_inventory VALUES ('30321', '101', 2000, 1500, 2500, NULL, NULL);
INSERT INTO s_inventory VALUES ('30326', '101', 2100, 2000, 3500, NULL, NULL);
INSERT INTO s_inventory VALUES ('30421', '101', 1822, 1800, 3150, NULL, NULL);
INSERT INTO s_inventory VALUES ('30426', '101', 2250, 2000, 3500, NULL, NULL);
INSERT INTO s_inventory VALUES ('30433', '101', 650, 600, 1050, NULL, NULL);
INSERT INTO s_inventory VALUES ('32779', '101', 2120, 1250, 2200, NULL, NULL);
INSERT INTO s_inventory VALUES ('32861', '101', 505, 500, 875, NULL, NULL);
INSERT INTO s_inventory VALUES ('40421', '101', 578, 350, 600, NULL, NULL);
INSERT INTO s_inventory VALUES ('40422', '101', 0, 350, 600, 'Phenomenal sales...',
'08-FEB-93');
INSERT INTO s_inventory VALUES ('41010', '101', 250, 250, 437, NULL, NULL);
INSERT INTO s_inventory VALUES ('41020', '101', 471, 450, 750, NULL, NULL);
INSERT INTO s_inventory VALUES ('41050', '101', 501, 450, 750, NULL, NULL);
INSERT INTO s_inventory VALUES ('41080', '101', 400, 400, 700, NULL, NULL);
INSERT INTO s_inventory VALUES ('41100', '101', 350, 350, 600, NULL, NULL);
INSERT INTO s_inventory VALUES ('50169', '101', 2530, 1500, 2600, NULL, NULL);
INSERT INTO s_inventory VALUES ('50273', '101', 233, 200, 350, NULL, NULL);
INSERT INTO s_inventory VALUES ('50417', '101', 518, 500, 875, NULL, NULL);
INSERT INTO s_inventory VALUES ('50418', '101', 244, 100, 275, NULL, NULL);
INSERT INTO s_inventory VALUES ('50419', '101', 230, 120, 310, NULL, NULL);
INSERT INTO s_inventory VALUES ('50530', '101', 669, 400, 700, NULL, NULL);
INSERT INTO s_inventory VALUES ('50532', '101', 0, 100, 175, 'Wait for Spring.',
'12-APR-93');
INSERT INTO s_inventory VALUES ('50536', '101', 173, 100, 175, NULL, NULL);
INSERT INTO s_inventory VALUES ('20106', '201', 220, 150, 260, NULL, NULL);
INSERT INTO s_inventory VALUES ('20108', '201', 166, 150, 260, NULL, NULL);
INSERT INTO s_inventory VALUES ('20201', '201', 320, 200, 350, NULL, NULL);
INSERT INTO s_inventory VALUES ('20510', '201', 175, 100, 175, NULL, NULL);
INSERT INTO s_inventory VALUES ('20512', '201', 162, 100, 175, NULL, NULL);
INSERT INTO s_inventory VALUES ('30321', '201', 96, 80, 140, NULL, NULL);
INSERT INTO s_inventory VALUES ('30326', '201', 147, 120, 210, NULL, NULL);
INSERT INTO s_inventory VALUES ('30421', '201', 102, 80, 140, NULL, NULL);
INSERT INTO s_inventory VALUES ('30426', '201', 200, 120, 210, NULL, NULL);
INSERT INTO s_inventory VALUES ('30433', '201', 130, 130, 230, NULL, NULL);
INSERT INTO s_inventory VALUES ('32779', '201', 180, 150, 260, NULL, NULL);
INSERT INTO s_inventory VALUES ('32861', '201', 132, 80, 140, NULL, NULL);
INSERT INTO s_inventory VALUES ('50169', '201', 225, 220, 385, NULL, NULL);
INSERT INTO s_inventory VALUES ('50273', '201', 75, 60, 100, NULL, NULL);
INSERT INTO s_inventory VALUES ('50417', '201', 82, 60, 100, NULL, NULL);
INSERT INTO s_inventory VALUES ('50418', '201', 98, 60, 100, NULL, NULL);
INSERT INTO s_inventory VALUES ('50419', '201', 77, 60, 100, NULL, NULL);
INSERT INTO s_inventory VALUES ('50530', '201', 62, 60, 100, NULL, NULL);
INSERT INTO s_inventory VALUES ('50532', '201', 67, 60, 100, NULL, NULL);
INSERT INTO s_inventory VALUES ('50536', '201', 97, 60, 100, NULL, NULL);
INSERT INTO s_inventory VALUES ('20510', '301', 69, 40, 100, NULL, NULL);
INSERT INTO s_inventory VALUES ('20512', '301', 28, 20, 50, NULL, NULL);
INSERT INTO s_inventory VALUES ('30321', '301', 85, 80, 140, NULL, NULL);
INSERT INTO s_inventory VALUES ('30421', '301', 102, 80, 140, NULL, NULL);
INSERT INTO s_inventory VALUES ('30433', '301', 35, 20, 35, NULL, NULL);
INSERT INTO s_inventory VALUES ('32779', '301', 102, 95, 175, NULL, NULL);
INSERT INTO s_inventory VALUES ('32861', '301', 57, 50, 100, NULL, NULL);
INSERT INTO s_inventory VALUES ('40421', '301', 70, 40, 70, NULL, NULL);
INSERT INTO s_inventory VALUES ('40422', '301', 65, 40, 70, NULL, NULL);
INSERT INTO s_inventory VALUES ('41010', '301', 59, 40, 70, NULL, NULL);
INSERT INTO s_inventory VALUES ('41020', '301', 61, 40, 70, NULL, NULL);
INSERT INTO s_inventory VALUES ('41050', '301', 49, 40, 70, NULL, NULL);
INSERT INTO s_inventory VALUES ('41080', '301', 50, 40, 70, NULL, NULL);
INSERT INTO s_inventory VALUES ('41100', '301', 42, 40, 70, NULL, NULL);
INSERT INTO s_inventory VALUES ('20510', '401', 88, 50, 100, NULL, NULL);
```

```
INSERT INTO s_inventory VALUES ('20512', '401', 75, 75, 140, NULL, NULL);
INSERT INTO s_inventory VALUES ('30321', '401', 102, 80, 140, NULL, NULL);
INSERT INTO s_inventory VALUES ('30326', '401', 113, 80, 140, NULL, NULL);
INSERT INTO s_inventory VALUES ('30421', '401', 85, 80, 140, NULL, NULL);
INSERT INTO s_inventory VALUES ('30426', '401', 135, 80, 140, NULL, NULL);
INSERT INTO s_inventory VALUES ('30433', '401', 0, 100, 175, NULL, NULL );
INSERT INTO s_inventory VALUES ('32779', '401', 135, 100, 175, NULL, NULL);
INSERT INTO s_inventory VALUES ('32861', '401', 250, 150, 250, NULL, NULL);
INSERT INTO s_inventory VALUES ('40421', '401', 47, 40, 70, NULL, NULL);
INSERT INTO s_inventory VALUES ('40422', '401', 50, 40, 70, NULL, NULL);
INSERT INTO s_inventory VALUES ('41010', '401', 80, 70, 220, NULL, NULL);
INSERT INTO s_inventory VALUES ('41020', '401', 91, 70, 220, NULL, NULL);
INSERT INTO s_inventory VALUES ('41050', '401', 169, 70, 220, NULL, NULL);
INSERT INTO s_inventory VALUES ('41080', '401', 100, 70, 220, NULL, NULL);
INSERT INTO s_inventory VALUES ('41100', '401', 75, 70, 220, NULL, NULL);
INSERT INTO s_inventory VALUES ('50169', '401', 240, 200, 350, NULL, NULL);
INSERT INTO s_inventory VALUES ('50273', '401', 224, 150, 280, NULL, NULL);
INSERT INTO s_inventory VALUES ('50417', '401', 130, 120, 210, NULL, NULL);
INSERT INTO s_inventory VALUES ('50418', '401', 156, 100, 175, NULL, NULL);
INSERT INTO s_inventory VALUES ('50419', '401', 151, 150, 280, NULL, NULL);
INSERT INTO s_inventory VALUES ('50530', '401', 119, 100, 175, NULL, NULL);
INSERT INTO s_inventory VALUES ('50532', '401', 233, 200, 350, NULL, NULL);
INSERT INTO s_inventory VALUES ('50536', '401', 138, 100, 175, NULL, NULL);
INSERT INTO s_inventory VALUES ('10012', '10501', 300, 300, 525, NULL, NULL);
INSERT INTO s_inventory VALUES ('10013', '10501', 314, 300, 525, NULL, NULL);
INSERT INTO s_inventory VALUES ('10022', '10501', 502, 300, 525, NULL, NULL);
INSERT INTO s_inventory VALUES ('10023', '10501', 500, 300, 525, NULL, NULL);
INSERT INTO s_inventory VALUES ('20106', '10501', 150, 100, 175, NULL, NULL);
INSERT INTO s_inventory VALUES ('20108', '10501', 222, 200, 350, NULL, NULL);
INSERT INTO s_inventory VALUES ('20201', '10501', 275, 200, 350, NULL, NULL);
INSERT INTO s_inventory VALUES ('20510', '10501', 57, 50, 87, NULL, NULL);
INSERT INTO s_inventory VALUES ('20512', '10501', 62, 50, 87, NULL, NULL);
INSERT INTO s_inventory VALUES ('30321', '10501', 194, 150, 275, NULL, NULL);
INSERT INTO s_inventory VALUES ('30326', '10501', 277, 250, 440, NULL, NULL);
INSERT INTO s_inventory VALUES ('30421', '10501', 190, 150, 275, NULL, NULL);
INSERT INTO s_inventory VALUES ('30426', '10501', 423, 250, 450, NULL, NULL);
INSERT INTO s_inventory VALUES ('30433', '10501', 273, 200, 350, NULL, NULL);
INSERT INTO s_inventory VALUES ('32779', '10501', 280, 200, 350, NULL, NULL);
INSERT INTO s_inventory VALUES ('32861', '10501', 288, 200, 350, NULL, NULL);
INSERT INTO s_inventory VALUES ('40421', '10501', 97, 80, 140, NULL, NULL);
INSERT INTO s_inventory VALUES ('40422', '10501', 90, 80, 140, NULL, NULL);
INSERT INTO s_inventory VALUES ('41010', '10501', 151, 140, 245, NULL, NULL);
INSERT INTO s_inventory VALUES ('41020', '10501', 224, 140, 245, NULL, NULL);
INSERT INTO s_inventory VALUES ('41050', '10501', 157, 140, 245, NULL, NULL);
INSERT INTO s_inventory VALUES ('41080', '10501', 159, 140, 245, NULL, NULL);
INSERT INTO s_inventory VALUES ('41100', '10501', 141, 140, 245, NULL, NULL);
COMMIT;

prompt Finished populating the table s_inventory - processing continues
prompt

prompt creating table s_item
Rem************* S_ITEM TABLE *******************************
Rem******************************************************************

DROP TABLE s_item CASCADE CONSTRAINTS;
CREATE TABLE s_item
(ord_id           VARCHAR2(3) CONSTRAINT s_item_ord_id_nn NOT NULL,
 item_id          VARCHAR2(7) CONSTRAINT s_item_item_id_nn NOT NULL,
 product_id       VARCHAR2(7) CONSTRAINT s_item_product_id_nn NOT NULL,
 price            NUMBER(11, 2),
```

```
    quantity                NUMBER(9),
    quantity_shipped        NUMBER(9),
    CONSTRAINT s_item_ordid_itemid_pk PRIMARY KEY (ord_id, item_id),
    CONSTRAINT s_item_ordid_prodid_uk UNIQUE (ord_id, product_id)
);

prompt populating table s_item

INSERT INTO s_item VALUES ('100', '1', '10011', 135, 500, 500);
INSERT INTO s_item VALUES ('100', '2', '10013', 380, 400, 400);
INSERT INTO s_item VALUES ('100', '3', '10021', 14, 500, 500);
INSERT INTO s_item VALUES ('100', '5', '30326', 582, 600, 600);
INSERT INTO s_item VALUES ('100', '7', '41010', 8, 250, 250);
INSERT INTO s_item VALUES ('100', '6', '30433', 20, 450, 450);
INSERT INTO s_item VALUES ('100', '4', '10023', 36, 400, 400);
INSERT INTO s_item VALUES ('101', '1', '30421', 16, 15, 15);
INSERT INTO s_item VALUES ('101', '3', '41010', 8, 20, 20);
INSERT INTO s_item VALUES ('101', '5', '50169', 4.29, 40, 40);
INSERT INTO s_item VALUES ('101', '6', '50417', 80, 27, 27);
INSERT INTO s_item VALUES ('101', '7', '50530', 45, 50, 50);
INSERT INTO s_item VALUES ('101', '4', '41100', 45, 35, 35);
INSERT INTO s_item VALUES ('101', '2', '40422', 50, 30, 30);
INSERT INTO s_item VALUES ('102', '1', '20108', 28, 100, 100);
INSERT INTO s_item VALUES ('102', '2', '20201', 123, 45, 45);
INSERT INTO s_item VALUES ('103', '1', '30433', 20, 15, 15);
INSERT INTO s_item VALUES ('103', '2', '32779', 7, 11, 11);
INSERT INTO s_item VALUES ('104', '1', '20510', 9, 7, 7);
INSERT INTO s_item VALUES ('104', '4', '30421', 16, 35, 35);
INSERT INTO s_item VALUES ('104', '2', '20512', 8, 12, 12);
INSERT INTO s_item VALUES ('104', '3', '30321', 1669, 19, 19);
INSERT INTO s_item VALUES ('105', '1', '50273', 22.89, 16, 16);
INSERT INTO s_item VALUES ('105', '3', '50532', 47, 28, 28);
INSERT INTO s_item VALUES ('105', '2', '50419', 80, 13, 13);
INSERT INTO s_item VALUES ('106', '1', '20108', 28, 46, 46);
INSERT INTO s_item VALUES ('106', '4', '50273', 22.89, 75, 75);
INSERT INTO s_item VALUES ('106', '5', '50418', 75, 98, 98);
INSERT INTO s_item VALUES ('106', '6', '50419', 80, 27, 27);
INSERT INTO s_item VALUES ('106', '2', '20201', 123, 21, 21);
INSERT INTO s_item VALUES ('106', '3', '50169', 4.29, 125, 125);
INSERT INTO s_item VALUES ('107', '1', '20106', 11, 50, 50);
INSERT INTO s_item VALUES ('107', '3', '20201', 115, 130, 130);
INSERT INTO s_item VALUES ('107', '5', '30421', 16, 55, 55);
INSERT INTO s_item VALUES ('107', '4', '30321', 1669, 75, 75);
INSERT INTO s_item VALUES ('107', '2', '20108', 28, 22, 22);
INSERT INTO s_item VALUES ('108', '1', '20510', 9, 9, 9);
INSERT INTO s_item VALUES ('108', '6', '41080', 35, 50, 50);
INSERT INTO s_item VALUES ('108', '7', '41100', 45, 42, 42);
INSERT INTO s_item VALUES ('108', '5', '32861', 60, 57, 57);
INSERT INTO s_item VALUES ('108', '2', '20512', 8, 18, 18);
INSERT INTO s_item VALUES ('108', '4', '32779', 7, 60, 60);
INSERT INTO s_item VALUES ('108', '3', '30321', 1669, 85, 85);
INSERT INTO s_item VALUES ('109', '1', '10011', 140, 150, 150);
INSERT INTO s_item VALUES ('109', '5', '30426', 18.25, 500, 500);
INSERT INTO s_item VALUES ('109', '7', '50418', 75, 43, 43);
INSERT INTO s_item VALUES ('109', '6', '32861', 60, 50, 50);
INSERT INTO s_item VALUES ('109', '4', '30326', 582, 1500, 1500);
INSERT INTO s_item VALUES ('109', '2', '10012', 175, 600, 600);
INSERT INTO s_item VALUES ('109', '3', '10022', 21.95, 300, 300);
INSERT INTO s_item VALUES ('110', '1', '50273', 22.89, 17, 17);
INSERT INTO s_item VALUES ('110', '2', '50536', 50, 23, 23);
INSERT INTO s_item VALUES ('111', '1', '40421', 65, 27, 27);
```

```
INSERT INTO s_item VALUES ('111', '2', '41080', 35, 29, 29);
INSERT INTO s_item VALUES ('97', '1', '20106', 9, 1000, 1000);
INSERT INTO s_item VALUES ('97', '2', '30321', 1500, 50, 50);
INSERT INTO s_item VALUES ('98', '1', '40421', 85, 7, 7);
INSERT INTO s_item VALUES ('99', '1', '20510', 9, 18, 18);
INSERT INTO s_item VALUES ('99', '2', '20512', 8, 25, 25);
INSERT INTO s_item VALUES ('99', '3', '50417', 80, 53, 53);
INSERT INTO s_item VALUES ('99', '4', '50530', 45, 69, 69);
INSERT INTO s_item VALUES ('112', '1', '20106', 11, 50, 50);
COMMIT;

prompt Finished populating the s_item table - processing continues
prompt

prompt creating table s_ord
Rem************* S_ORD TABLE ******************************
Rem********************************************************************

DROP TABLE s_ord CASCADE CONSTRAINTS;
CREATE TABLE s_ord
(id                      VARCHAR2(3) CONSTRAINT s_ord_id_nn NOT NULL,
 customer_id             VARCHAR2(3) CONSTRAINT s_ord_customer_id_nn NOT NULL,
 date_ordered            DATE CONSTRAINT s_ord_date_ordered_nn NOT NULL,
 date_shipped            DATE,
 sales_rep_id            VARCHAR2(3),
 total                   NUMBER(11, 2),
 payment_type            VARCHAR2(6) CONSTRAINT s_ord_payment_type_nn NOT NULL,
 order_filled            VARCHAR2(1),
 CONSTRAINT s_ord_id_pk PRIMARY KEY (id),
 CONSTRAINT s_ord_payment_type_ck CHECK (payment_type in ('CASH', 'CREDIT')),
 CONSTRAINT s_ord_order_filled_ck CHECK (order_filled in ('Y', 'N'))
);

prompt populating table s_ord

INSERT INTO s_ord VALUES ('100', '204', TO_DATE('31-AUG-1992','DD-MON-YYYY'),
TO_DATE('10-SEP-1992','DD-MON-YYYY'),'11', 601100, 'CREDIT', 'Y');
INSERT INTO s_ord VALUES ('101', '205', TO_DATE('31-AUG-1992','DD-MON-YYYY'),
TO_DATE('15-SEP-1992','DD-MON-YYYY'),'14', 8056.6, 'CREDIT', 'Y');
INSERT INTO s_ord VALUES ('102', '206', TO_DATE('01-SEP-1992','DD-MON-YYYY'),
TO_DATE('08-SEP-1992','DD-MON-YYYY'),'12', 8335, 'CREDIT', 'Y');
INSERT INTO s_ord VALUES ('103', '208', TO_DATE('02-SEP-1992', 'DD-MON-YYYY'),
TO_DATE('22-SEP-1992','DD-MON-YYYY'),'11', 377, 'CASH', 'Y');
INSERT INTO s_ord VALUES ('104', '208', TO_DATE('03-SEP-1992','DD-MON-YYYY'),
TO_DATE('23-SEP-1992','DD-MON-YYYY'),'13', 32430, 'CREDIT', 'Y');

INSERT INTO s_ord VALUES ('105', '209', TO_DATE('04-SEP-1992','DD-MON-YYYY'),
TO_DATE('18-SEP-1992','DD-MON-YYYY'),'11', 2722.24, 'CREDIT', 'Y');
INSERT INTO s_ord VALUES ('106', '210', TO_DATE('07-SEP-1992','DD-MON-YYYY'),
TO_DATE('15-SEP-1992','DD-MON-YYYY'),'12', 15634, 'CREDIT', 'Y');
INSERT INTO s_ord VALUES ('107', '211', TO_DATE('07-SEP-1992','DD-MON-YYYY'),
TO_DATE('21-SEP-1992','DD-MON-YYYY'),'14', 142171, 'CREDIT', 'Y');
INSERT INTO s_ord VALUES ('108', '212', TO_DATE('07-SEP-1992','DD-MON-YYYY'),
TO_DATE('10-SEP-1992','DD-MON-YYYY'),'13', 149570, 'CREDIT', 'Y');
INSERT INTO s_ord VALUES ('109', '213', TO_DATE('08-SEP-1992','DD-MON-YYYY'),
TO_DATE('28-SEP-1992','DD-MON-YYYY'),'11', 1020935, 'CREDIT', 'Y');

INSERT INTO s_ord VALUES ('110', '214', TO_DATE('09-SEP-1992', 'DD-MON-YYYY'),
TO_DATE('21-SEP-1992','DD-MON-YYYY'),'11', 1539.13, 'CASH', 'Y');
INSERT INTO s_ord VALUES ('111', '204', TO_DATE('09-SEP-1992', 'DD-MON-YYYY'),
TO_DATE('21-SEP-1992','DD-MON-YYYY'),'11', 2770, 'CASH', 'Y');
```

```
INSERT INTO s_ord VALUES ('97', '201', TO_DATE('28-AUG-1992','DD-MON-YYYY'),
TO_DATE('17-SEP-1992','DD-MON-YYYY'),'12', 84000, 'CREDIT', 'Y');
INSERT INTO s_ord VALUES ('98', '202', TO_DATE('31-AUG-1992','DD-MON-YYYY'),
TO_DATE('10-SEP-1992','DD-MON-YYYY'),'14', 595, 'CASH', 'Y');
INSERT INTO s_ord VALUES ('99', '203', TO_DATE('31-AUG-1992','DD-MON-YYYY'),
TO_DATE('18-SEP-1992','DD-MON-YYYY'),'14', 7707, 'CREDIT', 'Y');
INSERT INTO s_ord VALUES ('112', '210', TO_DATE('31-AUG-1992','DD-MON-YYYY'),
TO_DATE('10-SEP-1992','DD-MON-YYYY'),'12', 550, 'CREDIT', 'Y');
COMMIT;

prompt Finished populating the s_ord table - Processing continues
prompt

prompt creating table s_product
Rem************* S_PRODUCT TABLE *********************************
Rem***************************************************************

DROP TABLE s_product CASCADE CONSTRAINTS;
CREATE TABLE s_product
(id                      VARCHAR2(7)  CONSTRAINT s_product_id_nn NOT NULL,
 name                    VARCHAR2(25) CONSTRAINT s_product_name_nn NOT NULL,
 short_desc              VARCHAR2(255),
 suggested_whlsl_price   NUMBER(11, 2),
 whlsl_units             VARCHAR2(10),
 CONSTRAINT s_product_id_pk PRIMARY KEY (id),
 CONSTRAINT s_product_name_uk UNIQUE (name)
);

prompt populating table s_product

INSERT INTO s_product VALUES ('10011', 'Bunny Boot', 'Beginner''s ski boot',150,
NULL);
INSERT INTO s_product VALUES ('10012', 'Ace Ski Boot', 'Intermediate ski boot',200,
NULL);
INSERT INTO s_product VALUES ('10013', 'Pro Ski Boot', 'Advanced ski boot',410,
NULL);
INSERT INTO s_product VALUES ('10021', 'Bunny Ski Pole', 'Beginner''s ski
pole',16.25, NULL);
INSERT INTO s_product VALUES ('10022', 'Ace Ski Pole', 'Intermediate ski pole',21.95,
NULL);
INSERT INTO s_product VALUES ('10023', 'Pro Ski Pole', 'Advanced ski pole',40.95,
NULL);
INSERT INTO s_product VALUES ('20106', 'Junior Soccer Ball', 'Junior soccer ball',11,
NULL);
INSERT INTO s_product VALUES ('20108', 'World Cup Soccer Ball', 'World cup soccer
ball',28, NULL);
INSERT INTO s_product VALUES ('20201', 'World Cup Net', 'World cup net',123, NULL);
INSERT INTO s_product VALUES ('20510', 'Black Hawk Knee Pads', 'Knee pads, pair',9,
NULL);
INSERT INTO s_product VALUES ('20512', 'Black Hawk Elbow Pads', 'Elbow pads, pair',8,
NULL);
INSERT INTO s_product VALUES ('30321', 'Grand Prix Bicycle', 'Road bicycle',1669,
NULL);
INSERT INTO s_product VALUES ('30326', 'Himalaya Bicycle', 'Mountain bicycle',582,
NULL);
INSERT INTO s_product VALUES ('30421', 'Grand Prix Bicycle Tires', 'Road bicycle
tires',16, NULL);
INSERT INTO s_product VALUES ('30426', 'Himalaya Tires', 'Mountain bicycle
tires',18.25, NULL);
INSERT INTO s_product VALUES ('30433', 'New Air Pump', 'Tire pump',20, NULL);
```

```
INSERT INTO s_product VALUES ('32779', 'Slaker Water Bottle','Water bottle',7,
NULL);
INSERT INTO s_product VALUES ('32861', 'Safe-T Helmet','Bicycle helmet',60, NULL);
INSERT INTO s_product VALUES ('40421', 'Alexeyer Pro Lifting Bar','Straight bar',65,
NULL);
INSERT INTO s_product VALUES ('40422', 'Pro Curling Bar','Curling bar',50, NULL);
INSERT INTO s_product VALUES ('41010', 'Prostar 10 Pound Weight','Ten pound
weight',8, NULL);
INSERT INTO s_product VALUES ('41020', 'Prostar 20 Pound Weight','Twenty pound
weight',12, NULL);
INSERT INTO s_product VALUES ('41050', 'Prostar 50 Pound Weight','Fifty pound
weight',25, NULL);
INSERT INTO s_product VALUES ('41080', 'Prostar 80 Pound Weight','Eighty pound
weight',35, NULL);
INSERT INTO s_product VALUES ('41100', 'Prostar 100 Pound Weight','One hundred pound
weight',45, NULL);
INSERT INTO s_product VALUES ('50169', 'Major League Baseball','Baseball',4.29,
NULL);
INSERT INTO s_product VALUES ('50273', 'Chapman Helmet','Batting helmet',22.89,
NULL);
INSERT INTO s_product VALUES ('50417', 'Griffey Glove','Outfielder''s glove',80,
NULL);
INSERT INTO s_product VALUES ('50418', 'Alomar Glove','Infielder''s glove',75,
NULL);
INSERT INTO s_product VALUES ('50419', 'Steinbach Glove','Catcher''s glove',80,
NULL);
INSERT INTO s_product VALUES ('50530', 'Cabrera Bat','Thirty inch bat',45, NULL);
INSERT INTO s_product VALUES ('50532', 'Puckett Bat','Thirty-two inch bat',47,
NULL);
INSERT INTO s_product VALUES ('50536', 'Winfield Bat','Thirty-six inch bat',50,
NULL);
COMMIT;

prompt Finished populating the s_product table - Processing continues
prompt

prompt creating table s_region
Rem************* S_REGION TABLE ******************************
Rem******************************************************************

DROP TABLE s_region CASCADE CONSTRAINTS;
CREATE TABLE s_region
(id          VARCHAR2(3)  CONSTRAINT s_region_id_nn NOT NULL,
 name        VARCHAR2(26) CONSTRAINT s_region_name_nn NOT NULL,
 CONSTRAINT s_region_id_pk PRIMARY KEY (id),
 CONSTRAINT s_region_name_uk UNIQUE (name)
);

prompt populating table s_region

INSERT INTO s_region VALUES ('1', 'North America');
INSERT INTO s_region VALUES ('2', 'South America');
INSERT INTO s_region VALUES ('3', 'Africa / Middle East');
INSERT INTO s_region VALUES ('4', 'Asia');
INSERT INTO s_region VALUES ('5', 'Europe');
INSERT INTO s_region VALUES ('6', 'Central America /Caribbean');
COMMIT;

prompt Finished populating the s_region table - Processing continues
prompt
```

```
prompt creating table s_title
Rem************** S_TITLE TABLE ********************************
Rem************************************************************

DROP TABLE s_title CASCADE CONSTRAINTS;
CREATE TABLE s_title
(title         VARCHAR2(25) CONSTRAINT s_title_title_nn NOT NULL,
 CONSTRAINT s_title_title_pk PRIMARY KEY (title)
);


prompt populating table s_title
INSERT INTO s_title VALUES ('President');
INSERT INTO s_title VALUES ('Sales Representative');
INSERT INTO s_title VALUES ('Stock Clerk');
INSERT INTO s_title VALUES ('VP, Administration');
INSERT INTO s_title VALUES ('VP, Finance');
INSERT INTO s_title VALUES ('VP, Operations');
INSERT INTO s_title VALUES ('VP, Sales');
INSERT INTO s_title VALUES ('Warehouse Manager');
COMMIT;


prompt Finished populating the s_title table - Processing continues


Rem************** S_WAREHOUSE TABLE ********************************
Rem************************************************************
prompt
prompt creating table s_warehouse

DROP TABLE s_warehouse CASCADE CONSTRAINTS;
CREATE TABLE s_warehouse
(id            VARCHAR2(7) CONSTRAINT s_warehouse_id_nn NOT NULL,
 region_id     VARCHAR2(3) CONSTRAINT s_warehouse_region_id_nn NOT NULL,
 address       VARCHAR2(20),
 city          VARCHAR2(20),
 state         VARCHAR2(15),
 country       VARCHAR2(20),
 zip_code      VARCHAR2(15),
 phone         VARCHAR2(20),
 manager_id    VARCHAR2(3),
 CONSTRAINT s_warehouse_id_pk PRIMARY KEY (id)
);


prompt populating table s_warehouse
INSERT INTO s_warehouse VALUES ('101', '1','283 King Street','Seattle', 'WA', 'US',
NULL,
NULL, '6');
INSERT INTO s_warehouse VALUES ('10501', '5','5 Modrany','Bratislava', NULL,
'Slovakia',
NULL, NULL, '10');
INSERT INTO s_warehouse VALUES ('201', '2','68 Via Centrale','Sao Paolo', NULL,
'Brazil',NULL,
NULL, '7');
INSERT INTO s_warehouse VALUES ('301', '3','6921 King Way','Lagos', NULL,
'Nigeria',NULL,
NULL, '8');
INSERT INTO s_warehouse VALUES ('401', '4','86 Chu Street','Hong Kong', NULL,
NULL,NULL,
NULL, '9');
COMMIT;
```

```
prompt Finished populating the s_warehouse table - Processing continues

Rem ADD FOREIGN KEYS AND CONSTRAINTS - PLEASE READ NOTE BELOW.

prompt
prompt altering tables to add foreign key constraints
Rem    **************************************************************
Rem    **************************************************************
Rem    THE FOLLOWING CONSTRAINTS SHOULD BE INCLUDED
Rem    AS PART OF THE SPORTING GOODS (SG)SCRIPT. THEY SHOULD
Rem    NOT BE PART OF THE SG_NO_CONSTRAINTS.
Rem    **************************************************************
Rem    ********************* CONSTRAINTS *********************

ALTER TABLE s_dept
    ADD CONSTRAINT s_dept_region_id_fk
    FOREIGN KEY (region_id) REFERENCES s_region (id);
ALTER TABLE s_emp
    ADD CONSTRAINT s_emp_manager_id_fk
    FOREIGN KEY (manager_id) REFERENCES s_emp (id);
ALTER TABLE s_emp
    ADD CONSTRAINT s_emp_dept_id_fk
    FOREIGN KEY (dept_id) REFERENCES s_dept (id);
ALTER TABLE s_emp
    ADD CONSTRAINT s_emp_title_fk
    FOREIGN KEY (title) REFERENCES s_title (title);
ALTER TABLE s_customer
    ADD CONSTRAINT s_sales_rep_id_fk
    FOREIGN KEY (sales_rep_id) REFERENCES s_emp (id);
ALTER TABLE s_customer
    ADD CONSTRAINT s_customer_region_id_fk
    FOREIGN KEY (region_id) REFERENCES s_region (id);
ALTER TABLE s_ord
    ADD CONSTRAINT s_ord_customer_id_fk
    FOREIGN KEY (customer_id) REFERENCES s_customer (id);
ALTER TABLE s_ord
    ADD CONSTRAINT s_ord_sales_rep_id_fk
    FOREIGN KEY (sales_rep_id) REFERENCES s_emp (id);
ALTER TABLE s_item
    ADD CONSTRAINT s_item_ord_id_fk
    FOREIGN KEY (ord_id) REFERENCES s_ord (id);
ALTER TABLE s_item
    ADD CONSTRAINT s_item_product_id_fk
    FOREIGN KEY (product_id) REFERENCES s_product (id);
ALTER TABLE s_warehouse
    ADD CONSTRAINT s_warehouse_manager_id_fk
    FOREIGN KEY (manager_id) REFERENCES s_emp (id);
ALTER TABLE s_warehouse
    ADD CONSTRAINT s_warehouse_region_id_fk
    FOREIGN KEY (region_id) REFERENCES s_region (id);
ALTER TABLE s_inventory
    ADD CONSTRAINT s_inventory_product_id_fk
    FOREIGN KEY (product_id) REFERENCES s_product (id);
ALTER TABLE s_inventory
    ADD CONSTRAINT s_inventory_warehouse_id_fk
    FOREIGN KEY (warehouse_id) REFERENCES s_warehouse (id);

prompt
prompt Creation and population of database has been completed.
set feedback on
```

Other Database Scripts Used

```
REM MULT.SQL
create table mult
(
        first  number,
        secondnumber
);

insert into mult
values (987,2);
insert into mult
values (22,NULL);
insert into mult
values (NULL,35);
insert into mult
values (5,4);
```

```
REM NAMES.SQL
create table NAMES (
FirstName      varchar2(25),
LastName       varchar2(25)
);
insert into NAMES (FirstName, LastName)
values ('THOMAS', 'JEFFERSON');
insert into NAMES (FirstName, LastName)
values (NULL, 'SOCRATES');
```

```
REM PAY_PERIODS.SQL
create table PAY_PERIODS(
first_check   date,
second_check  date
);
insert into PAY_PERIODS(first_check,second_check)
values ('14-JAN-00','28-JAN-00');
insert into PAY_PERIODS(first_check,second_check)
values ('16-FEB-00','29-FEB-00');
insert into PAY_PERIODS(first_check,second_check)
values ('16-MAR-00','30-MAR-00');
insert into PAY_PERIODS(first_check,second_check)
values ('14-APR-00','28-APR-00');
insert into PAY_PERIODS(first_check,second_check)
values ('16-MAY-00','30-MAY-00');
insert into PAY_PERIODS(first_check,second_check)
values ('16-JUN-00','30-JUN-00');
insert into PAY_PERIODS(first_check,second_check)
values ('14-JUL-00','28-JUL-00');
insert into PAY_PERIODS(first_check,second_check)
values ('16-AUG-00','30-AUG-00');
insert into PAY_PERIODS(first_check,second_check)
values ('15-SEP-00','29-SEP-00');
```

```
insert into PAY_PERIODS(first_check,second_check)
values ('16-OCT-00','30-OCT-00');
insert into PAY_PERIODS(first_check,second_check)
values ('16-NOV-00','30-NOV-00');
insert into PAY_PERIODS(first_check,second_check)
values ('15-DEC-00','29-DEC-00');
```

```
REM PROGRAMMER.SQL
Create table Programmer
(EmpNo Varchar2(3)                          PRIMARY KEY,
 Last_Name Varchar2(25)      NOT NULL,
 First_Name Varchar2(25),
 Hire_Date Date,
 Project Varchar2(3),
 Language Varchar2(15),
 TaskNo Number(2),
 Clearance Varchar2(25)
);
INSERT INTO programmer (EmpNo, Last_Name, First_Name, Hire_Date,
        Project, Language, TaskNo, Clearance)
Values('201','Campbell', 'John', '1-JAN-95',
        'NPR', 'VB',52, 'Secret');
INSERT INTO programmer (EmpNo, Last_Name, First_Name, Hire_Date,
        Project, Language, TaskNo, Clearance)
Values('390', 'Bell', 'Randall', '1-MAY-93',
        'KCW', 'Java', 11, 'Top Secret');
INSERT INTO programmer (EmpNo, Last_Name, First_Name, Hire_Date,
        Project, Language, TaskNo, Clearance)
Values('789', 'Hixon', 'Richard', '31-AUG-98',
        'RNC', 'VB', 11, 'Secret');
INSERT INTO programmer (EmpNo, Last_Name, First_Name, Hire_Date,
        Project, Language, TaskNo, Clearance)
Values('134','McGurn', 'Robert', '15-JUL-95',
        'TIP','C++',52, 'Secret');
INSERT INTO programmer (EmpNo, Last_Name, First_Name, Hire_Date,
        Project, Language, TaskNo, Clearance)
Values('896','Sweet', 'Jan', '15-JUN-97',
        'KCW','Java',10, 'Top Secret');
INSERT INTO programmer (EmpNo, Last_Name, First_Name, Hire_Date,
        Project, Language, TaskNo, Clearance)
Values('345',' Rowlett', 'Sid', '15-NOV-99',
        'TIP','Java',52, NULL);
INSERT INTO programmer (EmpNo, Last_Name, First_Name, Hire_Date,
        Project, Language, TaskNo, Clearance)
Values('563', 'Reardon', 'Andy', '15-AUG-94',
        'NIT', 'C++', 89, 'Confidential');
```

```
REM STATS.SQL
CREATE TABLE stats
( even        number,
  odd         number
);
insert into stats values(2,1);
```

```
insert into stats values(NULL,3);
insert into stats values(6,5);
insert into stats values(8, NULL);
insert into stats values(10,9);
insert into stats values(NULL,11);
insert into stats values(14,NULL);
insert into stats values(16,15);
```

```
REM TRYNUM.SQL
create table trynum
(
        first number,
        second number,
        third number
);

insert into trynum
values (987,987,987);
insert into trynum
values (987.222,987,987.23);
insert into trynum
values (98.5,99,98.5);
insert into trynum
values (98765,98765,98765);
insert into trynum
values (23.987,24,23.99);
insert into trynum
values (.00003,0,0);
insert into trynum
values (100.9,101,100.9);
insert into trynum
values (.00005,0,0);
insert into trynum
values (1.9,2,1.9);
insert into trynum
values (10.1,10,10);
```

```
REM WORLD_CITIES.SQL
create table World_Cities (
City          varchar2(25),
Country       varchar2(25),
Continent     varchar2(25),
Latitude      number,
NorthSouth    char(1),
Longitude     number,
EastWest      char(1)
);
insert into World_Cities (City,Country,Continent,Latitude,
                    NorthSouth,Longitude,EastWest)
values ('ATHENS','GREECE','EUROPE',37.59,'N',23.44,'E');
insert into World_Cities (City,Country,Continent,Latitude,
                    NorthSouth,Longitude,EastWest)
```

```
values ('ATLANTA','UNITED STATES','NORTH AMERICA' ,
       33.45,'N',84.23,'W');
insert into World_Cities (City,Country,Continent,Latitude,
                    NorthSouth,Longitude,EastWest)
values ('DALLAS','UNITED STATES','NORTH AMERICA',
       32.47,'N',96.47,'W');
insert into World_Cities (City,Country,Continent,Latitude,
                    NorthSouth,Longitude,EastWest)
values ('NASHVILLE','UNITED STATES','NORTH AMERICA',
       36.09,'N',86.46,'W');
insert into World_Cities (City,Country,Continent,Latitude,
                    NorthSouth,Longitude,EastWest)
values ('VICTORIA','CANADA','NORTH AMERICA',
       48.25,'N',123.21,'W');
insert into World_Cities (City,Country,Continent,Latitude,
                    NorthSouth,Longitude,EastWest)
values ('PETERBOROUGH','CANADA','NORTH AMERICA',
       44.18,'N',79.18,'W');
insert into World_Cities (City,Country,Continent,Latitude,
                    NorthSouth,Longitude,EastWest)
values ('VANCOUVER','CANADA','NORTH AMERICA',
       49.18,'N',123.04,'W');
insert into World_Cities (City,Country,Continent,Latitude,
                    NorthSouth,Longitude,EastWest)
values ('TOLEDO','UNITED STATES','NORTH AMERICA',
       41.39,'N',83.82,'W');
insert into World_Cities (City,Country,Continent,Latitude,
                    NorthSouth,Longitude,EastWest)
values ('WARSAW','POLAND','EUROPE',52.15,'N',21.00,'E');
insert into World_Cities (City,Country,Continent,Latitude,
                    NorthSouth,Longitude,EastWest)
values ('LIMA','PERU','SOUTH AMERICA',12.03,'S',77.03,'W');
insert into World_Cities (City,Country,Continent,Latitude,
                    NorthSouth,Longitude,EastWest)
values ('RIO DE JANEIRO','BRAZIL','SOUTH AMERICA',
       22.43,'S',43.13,'W');
insert into World_Cities (City,Country,Continent,Latitude,
                    NorthSouth,Longitude,EastWest)
values ('SANTIAGO','CHILE','SOUTH AMERICA',33.27,'S',70.40,'W');
insert into World_Cities (City,Country,Continent,Latitude,
                    NorthSouth,Longitude,EastWest)
values ('BOGOTA','COLOMBIA','SOUTH AMERICA',
       04.36,'N',74.05,'W');
insert into World_Cities (City,Country,Continent,Latitude,
                    NorthSouth,Longitude,EastWest)
values ('BUENOS AIRES','ARGENTINA','SOUTH AMERICA',
       34.36,'S',58.28,'W');
insert into World_Cities (City,Country,Continent,Latitude,
                    NorthSouth,Longitude,EastWest)
values ('QUITO','ECUADOR','SOUTH AMERICA',00.13,'S',78.30,'W');
insert into World_Cities (City,Country,Continent,Latitude,
                    NorthSouth,Longitude,EastWest)
values ('CARACAS','VENEZUELA','SOUTH AMERICA',
       10.30,'N',66.56,'W');
insert into World_Cities (City,Country,Continent,Latitude,
```

```
                  NorthSouth,Longitude,EastWest)
values ('MADRAS','INDIA','ASIA',13.05,'N',80.17,'E');
insert into World_Cities (City,Country,Continent,Latitude,
                  NorthSouth,Longitude,EastWest)
values ('NEW DEHLI','INDIA','ASIA',28.36,'N',77.12,'E');
insert into World_Cities (City,Country,Continent,Latitude,
                  NorthSouth,Longitude,EastWest)
values ('BOMBAY','INDIA','ASIA',18.58,'N',72.50,'E');
insert into World_Cities (City,Country,Continent,Latitude,
                  NorthSouth,Longitude,EastWest)
values ('MANCHESTER','ENGLAND','EUROPE',53.30,'N',2.15,'W');
insert into World_Cities (City,Country,Continent,Latitude,
                  NorthSouth,Longitude,EastWest)
values ('LONDON','ENGLAND','EUROPE',51.30,'N',0.0,NULL);
insert into World_Cities (City,Country,Continent,Latitude,
                  NorthSouth,Longitude,EastWest)
values ('MOSCOW','RUSSIA','EUROPE',55.45,'N',37.35,'E');
insert into World_Cities (City,Country,Continent,Latitude,
                  NorthSouth,Longitude,EastWest)
values ('PARIS','FRANCE','EUROPE',48.52,'N',2.20,'E');
insert into World_Cities (City,Country,Continent,Latitude,
                  NorthSouth,Longitude,EastWest)
values ('SHENYANG','CHINA','ASIA',41.48,'N',123.27,'E');
insert into World_Cities (City,Country,Continent,Latitude,
                  NorthSouth,Longitude,EastWest)
values ('CAIRO','EGYPT','AFRICA',30.03,'N',31.15,'E');
insert into World_Cities (City,Country,Continent,Latitude,
                  NorthSouth,Longitude,EastWest)
values ('TRIPOLI','LYBIA','AFRICA',32.54,'N',13.11,'E');
insert into World_Cities (City,Country,Continent,Latitude,
                  NorthSouth,Longitude,EastWest)
values ('BEIJING','CHINA','ASIA',39.56,'N',116.24,'E');
insert into World_Cities (City,Country,Continent,Latitude,
                  NorthSouth,Longitude,EastWest)
values ('ROME','ITALY','EUROPE',41.54,'N',12.29,'E');
insert into World_Cities (City,Country,Continent,Latitude,
                  NorthSouth,Longitude,EastWest)
values ('TOKYO','JAPAN','ASIA',35.42,'N',139.46,'E');
insert into World_Cities (City,Country,Continent,Latitude,
                  NorthSouth,Longitude,EastWest)
values ('SYDNEY','AUSTRALIA','AUSTRALIA',33.52,'S',151.13,'E');
insert into World_Cities (City,Country,Continent,Latitude,
                  NorthSouth,Longitude,EastWest)
values ('SPARTA','GREECE','EUROPE',37.05,'N',22.27,'E');
insert into World_Cities (City,Country,Continent,Latituden,
                  NorthSouth,Longitude,EastWest)
values ('MADRID','SPAIN','EUROPE',40.24,'N',3.41,'W');
```

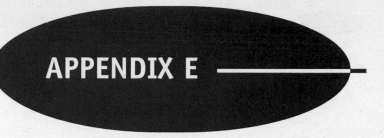

APPENDIX E

Creating Reports Using SQL*Plus

In Chapter 2 we studied some system variables and the use of the COLUMN command to change headings while displaying query results. Through the use of additional capabilities of SQL*Plus, it is possible to produce reports with formatted headings and column data. In this appendix we will concentrate on producing reports using SQL*Plus.

System Variables and the SET Command

As we saw in Appendix A, the SET command can be used to set assign values to the system or environment variables (sysvars). Table E-1 shows some of the most useful system variables for producing reports or queries.

Table E-1. Partial list of useful system variables for formatting reports.

System Variable	Can Be Used to Set the
LINESIZE	Maximum number of characters in a line before wrapping occurs. Default value is 80.
PAGESIZE	Maximum number of lines to be displayed in a single page. Default value is 24.
NEWPAGE	Number of lines to before top line of a page. Default value is 1.
NUMWIDTH	Default column width for numeric values.
SPACE	Number of spaces between columns in a report. The maximum value allowed is 10.

The syntax to assign a value to a system variable is shown next.

```
SET system-variable new-value
```

Formatting Commands

In addition to the system variables, there are some SQL*Plus commands that are also helpful when creating a report. Table E-2 shows a partial list of these commands. All these commands *must* precede the query that defines the report.

Table E-2.   Partial list of useful SQL*Plus commands.

Commands	Description
BTITLE [title | system var]	Places title or system variable at the bottom of a page.
TTITLE [title | system var]	Places title or system variable at the top of a page.
BREAK	Specifies where and how formatting will change in a report. Explained below.
COMPUTE	Calculates and print summary lines on subsets of rows. Explained below.

The following example illustrates the use of some of these commands.

EXAMPLE 1

Display the result of the query shown below. Make sure that the title heading at the top of the page reads "Sales Representatives of the SG Company".

```
SELECT first_name, last_name, dept_id AS "Dpt"

FROM s_emp  ◄───────────────────────────  Use this query in this example.

WHERE title = 'Sales Representative';
```

To produce the required title heading, it is necessary to use the **TTITLE** command, as shown below. Notice that the title is surrounded by single quotes. As mentioned before, the TTITLE command must precede the execution of the query. The result of executing the query and the effect of the TTITLE command are shown below. We have formatted the result to fit the width of this page.

```
SET LINESIZE 80

TTITLE ' Sales Representatives of the SG Company'

SELECT first_name, last_name, dept_id AS "Dpt"

FROM s_emp

WHERE title = 'Sales Representative';
```

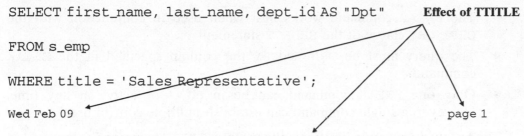

```
Wed Feb 09                                              page 1

            Sales Representatives of the SG Company

FIRST_NAME           LAST_NAME            Dpt
-------------------- -------------------- ---
Colin                Henderson            31
Sam                  Gilson               32
Jason                Sanders              33
Andre                Dameron              35
```

Observe that in addition to the given title heading the `TTITLE` command displays, by default, the system date at the top left of the page and the page number at the top right side of the page as displayed.

Using the BREAK Command[1]

The **BREAK** command is used to control the appearance of a report, since it allows us to define a control break on a column. A *control break* occurs whenever the value of the *control column* changes—that is, when the value on one line is different from the corresponding value on the previous line for the variable that has been chosen as the control variable.

The basic syntax of this command is as follows:

> **BREAK ON report-element [action [action]......]**

Where report-element requires the following syntax:

> **{column | expression | REPORT}**

Where Action requires the following syntax:

> **[SKIP n | SKIP PAGE] [NO DUPLICATES | DUPLICATES]**

---

[1] The reader should refresh the SG database before attempting the queries of this sections and the next.

A BREAK command remains "in effect" until it is redefined with another BREAK or it is rendered ineffective with a CLEAR BREAKS command. The user should keep in mind the following guidelines whenever creating a report with the BREAK command:

- The BREAK command works best when used in conjunction with the ORDER BY clause of the SELECT statement.

- The query must be ORDERed BY the column specified in the BREAK command.

- Only one BREAK command can be in effect or active at any time. However, a single command can establish multiple control breaks.

The following example illustrates the use of a BREAK command when used in conjunction with a query ordered by the column that defines the break.

EXAMPLE 2
Display the names of all customers, along with their city and country, and the region of the SG database. Group customers by region.

The query and its result are shown below. The result has been formatted for explanation purposes and to fit the width of the page.

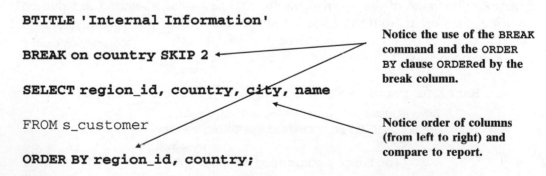

```
TTITLE ' Location of the customers of the SG Company'

BTITLE 'Internal Information'

BREAK on country SKIP 2

SELECT region_id, country, city, name

FROM s_customer

ORDER BY region_id, country;
```

Notice the use of the BREAK command and the ORDER BY clause ORDERed by the break column.

Notice order of columns (from left to right) and compare to report.

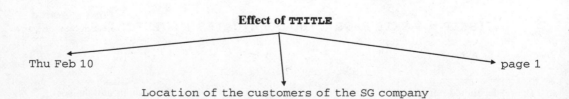

Effect of TTITLE

Thu Feb 10   page 1

Location of the customers of the SG company

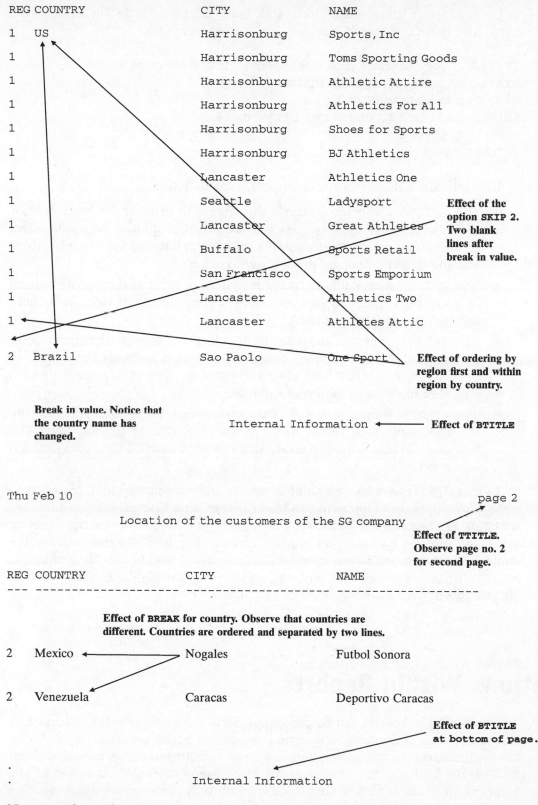

REG	COUNTRY	CITY	NAME
1	US	Harrisonburg	Sports, Inc
1		Harrisonburg	Toms Sporting Goods
1		Harrisonburg	Athletic Attire
1		Harrisonburg	Athletics For All
1		Harrisonburg	Shoes for Sports
1		Harrisonburg	BJ Athletics
1		Lancaster	Athletics One
1		Seattle	Ladysport
1		Lancaster	Great Athletes
1		Buffalo	Sports Retail
1		San Francisco	Sports Emporium
1		Lancaster	Athletics Two
1		Lancaster	Athletes Attic
2	Brazil	Sao Paolo	One Sport

Effect of the option SKIP 2. Two blank lines after break in value.

Effect of ordering by region first and within region by country.

Break in value. Notice that the country name has changed.

Internal Information ←———— **Effect of BTITLE**

Thu Feb 10   page 2

Location of the customers of the SG company

Effect of TTITLE. Observe page no. 2 for second page.

REG	COUNTRY	CITY	NAME
---	-------------------	--------------------	-------------------

Effect of BREAK for country. Observe that countries are different. Countries are ordered and separated by two lines.

2	Mexico	Nogales	Futbol Sonora
2	Venezuela	Caracas	Deportivo Caracas

Effect of BTITLE at bottom of page.

.

.

Internal Information

25 rows selected.

Let's examine these commands and their effects a little bit closer. We reproduce these commands here for explanation purposes.

```
TTITLE ' Location of the customers of the SG company'
BTITLE 'Internal Information'
BREAK on country SKIP 2
SELECT region_id, country, city, name
FROM s_customer
ORDER BY region_id, country;
```

The individual effect of each command is explained here:

- The TTITLE command instructs the system to print at the beginning or top of every page the heading enclosed in single quotes. As a side effect of this command, the system prints the system date on the top left corner and the page number on the top right corner.

- The BTITLE command instructs the system to print at the end or bottom of every page the message enclosed in single quotes, provided that there are PAGESIZE lines printed.

- The BREAK command, through the ON clause, indicates that the *country* column is the break-column. The SKIP 2 option instructs the system to print (skip) two blank lines after every break—that is, whenever there is a change in value in the break-column.

- The SELECT statement instructs the system to retrieve the values for the columns mentioned in the SELECT clause FROM the S_EMP table. The ORDER BY clause is used to establish a row sequence for the break-column (country).

To make the reports more readable, always choose columns that, from left to right, go from higher hierarchies to lower hierarchies. For instance, in this case we chose regions as the top hierarchy because regions contain countries; then we selected countries because they contain cities. After that, we chose cities. We could have continued by choosing something like neighborhoods within the cities. Within neighborhoods we may choose blocks; within blocks, we may choose streets, and so on.

Calculations Within Reports

The COMPUTE command can be used to perform calculations within a report. A calculation can be performed whenever a control break occurs. The COMPUTE command works in conjunction with the BREAK command and is useless without it. Therefore, the COMPUTE command *must* follow a BREAK command. The calculations of the COMPUTE command are generally performed using a function (see Table E-3).

The basic form of this command is as follows:

```
COMPUTE [function ] OF {column | alias} ON {break-column | REPORT}...]
```

A partial list of the most common functions used within a COMPUTE command is shown in Table E-3.

Table E-3. Partial list of common functions used within a COMPUTE command.

Function Name	Used to Compute	Data Type that This Function Applies
AVG	Average of non-null values	NUMBER
COUNT	Count of non-null values	All types
MAXIMUM	Maximum value	NUMBER / CHARACTER
MINIMUM	Minimum value	NUMBER / CHARACTER
SUM	Sum of non-null values	NUMBER

The user can always verify if there is an active compute or get rid of any active compute by issuing the following commands at the sequel prompt:

COMPUTE
or
CLEAR COMPUTES

EXAMPLE 3
Display the job title, last name, and salary of all employees of the S_EMP table. Compute the subtotals for each group of titles. Assume that the environmental settings in Fig. E-1 are active.

```
TTITLE 'Employee Salaries by Title'
BTITLE 'For Internal Use Only'
COLUMN salary HEADING 'Salary' FORMAT $99,999.99
```

Fig. E-1. Environmental settings.

The corresponding BREAK and COMPUTE commands to produce the required report, the SQL query, and a partial result are shown below. Observe the combined effect of the BREAK and COMPUTE commands. This result has been formatted to fit the width of the page and for explanation purposes.

```
CLEAR COMPUTES
BREAK ON title SKIP 2
COMPUTE SUM OF salary on TITLE
SELECT title, last_name, salary
FROM s_emp
ORDER BY title, last_name, salary
```

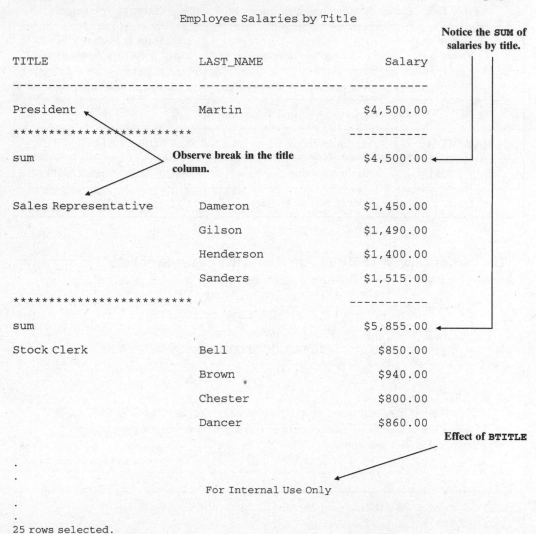

Thu Feb 10   page 1

                          Employee Salaries by Title

                                                          Notice the SUM of
                                                          salaries by title.

TITLE   LAST_NAME   Salary
------------------------- -------------------- -----------

President   Martin $4,500.00

*************************   -----------
sum   Observe break in the title $4,500.00
                          column.

Sales Representative   Dameron $1,450.00

                          Gilson $1,490.00

                          Henderson $1,400.00

                          Sanders $1,515.00

************************   -----------
sum $5,855.00

Stock Clerk   Bell $850.00

                          Brown $940.00

                          Chester $800.00

                          Dancer $860.00

                                                          Effect of BTITLE
.
.
                          For Internal Use Only
.
.
25 rows selected.

The command CLEAR COMPUTES is necessary to get rid of any COMPUTE that may be in effect. There is no need for a CLEAR BREAKS command because, as we indicated before, only one BREAK command is active at any given time. Therefore, this new BREAK command redefines any previously active BREAK command.

Let's look a little closer at the following COMPUTE command for sake of explanation.

COMPUTE SUM OF salary on TITLE

In this command we can observe the following:

- The function SUM indicates the type of calculation to be performed.
- The clause OF salary indicates the column to be summarized
- The clause ON TITLE indicates the column on which the control break occurs.

In summary, this command calculates (computes) the SUM of the salaries of the employees that have a common title every time the value of the title columns changes (a break). Notice that in this report there is no salary grand total. By a *grand total*, we mean the total sum of a quantity; this total is included at the end of the report. For instance, if there were a salary grand total in this report, the grand total would have been the sum of all salaries. If there is a need to obtain a grand total, the user *must* use the **REPORT** option in both the BREAK and COMPUTE commands, as illustrated below. Only these two commands are shown because we are assuming that the remaining statements of the previous query are the same.

BREAK ON title SKIP 2 **ON REPORT** ◄————————   Notice the use of the REPORT clause on both the BREAK and COMPUTE commands.

COMPUTE SUM OF salary **ON TITLE REPORT**

A partial output of the last page of the report is shown below to illustrate the use of the REPORT option on both the BREAK and the COMPUTE command. Observe that this result has been formatted to fit the width of the page.

```
Thu Feb 10                                                        page 4

                        Employee Salaries by Title
                                          Grand total produced by the use
                                          of the REPORT on both the
                                          COMPUTE and BREAK commands.

TITLE                    LAST_NAME              Salary
------------------------ -------------------- ----------

Warehouse Manager        Hawkins              $1,650.00
                         Jackson              $1,507.00
***********************                       ----------
sum                                           $7,957.00
```

Subtotal of the salary of all warehouse managers. Notice that the list of managers is incomplete.

```
                                              ----------
sum                                          $38,562.00 ◄
```

Additional Features of the `TTITLE` and `BTITLE` Commands

So far, whenever we have used the `TTITLE` and `BTITLE` command we have used the system default values. Table E-4 shows some of the options that can be used with these title commands to exert more control on the appearance of a heading.

Table E-4. Partial list of options of the `TTITLE` and `BTITLE` commands.

Option	Description
COL n	Go to column *n*.
SKIP n	Leave *n* blank lines before printing next character.
LEFT	Left-align next sequence of characters.
CENTER	Center the sequence of characters.
RIGHT	Right-align next sequence of characters.

Sometimes, the heading that we need to write may exceed more than 80 characters, and it may be necessary to continue writing it on the next line. To do this, we can use a hyphen to let the system know that the current line continues on the next line.

One side effect of using any of the options of Table E-4 with the title commands is that the system no longer prints the system date and the page number at top or bottom of the page. To display the page number, we need to include, as part of the `TTITLE` command, the system variable `SQL.PNO`. How to include the system date in the report will be explained later in this appendix. The following commands illustrate the use of some of the system variables and some of the options of Table E-4.

```
TTITLE CENTER 'CUSTOMER AND THEIR LOCATION' SKIP 1 -
CENTER '==============================' SKIP 1 -
LEFT 'Internal Report' RIGHT 'Sales Department' SKIP 2
BTITLE CENTER 'Confidential' RIGHT SQL.PNO
```

A partial output of the top and bottom sections of the first page of the report is shown next. We are assuming that the query of Example 2 of this Appendix and all other settings are still in effect. Notice that the report has been formatted to fit the width of the page.

```
                      CUSTOMER AND THEIR LOCATION
                      ==============================
Internal Report                                  Sales Department
.
.
.
.  Effect of the TTITLE command and
.  the CENTRE, LEFT, and RIGHT
   options.                         Confidential                    1
```

Effect of the **BTITLE** command
and the **SQL.PNO** sysvar.

Observe that there is only one TTITLE command even though it spreads over three lines. In this case we have used a hyphen to indicate that the command continues on the next line. The option CENTER followed by twenty-eight = characters allows us to obtain the effect of underlining the main heading of the report. The combined effect of the LEFT and RIGHT options produces the second line of the heading. The SKIP option allows us to print this heading in more than one line. The use of the system variable SQL.PNO as part of the BTTITLE allows us to print the page number.

Printing the system date when using the TTTILE of BTITLE command is a little bit more complicated than using the sysvar SQL.PNO. To print the system date, we need to use simultaneously the NEW_VALUE command, a couple of new options of the COLUMN command, and table aliases. Consider the following sequence of commands. Notice that only those instructions that are being affected are shown. The remaining commands and options are still in effect.

```
COLUMN today_date NEW_VALUE today NOPRINT FORMAT A1 TRUNC
BTITLE CENTER 'Confidential' RIGHT today


.
.

.
SELECT title, last_name, salary, TO_CHAR(SysDate) "Today_date"
FROM s_emp
ORDER BY title, last_name, salary;
```

First of all, observe that the SysDate system variable is printed as a pseudocolumn of the SELECT statement. In this case, we are converting it to a character variable before printing it. We have given this pseudocolumn the alias today_date. In addition, observe the use of this alias in the COLUMN command. The SQL*Plus NEW_VALUE command is used to assign the value of the today_date column to a user variable called today. The latter variable is then used as part of the BTITLE command. The NOPRINT option instructs the system *not* to print the value of the column today_date when it prints the result of the query. Finally, observe the use of TRUNC in the formatting clause FORMAT A1 TRUNC. The use of this option and FORMAT A1 requires some explanation. The reader should be aware that when dates get formatted with the TO_CHAR function, the system uses a default column width of 100 characters. Therefore, it is necessary to fool the system so it does not take into account the width of the today column when determining whether or not the value of LINESIZE has been exceeded. The options FORMAT A1 TRUNC trick the system into using as many characters as are indicated in the format of the TO_CHAR instead of the system default.

The effect of these statements in the BTITLE command is shown below. Observe that only the bottom section of the last page of the report is shown here.

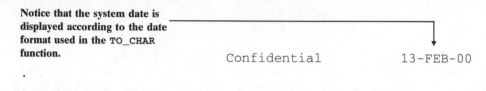

Notice that the system date is displayed according to the date format used in the TO_CHAR function.

```
                                  Confidential          13-FEB-00
  .

  .
25 rows selected.
```

Sometimes, when writing a report we may find necessary to use a more descriptive and longer title. In these occasions, we can always use the hyphen to continue on the next line. However, if the titles are very long, the TTITLE or BTITLE commands may not be easy to read. We can alleviate this situation by breaking the titles into smaller pieces and using the SQL*Plus DEFINE command to place each piece into a *user-defined variable*. These variables can then be referenced in a TTITLE or BTITLE command. The basic syntax of the DEFINE command is illustrated with the following section of code.

```
DEFINE FirstLine = ' This line is one of several pieces'
DEFINE SecondLine = ' second line of a very long title'
DEFINE ThirdLine = ' As you can see we are using three user
defined variables in this example'
TITLE LEFT FirstLine CENTER SecondLine RIGHT ThirdLine SKIP
```

Entering Top and Bottom Titles Interactively

In a report, it is possible to enter the top and bottom headings interactively using substitution variables and the PROMPT and the ACCEPT commands. A substitution variable is a user variable that begins with one or two ampersands (&). As it will be explained later, the use of one or two ampersands makes a difference in the behavior of a substitution variable.

The **PROMPT** command is used to display messages to users. The basic syntax of this command is shown below.

```
          PROMPT text-to-be-displayed-to-user
```

The **ACCEPT** command serves a dual purpose. First, it prompts the user with a message. This message is generally to instruct the user to type a value. Second, it stores the value typed by the user into a substitution variable. The basic syntax of this command is as follows:

```
ACCEPT substitution-variable PROMPT text-to-user
```

The following example illustrates the use of these commands.

EXAMPLE 4
Write a report that lists the names of all employees of the SG company. Group the employees by department. Enter the title report interactively.

We have divided the commands into two groups. The first of the two groups contains the PROMPT and ACCEPT commands. The second group contains the BREAK command and the query to create the report. We will only explain the commands of the first group.

```
CLEAR COLUMNS
PROMPT Please enter a title of 30 characters or less;
ACCEPT title_var PROMPT 'enter title:';
TTITLE CENTER title_var RIGHT SQL.PNO SKIP 2;

BREAK on department SKIP
SELECT D.name, E.last_name, E.first_name
FROM s dept D, s_emp E
WHERE E.dept_id = D.id
ORDER BY D.name;
```

The PROMPT instruction displays a message informing the user of the maximum number of characters that he or she can enter in the top title. For this example, we chose the value of 30 characters, but we could have chosen any other convenient value.

The ACCEPT command instructs the user to enter a title. The title entered by the user is then stored into the substitution variable title_var. This variable is then used in the TTITLE command.

To enter data interactively into a table, the user may preceed a substitution variable with one or two ampersands (&). The use of an ampersand at the beginning of a substitution variable forces the system to ask the user to enter a value. Using a double ampersand at the beginning of substitution variable forces the system to ask the user for a value the first time it encounters the system variable. After that, every time the system encounters the same variable preceded by the double ampersand, it uses the current value rather than asking the user for a new value. Notice that there is a significant difference between using one or two ampersands. If the variable begins with a single ampersand, the system will always ask the user for a value regardless of how many values the user has entered for the same variable. Variables that begin with a double ampersand force the system to ask for a value only once. After that, the system uses the current value of the variable.

Whenever we need to enter character data into a substitution variable, it is necessary to enclose the data in single quotes. The user can avoid the tedious task entering single quotes if he or she encloses the substitution variable in single quotes. This feature of the substitution variables is particularly useful when entering data into a table. The following example illustrates the use of substitution variables when entering data.

EXAMPLE 5
Insert data into the table s_dept using substitution variables.

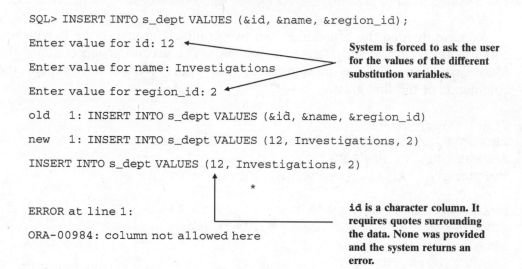

```
SQL> INSERT INTO s_dept VALUES (&id, &name, &region_id);

Enter value for id: 12

Enter value for name: Investigations

Enter value for region_id: 2

old   1: INSERT INTO s_dept VALUES (&id, &name, &region_id)

new   1: INSERT INTO s_dept VALUES (12, Investigations, 2)

INSERT INTO s_dept VALUES (12, Investigations, 2)

                                          *

ERROR at line 1:

ORA-00984: column not allowed here
```

System is forced to ask the user for the values of the different substitution variables.

id is a character column. It requires quotes surrounding the data. None was provided and the system returns an error.

Notice that, when entering data, the system shows the *old value* and *new value* of all substitution variables. This is the VERIFY feature of Oracle. The user can turn this feature off by issuing the command SET VERIFY off. Observe the effect of using single quotes around the substitution variables when entering character

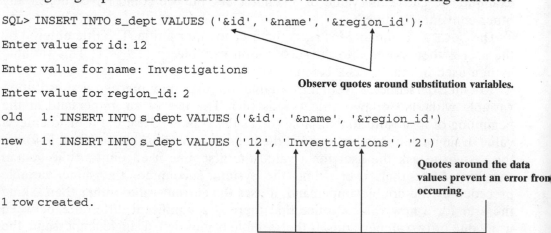

```
SQL> INSERT INTO s_dept VALUES ('&id', '&name', '&region_id');

Enter value for id: 12

Enter value for name: Investigations

Enter value for region_id: 2

old   1: INSERT INTO s_dept VALUES ('&id', '&name', '&region_id')

new   1: INSERT INTO s_dept VALUES ('12', 'Investigations', '2')
```

Observe quotes around substitution variables.

Quotes around the data values prevent an error from occurring.

```
1 row created.
```

INDEX